WHEN GOD SCRAMBLES YOUR PLANS

and 49 Other Complete Lessons for Youth Bible Study

Compiled and edited by

Ann B. Cannon

ABINGDON PRESS

Nashville

WHEN GOD SCRAMBLES YOUR PLANS
AND 49 OTHER COMPLETE LESSONS FOR YOUTH BIBLE STUDY

Copyright © 1997 by Abingdon Press

This book is printed on acid-free, recycled paper.

Library of Congress Cataloging-in-Publication Data

When God scrambles your plans— : and 49 other complete lessons for youth Bible study / compiled and edited by Ann B. Cannon.
    p.   cm. — (Essentials for Christian youth)
    "This resource was created using Bible study sessions written from 1993 to 1995 and published in 'TREK' and 'Bible lessons for youth' "—Introd.
    Includes index.
    ISBN 0-687-02599-0 (alk. paper)
    1. Church group work with teenagers. 2. Bible—Study and teaching. I. Cannon, Ann. II. Series.
    BV4447.W53   1997
    268'.433—dc21
                                       96-24114
                                          CIP

God scrambled my plans the year I worked on this book. So, it is to my dad, Marcus Bartlett, and to my husband, Cecil, that I dedicate this book.
I'm glad you both are still around to see it.

97 98 99 00 01 02 03 04 05 06—10 9 8 7 6 5 4 3 2 1

MANUFACTURED IN THE UNITED STATES OF AMERICA

CONTENTS

Chapter 5
Real Relationships

Chapter 6
The gods of Society

Chapter 7
Transitions

INTRODUCTION

Welcome to the Wonderful, Wacky, Worthwhile World of Teaching Teenagers

It's been said that the devil doesn't have to do away with the Bible; he's already enlisted boring Bible study teachers. *Congratulations! You're not one of them!* The fact that you picked up this book indicates that you refuse to be a boring Bible teacher. You know that Bible study with teenagers can be fun, informative, and a little bit wacky. So, use this book as a resource in facing that roomful of wiggling energy, raging hormones, and rapidly growing bodies commonly called teenagers. Hold up God's eternal truths through exciting, relevant expression that gets teenagers involved.

Teenagers want practical help to deal with everyday issues. What a great compliment to a Bible study leader when a teenager shares how he used a Bible study challenge at school, or how she held her temper with her family, or how they stood up against negative peer pressure.

This resource was created using Bible study sessions written from 1993 to 1995 and published in *TREK* and *Bible Lessons for Youth*. I applaud the talented writers of these curriculum pieces who contributed many of the procedures suggested here.

Where to Use This Book

This book is designed with flexibility in mind so that you can use the sessions in any setting where you want to offer thought-provoking Bible study for teenagers. Consider these opportunities:

- Select a topic and teach the listed sessions at a weekend retreat.
- Use the related sessions of a topic for Bible study at summer camp.
- Select a key topic for a weekday Bible study.
- Prepare youth to lead the sessions in a weekly Bible study at school.
- Create a theme around a topic and plan an intense, daily Bible study during the summer (afternoons for younger youth, evenings for older youth).
- Supplement regular Bible study curriculum on Sunday morning.
- Establish appropriate Bible study in informal, neighborhood groups.
- Enlist teenagers who desire additional Bible study to meet regularly and work through the topics in the book.
- Publicize a topic and encourage teenagers to bring friends to an all-day event of fun, food, and Bible study.
- Use the sessions to train teachers in how to involve youth in Bible study while teaching a relevant subject.
- Pull out a session to meet a specific need (for example, to face the death of a teenage friend).

How to Use This Book

First, check out the Contents page. Pick a youth-related topic or issue. Each Bible study listed under a topic examines a different facet of the main topic. The key phrase at the beginning of each session offers direction for the Bible study. To help you share eternal truths related to the lives of youth, each session includes Bible study strongly integral to youth today.

Each session is built around a main teaching plan made up of these sections—STARTING, EXPLORING, and CONNECTING. This main teaching plan should take about an hour. OPTIONS in each teaching plan provide alternate teaching ideas. An option may replace a step in the main teaching plan. Or, it can complement the main teaching step, especially if you have more teaching time than an hour. OPTIONS were created to help you in various situations, like these:

- to relate to a specific age (younger or older youth);
- to use if you have unusual resources available, such as a TV and VCR;
- when you are willing to do extra preparation;
- to allow a teenager to lead a segment of the Bible study;
- to provide new procedures for teaching the same Scripture.

STARTING and CONNECTING always have an option. EXPLORING may offer one or more options. In addition, the "Bible Passages" listing in the back of this volume lets you select a Bible study based on a specific Bible passage.

How to Use Each Session

At the beginning of each session the topic, title, and related icon identify the area of study. The key phrase expresses what youth should accomplish during the study. Each session contains four main components:

✔ *Check Up!* provides basic commentary information related to the scripture being studied.
✔ *Check List* tells you the supplies to gather.
✔ *Check In* suggests teaching procedures to use in the session. If preparation is needed, it is explained at the beginning of a step. Each teaching plan is built around three essentials:

- STARTING captures the attention of teenagers and gets them involved immediately in the study. Allow 15 to 20 minutes for this step;
- EXPLORING lets youth focus on the Bible passage. Allow 20 to 30 minutes for the steps in this section;
- CONNECTING makes the Bible passage relevant to teenagers' lives. This step is designed to take 15 to 20 minutes.

The best way to use the material is to take the suggested ideas, evaluate the needs of your teenagers, and come up with your own teaching plan that meets those needs.

✔ *Check Out* is the last item in each session. It is designed to help youth think beyond the Bible study session. You can

- write the question or comment on a large poster as a session visual;
- state it as a final thought without expecting a response;
- use it in a closing prayer;
- write it on a bookmark or slip of paper for youth to carry home;
- suggest youth write it near the Bible passage studied that day;
- send it on a postcard to youth prior to the study as a way of creating interest.

My prayer is that through exciting Bible study teenagers will find Bible truths applicable, helpful, and full of hope. *"Because of our love for you we were ready to share with you not only the Good News from God but even our own lives"* (1 Thess. 2:8, GNB).

Blessings!

Ann B. Cannon

## CHAPTER 1

A LIFE
WORTH LIVING

1. AM I DIFFERENT OR ARE YOU?

Philemon 7-21

How God values all people in spite of our differences.

✔ CHECK UP!

As one of God's apostles, or someone appointed by God to go out and preach God's word, Paul wrote many letters during his tenure. In his letter to Philemon he uses an especially personal tone. Though it is addressed to Philemon and the church in his house, most of the letter centers on a specific issue—the return and the acceptance in faith of Onesimus, Philemon's runaway slave. Slavery was an accepted practice in biblical times. After running away from Philemon, his master, Onesimus is taken in and treated as an equal by Paul. Onesimus voluntarily spends time in service to Paul, and God transformed what could have been just a typical master-slave relationship into a relationship as close as that of two brothers or of a father and son. Philemon was at first an outsider in this triangle of the three men, since ordinarily he would not interact equally with a slave such as Onesimus. But through the grace of God, Philemon became an insider—a person who could see the potential in someone who was otherwise discounted or ignored.

The law of the day required that runaway slaves be returned. After a time Paul sent Onesimus back not only to deliver a letter to Philemon, but also to return to his master's house. Onesimus was probably apprehensive about this development, since the law allowed slaves to be severely punished or even executed for running away.

The bulk of the letter to Philemon concerns the welfare of Onesimus. Paul urged that the returning slave be received in a new context, that of the Christian faith, and that he be treated accordingly. Though Paul refused to use his position of authority to make demands on Philemon, he did promise to take responsibility for anything Onesimus might owe Philemon. Moreover, Paul clearly explained that he expected Philemon to choose to act with transforming love, the same love that transformed Onesimus from someone "useless" into a person of "useful" and generous service to Paul. One of the most important teachings of the book of Philemon is that God through Christ gives worth to every human life. Onesimus was a runaway slave who belonged to Philemon, but Paul saw himself as a father to Onesimus (v. 10) and pleaded with Philemon to accept his return without punishment. Onesimus, who was once a slave, became a son to Paul and a brother to Philemon (v. 16).

✔ CHECK LIST

STARTING
❑ Two colors of dots, or strips of paper in two colors, and safety pins.
❑ Bring refreshments.

EXPLORING
❑ Poster board markers, a box for each youth, or newsprint.

CONNECTING
❑ Paper, pencils.

OPTION 1
❑ Prepare two poster-board-sized graffiti sheets.
❑ Markers.

OPTION 2
❑ Enlist a youth.

OPTION 3
❑ Do background check.

 CHECK IN

STARTING

A "Different" Experience

Put a colored dot on each person's forehead, or pin a colored strip of paper on each person's outfit. Use only two colors. Order those wearing one color to do things like rearrange the chairs, hang up posters, pick up the trash, and so on. Offer cookies and soft drinks to the youth with the other color. Make a big deal about being nice to one group and abrupt with the other.

As you begin, ask:
▼ **What's been happening today since you arrived?**
▼ **What caused the different reactions to each of you?** *(Tell them about the colors, if they don't mention this.)*
▼ **How did you feel about the way you were treated?**
▼ **How did you feel about the way others were treated?**
▼ **In real life how do we react to people who are different from us?**
▼ **What influences the way we think about others?** *(Family, training, culture, beliefs, traditions.)*

Say: **Today we'll look at how personal prejudices keep us from seeing a very important truth.**

EXPLORING

Onesimus, This Is Your Life

Direct a youth to read Philemon 4-21. Explain the Bible background in Check Up! Tell youth to make up a storyboard of Onesimus' life. (A storyboard contains several frames where stick figures and basic dialogue tell the story from frame to frame.) Dialogue may include how Onesimus reacted when Paul told him he was going back to Philemon, Paul's explanation to Onesimus about the letter to Philemon, and Philemon's reaction to the returned slave. (If you have a large group, let youth work on more than one storyboard.)

Ask:
▼ **How do you think Onesimus felt about being sent back?**
▼ **What do you think caused Paul to send him back to Philemon?**
▼ **How do you think Philemon reacted when Onesimus returned with Paul's letter?**

OPTION 1

Recording Our Differences

PREPARATION: Make two graffiti sheets by writing *Ways We Are Different* in the middle of one of the sheets. In the middle of the other write *Ways We Are the Same.*

Hand youth the markers and tell them to write several comments on each sheet. Review the comments on both sheets of paper. Ask the last two questions under STARTING. Include the final comment.

OPTION 2

Director

Enlist a youth who is willing to do some outside study on Onesimus. Help this youth get information from a Bible commentary and other resources. During the session, ask this youth to share this research. Tell the youth to serve as the director of a skit based on the story. The director should tell others what to do and say as they reenact the story. Ask the questions under "Onesimus, This Is Your Life."

Barriers

Ask:

▼ **In the story of Onesimus what differences were involved?**

Direct youth to look at the other youth. Ask them to call out the differences among the group members. (These might include appearance, talents, taste in music, schools, grade levels, personality.)
Say: **A negative way to handle differences is to assume that people who are most like you, and who agree with you, are the "best." This attitude can lead to choosing one's friends only from this group and ignoring others who do not fit this description.**

Ask the youth to name persons or groups of persons who have suffered from prejudice and oppression in our society, similar to that endured by slaves and others in Philemon's day. Examine the reasons that people in one group feel free to discriminate or oppress persons of another group. Oppression is usually justified by the belief that some persons are of less value than the group of people doing the oppressing.

Ask:

▼ **How do differences create barriers?**
▼ **What barriers separate us from others?** *(Ethnic, social, economic, location, expectations)*

As youth identify these, write each on separate small boxes (shoeboxes, egg cartons, or other small box shapes) or on large newsprint. If you use boxes, build a barrier.

CONNECTING

Respect

Ask youth to define *respect*.

Ask:

▼ **Why should we respect one another?**
▼ **How can we respect one another when we are different?**
▼ **What does the Bible say about how God feels about people?**
▼ **How is God color-blind?**
▼ **How can we react positively toward one another to break down these barriers?** *(As youth name ways, remove the boxes or cross out the barriers on the list.)*

Hand out half-sheets of paper and pencils. Tell youth they are not going to share this information. Direct youth to write the name of someone they know who is different from them—someone at school, in the church, at work, in the neighborhood. Next, tell youth to write down one way that they can show that person respect. Challenge youth to carry out their statements this week.

 **CHECK OUT**

The first step to respecting others and accepting their differences is to respect ourselves.

OPTION 3

Putting Prejudice Away

PREPARATION: Check with the church missions committee or a local community social services organization to see how youth can be involved in a community project.

Depending on where you live, investigate helping in a soup kitchen, creating a project to help the homeless, or finding some other social outreach program in your area to participate in. Another idea is to take the first step in offering friendship to an "outsider" in school. Say: **These are some ways to bridge the gap between the outsider and the insider and to let God transform all your relationships.**

2. ATTITUDES ADJUSTED HERE

Luke 18:9-14

How the wrong attitude can give a false sense of security with God.

✔ CHECK UP!

Jesus told this parable to some people who trusted that they themselves were righteous and who regarded others with contempt. What it says is not addressed to just the Pharisees. It's addressed to anyone and everyone who thinks, "I'm cool. I can take care of myself. I'm self-sufficient." Sin has been described like this. Sin is like building little ledges of security where we can climb up and look down on other people and say, "Well, I have my faults, of course; everyone does. But at least I'm not like . . ." Sometimes, however, such people must scramble to find faults in another person. So they build their security ledge a little higher, saying, "Well, at least I don't . . ." The higher the ledge gets, the more they have to put down other people to feel secure. The only real security is in admitting we're sinful and throwing ourselves on the grace and mercy of God. And that's exactly what this parable is about.

The Pharisee prays to God, giving thanks that he's not like the people he sees around him in society. He defines his relationship with God in terms of what he hasn't done. He's not a thief, or a rogue, or an adulterer, or even a tax collector. He justifies himself by saying, "Well, at least I'm not like . . ." Next he defines himself positively: He fasts twice a week, he tithes on everything he earns. These are, in fact, good things. They are acts of piety and mercy. Fasting is a discipline that is more than just a weight-loss program. True fasting involves offering one's deprivation to God as a gift, and growing spiritually through that experience. Tithing was written into the Torah. One-tenth of everything belonged to God and was to be offered at the Temple during the harvest festival. The wealth thus accumulated was used to feed the poor and care for the sick in Israel. So the Pharisee is also defining himself in terms of his spiritual discipline. It would be a mistake for us to decide, because the parable frowns on the Pharisee, that we ought not to take up spiritual discipline. The Pharisee knows who he is and how safe he is. Of course, it's a false security, but he doesn't know that.

The tax collector stood apart, perhaps just barely inside the court of Israel in the Temple. Tax collectors were among the most hated people in Israel. They were agents of the Roman government, and they made their living by wringing every dime they could out of their fellow citizens. They were considered traitors to both nation and God. They could never be witnesses in a trial because their word was not considered trustworthy. The tax collector knows where he stands in the

✔ CHECK LIST

STARTING
❑ Index cards, pencils.

EXPLORING
❑ Bible dictionaries and commentaries.
❑ Prepare balloons.

CONNECTING
❑ Large paper bags, crayons or markers, slips of paper, large trash bags, washcloths, hand towels, a container of water.
❑ Make sign.

OPTION 1
❑ Large newsprint, marker.

OPTION 2
❑ Camera with self-developing film (optional).
❑ Standard dictionary.

OPTION 3
❑ Paper, pencils.

eyes of the world and, he assumes, in God's eyes. He won't even look up to heaven. Unlike us, people in ancient Israel prayed standing up, looking up, with their eyes open. That was considered the proper way to pray. Beating his breast as a sign of mourning and contrition, the tax collector's prayer is simple: *God be merciful to me, a sinner.* What else can anyone ever pray and be honest? The tax collector has no security in the world. His only security is in God, so he throws himself on God's mercy.

Here's the reality on a personal level. The more secure we try to make ourselves, the less secure we are. The more we're willing to let go, the more secure we are. And, Jesus says, it was the tax collector who went home justified, rather than the other man. The Pharisee justified himself, but God justified the tax collector. The Pharisee had just what he claimed for himself; but because he claimed nothing, the tax collector had everything. He was justified, made right with God. This is the way it is, Jesus said. Just because we have a lot of self-confidence, just because we keep the rules, doesn't mean we're right with God. It's only when we rely on God for our security that we have hope.

 # CHECK IN

STARTING

A Heavenly Application

Hand out index cards and pencils. Tell youth you will read a series of questions. They need to mark *Y* for *yes* or *N* for *no* on their cards. Urge youth to be honest, since they will not share this information. Read the following questions:

- Have you ever skipped church for reasons other than severe illness—for example, when you are out of town?
- Do you volunteer your time and talents to the church and to those in need?
- Have you kept all Ten Commandments without breaking any of them, including the one about lying? (Are you telling the truth? ____)
- Are you like Mary Poppins, "practically perfect" in every way?
- If we asked your enemies to verify the information on this application, would they agree that you are "practically perfect in every way"?
- Do you truly love your enemies and even pray for people who mistreat you?
- Do you read the Bible every day?
- Do you pray without ceasing?
- Do you have perfect control over your tongue, even when you hit your thumb with a hammer?
- Do you always honor your father and mother?
- Do you "do unto others"—particularly your brothers and sisters—"as you would have them do unto you"?
- Do you believe, on the basis of your answers, that your application should be accepted?
- Would you be willing to give your life so that someone else, whose application for heaven has been rejected, can be accepted into heaven?

OPTION 1

Apply Within

Ask:
▼ Have any of you applied for a credit card, checking account, college entrance exam, job, or other situation where you filled out an application?
▼ What requirements were listed on the application?

Tell youth to prepare an application blank for getting into heaven. Work as a large group to make up the application form.

Ask:
▼ What should be included on the application?
▼ What are the requirements?
▼ What does the applicant need to be able to do?

Write their suggestions on large newsprint. Read the concluding statement under STARTING to help youth see what is really required for entrance into heaven. Say: **Today we'll look at how our attitude sometimes leads us to believe we can earn our way into heaven.**

Say: **Count up your *Y*s and *N*s. If you have more *N*s than *Y*s, you would not make it into heaven by earthly standards. But, congratulations! Even though your application was not perfect in every way, someone else gave his life so that your application can be accepted.**

Ask:

▼ **Do you know who did that for you?**

Say, **Welcome to an everlasting and wonderful relationship with God! Hear the Good News:** *Through Christ, you are accepted!*

EXPLORING

Pharisee or Tax Collector?

PREPARATION: Have a balloon for each person. Inside half the balloons place slips of paper that say "Pharisee," and inside the other half place slips of paper that say "Tax Collector." Inflate and tie a knot in each balloon. Also borrow Bible dictionaries and commentaries from your minister or church library.

Give each youth a balloon. At your signal, have everyone pop their balloons and read the note inside to discover whether they will be Pharisees or tax collectors for the remainder of the lesson.

Tell the Pharisees team to look up the definitions of *tax collector* in the Bible commentaries and dictionaries and to investigate the tax collectors of Jesus' day. Encourage them to discover the following:

Which people were required to pay taxes?
How did they determine the amount of tax to be paid?
What government got the money?
Was collecting taxes an honorable profession? A well-paying profession?

Also, using commentaries and dictionaries, have the tax collectors investigate the Pharisees of Jesus' day to uncover the following:

What made the Pharisees different from other Jewish people?
What were some of their habits, beliefs, and customs?
What notable experiences did Jesus have with Pharisees?

Ask representatives from each team to report their findings to the entire group. Ask youth to pay special attention to the information about the team to which they are assigned, and about their attitudes toward the other group. Share information about the Pharisee and the tax collector from the Bible background in Check Up! Have youth "play their parts" during the rest of the session, reacting as they think their group would to each activity.

CONNECTING

A Self-Portrait

Give each of the "Pharisees" and "tax collectors" a paper grocery bag and a handful of crayons. Say: **Put your bag over your head. You may not make eye holes, but you may tear the sides of the bag a bit to fit it over your shoulders. You are going to draw self-portraits on these sacks as I give you instructions. And Pharisees, be sure to make yourselves look especially good!** When everyone has a bag on, say: **Without looking, pick up any crayon and draw a left ear on your sack.**

OPTION 2

Pride or Humility?

Invite two volunteers to create a sculpture entitled "Pride." Say: **Create the sculpture out of at least two persons in the group, who will become human mannequins and will hold the poses that the sculptors put them in. Do not create anything that is obscene, profane, or more than mildly embarrassing.** Give the sculptors a few minutes to think about pride before they begin their work. To define *pride,* provide a dictionary. Be sure that no one talks except the sculptors.

When the sculpture is completed, take a picture of the sculpture so that the participants may see it afterward.

Ask:

▼ **Tell us about your sculpture.**
▼ **What were you trying to say about pride?**
▼ **What did the rest of you see as the sculpture was created?**
▼ **What is pride?**
▼ **Is there more than one kind of pride? If so, what are some other kinds of pride?**
▼ **Is one kind of pride better than another? why? why not?**

Read aloud Luke 18:9-12.

Ask:

▼ **What kind of pride is described in the Scripture?**

Read aloud Luke 18:13. Tell youth about tax collectors, using the Bible background from Check Up!

Ask:

▼ **How would you describe the tax collector's attitude?**
▼ **Is humility something we learn, like a habit? Is it deeper than a habit? Are we born with humility? How does a person become humble?**

When everyone has finished the ear, give similar instructions for drawing each of the following in the order listed, having the youth pick up a new crayon each time: right eye, mouth, right ear, nose, left eye, right eyebrow, hair, beard (for boys) or earrings (for girls), left eyebrow.

When everyone is finished, ask the Pharisees to take off their bags and, without looking at them, place them face-down on the table. Have them look at the tax collectors' sacks, react as they wish (probably with laughter), and then explain to the tax collectors what is wrong with their sacks. Then, allow everyone to look at their own sacks.

Ask the Pharisees:
▼ **Were you surprised to see that your faces looked just as funny as the tax collectors'?**

Ask the tax collectors:
▼ **How did you feel about the Pharisees' judgment of your drawings?**

Say: **Being a Christian means comparing ourselves with God instead of with each other. In the biblical text the Pharisee's mistake was comparing himself with the tax collector. The tax collector was humbled because he compared his life with the holiness God expects from us. These bag faces symbolize how we picture our own mistakes as looking much nicer than God sees them. We view our sin as far less than everyone else's sin. Humility means getting outside ourselves to compare our life with God's measure of perfection, not with someone else's life, and repenting for the ways in which we fall short.**

Hand out slips of paper. Have youth write any sin that they want to confess on these slips of paper. Tell them to wad up the paper and throw it into their bags. Then, let youth wad up the sacks and stuff them all into a large trash bag with a sign that reads "Garbage from the past. Forgiven today, wiser—and more humble—tomorrow."

Experience Humility

Say: **Jesus taught the disciples to wash each other's feet as an act of servanthood. Today we will wash the hands of another person as a way to humble ourselves before that person.** Demonstrate the way you want the youth to wash each other's hands. Dip the washcloth in the water, squeeze the water over another person's hands, and then dry the hands with the towel. Begin by asking the Pharisees to wash the hands of the tax collectors. Repeat the process with the tax collectors washing the hands of the Pharisees. Close with a prayer asking God to give us an attitude of humility before our Creator and to help us measure ourselves by God's perfect example, instead of judging ourselves by others.

IECK OUT

attitude toward people who are not like you?
iveness have to do with pride and humility?

Use the same procedure outlined above to create a sculpture entitled "Humility."

When the people-sculpture is complete, take a picture of it. Invite the sculptors to tell about it.

Ask:
▼ **What did the sculpture say to you?**
▼ **How did you decide what the sculpture would look like?**
▼ **Some of you did not participate in making the sculpture. What did you see in the sculpture? How did you feel about it?**

OPTION 3
Prayer of Confession

Invite youth to write prayers of confession using the following guide. Say: **Let your humility meet God's grace. Think about your need to confess. Write your confession of sins in this way:**

▼ **Tell youth to ask for forgiveness for sins committed in the last week.**
▼ **Tell youth to confess acts that were wrong and unloving.**
▼ **Tell youth to confess thoughts that were wrong and unloving.**

Say: **As you confess your sins, you are like the tax collector, who knew the reality of his life and was willing to trust God to give him security.** Be sure the youth know that whatever they write is personal and that they will not be asked to read it. Encourage them to take these prayers home so that what they write will remain private.

Conclude the session with this prayer: **Forgive our sins, renew in us a desire to live as your children and give us the power to follow you, in the name of Jesus Christ. Amen.**

WHEN GOD SCRAMBLES YOUR PLANS

3. LIVING LIFE HAPPY

Matthew 5:1-12

Examining the advantages of living life guided by the Beatitudes.

 **CHECK UP!**

The familiar Beatitudes are the keynote of a new time of humanity which Jesus came to introduce. They are the basic notes for a life lived in harmony with our triune God. There is no new law introduced here, but rather the gift of a lifestyle which results in blessing and fulfillment. Jesus begins his Sermon on the Mount by sitting down, a signal that the rabbi will begin teaching. His sermon makes a relationship to God the essential basic in life. It describes to Jewish hearers and to us the lifestyle of a true disciple. The repeated word "blessed" is our middle C, our reference point, our center. "Blessed" burst forth as we might say "oh," as an expression of the happiness of being in the realm of God.

We might understand the virtues listed as notes in the chords of life played together to make a symphony. The symphony might be titled "The Promised Blessing of God Now and Later." A disciple will play all the notes in a lifetime. Let's look at the measures separately. "Blessed are the poor in spirit" may be read as those who accept the hardships and limitations of life without bitterness toward humans or God. In this way they place their lives in God's hands and will be blessed.

"Blessed are those who mourn, for they shall be comforted." Those who mourn are those who undergo life's hard experiences, crushing disappointments, and losses. Yet, intentionally or unintentionally they turn in faith to God for help. "Comforted" implies strengthening as well as consolation.

"Blessed are the meek, for they shall inherit the earth." Meek means more than gentle. It means being humble and trusting God. It is the opposite of brazen independence from God, and the trust lasts even when the conditions of life are difficult. "Inherit the earth" is a figure of speech for the kingdom of God where the faithful will know all the privileges of life with God.

"Blessed are those who hunger and thirst after righteousness." Just as we cannot continue to live in our human bodies without food and water, so do the faithful need to know and do God's will. Righteousness describes a life fully conformed to the will of God, a relationship harmonious in thought, word, and deed. One's whole life would be an act of worship.

"Blessed are the merciful, for they shall obtain mercy." Here Jesus

---

✔ CHECK LIST

STARTING
❏ Prepare matchup sheets.

EXPLORING
❏ Prepare copies of Scripture.
❏ Bring different Bible translations.
❏ Chalkboard or large newsprint, marker.

OPTION 1
❏ Prepare slips with *Bless You!*

OPTION 2
❏ Paper, pencils.

OPTION 3
❏ Prepare sentences on large sheets of newsprint, markers, index cards, pencils.

---

speaks of relationships with other people. Those who are gentle, understanding, and forgiving also receive mercy. Not only will other people treat kindly those who show them kindness, but God will deal mercifully with those who have shown mercy.

"Blessed are the pure in heart" refers to those who are single-mindedly devoted to God. They see God not in some rare, fleeting vision but in a life lived in full harmony with God.

"Blessed are the peacemakers," those whose attitudes, words, and actions preserve friendship where it exists and restore relationships where they have been destroyed by violence. This is a concrete action, not just a "be happy attitude." Making peace is a risky proposition. Jesus knows we need God at our center to do this.

"Blessed are you when you are persecuted for righteousness' sake" because of your relationship to God. The world is not heaven. When you live in the world dedicated to God's will, you are bound to confront evil. If you are hurt physically or emotionally in this confrontation, God will preserve you and welcome you into the Kingdom, for you are a living disciple.

Again and again we see real power in these Beatitudes. Jesus does not mean that we can earn our way into salvation. The final privilege of the kingdom of God is a blessing given by God. But faithfulness is a necessary quality for salvation. If we fall away from the relationship with God, we lose the source of our power. If we live in the blessedness of God's relationship, we will exhibit God's gifts.

 CHECK IN

STARTING

Making the Match

PREPARATION: Write the following words or phrases on twelve sheets of paper, one word or phrase to a sheet:

those who mourn	pleasure seeker
merciful	cruel
meek	aggressive
peacemaker	troublemaker
pure in heart	insincere
poor in spirit	proud

Ask for twelve volunteers and give one sheet to each. Then ask the volunteers to come to the front of the room, mingle, and find their opposites. Have them stand in pairs and display their words so that everyone can read the opposites. *(For a small group, place all the sheets on the floor or on a table and have youth match the opposites.)* Explain that youth will examine these key words and ideas in Bible study today.

Ask:
▼ **Which of these words or phrases are hard to understand?**

If youth don't name any, ask them to define the words. Place the words on the wall as you begin the session.

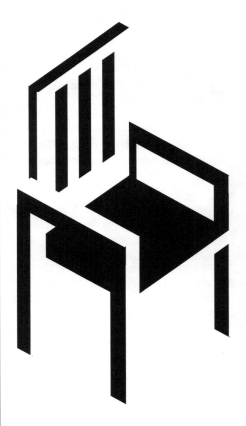

OPTION 1

Bless You!

PREPARATION: Write *Bless You!* on slips of paper. Place one in each chair before youth arrive.

Ask:
▼ **Did you notice anything different as you sat down?**
▼ **When do you hear "Bless You!" used?**
▼ **What does "Bless You!" mean?**

Explain that youth will look at how important it is to be blessed as they study the Bible today.

EXPLORING

Dig These Beatitudes

PREPARATION: Select a translation of the Beatitudes that is easy to read. Write out this translation and make copies so all youth will be reading from the same translation.

Pass out the copies of Matthew 5:1-12. Form two teams of youth. Direct youth to read these verses in the following manner. Read verses 1 and 2 aloud. Then invite the two groups to join together reading responsively verses 3-10, with Group 1 reading the "blessed" and Group 2 picking up with the word "*for* . . ." For verses 11-12, have Group 1 read verse 11, and Group 2 read verse 12.

Continue with the study by forming as many groups as you have different versions or translations of the Bible. Give a different version to each group. Ask participants to find Matthew 5:1-12 in their Bibles. Say: **The Bible was not originally written in English, so it has been translated into our language, as well as into other languages of the world. Different translations may use different words to express a particular thought.**

Beginning with verse 3, try to discover who will inherit the Kingdom. Ask a reader from each group to identify the version or translation from which he or she is reading and answer who will inherit the kingdom of heaven according to verse 3. After all groups have shared, ask everyone what words they would use to describe the "poor in spirit." Reach a consensus and write it under the heading "Sons and Daughters of God Are . . ." on the chalkboard or paper. Follow the same process with verses 4-10.

OPTION 2

Look at It in Another Way

Divide youth into small teams. Distribute Bibles, paper, and pencils. Instruct each group to read Matthew 5:1-12 and to write a reverse paraphrase for each Beatitude in verses 3 through 10. In other words, they should write verses that express the point of view opposite the one expressed in the Beatitudes—for example, verse 5 might be "Miserable are the proud, for they will lose everything." Bring the youth together to compare their ideas.

Ask:
▼ **How true are your reverse paraphrases?**
▼ **How often have you seen examples of your reverse paraphrases come true in life?**
▼ **How true are the Beatitudes?**
▼ **How often have you seen examples of their truth in life?**
▼ **What did you learn about the Beatitudes by working on your reverse paraphrases?**

CONNECTING
Media and the Beatitudes

Using the same small teams, invite each team to select a different popular television program. Ask each group to name two or three main characters in the television program and to evaluate how their lifestyle compares with the lifestyle described in Matthew 5:3-10. The youth may need to refer to the Scripture in order to keep in mind particular verses. Bring the groups together to report on their discussions.

Ask:
▼ How would you describe the lifestyles and the values of the characters on the television program you chose?
▼ How do the values of the world relate to the values of God's kingdom?
▼ Why are the values of the world and the values of God's kingdom so different?
▼ What would Jesus say to the television characters?

Focus

Lead youth in a prayer that expresses a desire to grow in grace and in the love of God. Say: **In order to be more effective it's often useful to focus on one thing.** Ask the youth to choose one of the Beatitudes and commit to making it more important in their personal lives. Allow a time of silence while youth name their chosen Beatitude in their hearts. Then thank God for the gracious gift of God's kingdom.

 **CHECK OUT**

How can I be happy when I'm so confused about what kind of person I want to be?

OPTION 3
The Reality of the Beatitudes

PREPARATION: Write each of the following sentences on separate sheets of large newsprint:

> **IN ORDER TO LIVE AS ONE OF THE MEEK, I NEED TO START BY . . .**
>
> **IN ORDER TO HUNGER AND THIRST FOR RIGHTEOUSNESS, I NEED TO START BY . . .**
>
> **IN ORDER TO BE MERCIFUL, I NEED TO START BY . . .**
>
> **IN ORDER TO BECOME PURE IN HEART, I NEED TO START BY . . .**
>
> **IN ORDER TO BECOME A PEACEMAKER, I NEED TO START BY . . .**
>
> **IN ORDER TO PREPARE MYSELF FOR PERSECUTION FOR RIGHTEOUSNESS' SAKE, I NEED TO START BY . . .**

Give each youth a marker. Tell them to complete three or four of the sentences. After youth have finished completing the sentences, read some of their comments. Urge youth to select one area to work on in living out the Beatitude during the coming week. (If you teach younger youth, they may participate better if they write responses on index cards first. Then, let them tape their cards to the related sentences.)

4. REMEMBER WHOSE YOU ARE

Exodus 20:1-20

How God's basic guidelines help us live as children of God.

 ✔ **CHECK UP!**

Faith stories tell us what life means. They tell us about who we are and whose we are, about how the world came to be the way it is, and about what God is doing in it. This text is one of those stories. It's about the covenant between God and Israel on Mount Sinai, a definitive event of what it means to be God's people. God, working through Moses and Aaron, led Israel out of slavery in Egypt, across the Red Sea, and brought them to this place. The covenant on Mount Sinai has made Israel a nation and also a people dedicated to God. The covenant ends with a reminder of what God has already done to bring Israel to this point. Reciting the history, telling the story, is a way of establishing identity. "Who am I? I am one of those whom God brought out of Egypt. Because of that I live in relationship with God."

Youth may say, "Yes, but God didn't bring me out of Egypt. That doesn't mean anything." Not so! When we become a part of God's family, all that God has done in the past becomes a part of our story, a part of who we are, and we begin to learn to live in relationship out of that story. How do we respond to what God has done? What claims does the covenant lay on us? The Ten Commandments follow immediately after the recital of what God has done. It would be easy to say that these are laws we have to follow. This would sound oppressive and harsh because we can't live up to them perfectly. But because it is God who has given the law, which is Torah (meaning "teaching" rather than "law"), we begin to see these words as responding to God's saving acts. Torah becomes a way of expressing our love and thanksgiving, not a way of whipping us into line. Even the law is a form of grace. Read how Israel relates to God in Exodus 20:3-11. There's only one God whom Israel and the church worship.

In the Jewish-Christian tradition, images, symbols, or representations of God are not objects of worship but reminders of the God we worship. What does it mean that God is a jealous God? Didn't our parents try to get jealousy out of our systems? Then we hear that God is jealous. On the one hand, the jealousy of God is about idolatry. God wants us to be single-minded in our devotion, giving ourselves only to God and not to idols. Jealousy is also related to God's holiness. The covenant means we are called to total obedience, and

God is jealous or passionate for that obedience. On the other hand, it's God's passion for God's people that keeps us safe and maintains the Kingdom. It is because God is jealous or passionate for us as people that we continue to be kept in God's care.

Knowing someone's name means you know something about that person's character, about the essential being of that person, and therefore, have a degree of power over him or her. That understanding is related to the commandment about not making wrongful use of the name of the Lord. There's more to this commandment than just a prohibition of swearing, though that certainly is a wrongful use of God's name. Whenever we talk lightly about God, whenever we make easy promises in God's name, like promising peace when there is no peace, we misuse the name of God.

God's people are called to remember the Sabbath and keep it holy. For Christians, the Sabbath is moved from Saturday to Sunday, but the principle is still the same. One day in seven is set apart to honor God. Verse 11 says the Sabbath is important because God rested on the Sabbath day and called it holy. "Holy" in the Bible most often means "consecrated" or "set apart." To make the Sabbath holy means to honor God, to deliberately make a break with the normal patterns of life for the sake of remembering God.

So far the commandments have all been about the way we relate to God. Now we find a series of one-liners in verses 12-17 about life in the community. On one level, these commandments are a foundation for morality. Any community needs to observe them in order to live in harmony as a community. In the light of the covenant, they remind us that harmony in the community is a divine gift that carries grave responsibility. To break any of these commandments is a violation of the covenant that threatens the integrity of the community. If marriage relationships, relationships between generations, truth, property, even life itself cannot be carried on without some confidence that our neighbors will not threaten that relationship or activity, there is no basis for community. God's covenant says that one foundation of society is that life is held in respect and, therefore, we can trust each other, at least minimally.

In verses 18-20 the people are afraid and don't want God to speak to them. Moses is all they can handle. Dealing with God can be scary. God is a holy God, and we're not holy. Perhaps it's better not to get too close. We have to change who we are and how we live in the world if we meet God. But the God of the Bible is a strange God, both living in eternity, and at the same time, shamelessly getting involved in the muck and pain of human life. God calls Israel to come to the holy mountain and enter into a covenant relationship. Our God is an awesome God, but also a God who comes near to us and invites us into relationship. Moses' reply in verse 20 is an interesting one, saying that God will help the people not to sin. It's almost as if their objection was, "We don't want to come into God's presence because we're only escaped slaves and we don't know how to act around God. We'd do something stupid, and God would punish us for it." It's safer to stay at a distance. But Moses says to them that this God is so incredibly open and gracious that God will help them act properly so they will not sin.

 CHECK IN

STARTING

A Game Without Rules

PREPARATION: Write the rules for the second game on a large sheet of newsprint. Do not display these rules before time for the game.

Say: **We are going to play a game in which the object is for each person to get as many balls of wadded paper into a trash can as possible.** Place the trash cans in random positions on the floor. Place the scrap paper on a table and yell "Go!" One of two things will probably happen: (1) The youth will begin to do anything they want, moving baskets, hoarding paper balls, yelling out scores, and so forth, or (2) they will sit around wondering what to do. Either reaction is all right. The object of this exercise is to demonstrate that it's hard to do anything—even play a simple game—without some basic rules.

After a few minutes of play, yell "freeze" to stop the game. Then give detailed instructions. Have the youth form two teams. Place the trash cans at opposite ends of the room and assign one trash can to each team. Wad and tape two paper balls. Give one to each team.

Say: **The object of this game is to "shoot" your paper ball into the opposing team's goal (trash can). Your team will receive one point for each goal scored. The trash can goals may not be moved. No one from a defending team can be within three feet of his or her team's goal (meaning no goalies), except to begin a play. To begin the game and after each successful goal, the ball must be thrown into play from behind your team's goal line and passed the length of the room in order to attempt a goal. Players may not move when they have the ball in their possession.** Allow the youth to play the game again with rules.

Ask:
▼ What was it like to play this game the first time? the second time?
▼ What made the difference?
▼ Did the rules or boundaries help or hinder your play?
▼ How do boundaries help give direction to our lives? to our relationships?

Say: **In this session we look at the importance of having a basic purpose and basic rules for living together. These help us understand our relationship to God and to each other. We know who we are and whose we are.**

OPTION 1

Starting a New Society

Say: **Imagine that you are space travelers. Your mission is to create a colony in a new world. What will be the basic social standards for the colony?** After 8 minutes, bring the group together.

Ask:
▼ **What is your basic purpose?**
▼ **On what standards, beliefs, or principles is your world built?**

Say: **In this lesson we look at the importance of having a basic purpose and basic rules for living together. These help us understand our relationship to God and to one another. From these we discover who we are and whose we are.**

EXPLORING
Take This Down, Moses

Select two volunteers to read or act out the parts of Moses and God in the following skit.

TAKE THIS DOWN, MOSES

GOD: Take this down, Moses . . .

MOSES: *(reaching into backpack)* Wait a minute, I can't find my pen!

GOD: This can't wait. Just grab one of those rocks over there and chisel it out.

MOSES: Ready. But go slow.

GOD: I am the Lord your God.

MOSES: Yeah, I know that. Now, what did you want me to write down?

GOD: Write down: I am the Lord your God!

MOSES: Oh . . .

GOD: You shall have no other gods before me.

MOSES: So you want to be Number One, huh? Isn't that a little egotistical?

GOD: Hey, when you're God . . .

MOSES: Yeah, maybe you deserve to be Number One!

GOD: You shall not make for yourself an idol, in the form of anything that is in heaven above, or that is . . .

MOSES: Slow down!

GOD: Just do your best. We'll edit this later.

MOSES: Maybe we should number these . . .

GOD: You shall not make wrongful use of the name of the Lord your God.

MOSES: Oh my Go . . . oops!

GOD: What was that?

MOSES: Nothing, go on.

GOD: Remember the Sabbath to keep it holy . . .

MOSES: Does that mean no more football games?

GOD: Honor your mother and father . . .

MOSES: *(under his breath)* Wait till the kids hear that one!

GOD: You shall not murder. You shall not commit adultery. You shall not steal.

MOSES: Aren't we getting a bit negative, here? You *do* want the people to obey these, don't you?

GOD: You've got to say no to some things, Moses.

MOSES: I just don't want people to think that you're a killjoy. Don't do this. Don't do that.

GOD: I'm only trying to protect life. The things that hurt people, that rob people of their dignity—that's what's out of bounds, don't you understand?

MOSES: Of course I understand, but will they?

GOD: I don't know. We'll have to see.

Ask:
▼ **How do you think Moses felt in this situation?**
▼ **How do you feel when someone gives you a list of rules to follow?**

OPTION 2
Commandments for Today

PREPARATION: Write *Then* at the top of a large sheet of paper and *Now* at the top of a second large sheet of paper.

After youth read Exodus 20:1-18, direct them to list in their own words the Ten Commandments under *Then*. Working with each commandment, challenge youth to list what the commandment means currently.

Ask:
▼ **How is this commandment lived out today?**
▼ **How is it not lived out today?**

Write their comments under *Now*.

Ask:
▼ **Which commandment is easy to keep? why?**
▼ **Which commandment is hardest to keep? why?**
▼ **Are these laws helpful or a source of guilt? how?**

Read Exodus 20:19-20. Explain these verses using Bible background from Check Up!

Ask:
▼ **How can God help you live by these commandments?**
▼ **How have you seen God working in your life lately?**

▼ How do you think the people of Israel felt when Moses came down from the mountain and told them about the Ten Commandments?
▼ Why do we need commandments?
▼ What do the commandments mean for today since we aren't Jewish?

Share Bible background from Check Up! especially the information on keeping the Ten Commandments as a response of love.

Lots of Do's and Don'ts

Say: **Some people think the Ten Commandments are all negative. True, there are a few don'ts, but God's law brings good things into our lives and helps us stay away from the bad.** Divide youth into teams of two or three. Hand out paper and pencils. Tell them to read Exodus 20:1-18 in their Bibles. Direct them to write these commandments in their own words, changing the negative commandments into positive language. For example, for "Do not murder" youth might write, "Honor each person God created and respect human life."

CONNECTING

Just Do It!

PREPARATION: At the top of one large sheet of paper write *Wills* and at the top of the other write *Won'ts*.

Say: **Our efforts to live within the bounds of God's laws don't make us God's children. In other words, we don't have to try to be good enough to earn God's love. God's love is a gift, freely given to us even before we ask for it. But our attempts to live by God's laws do help us to show other people that we know we are God's children, that we take the benefits and responsibilities of the covenant seriously.**

Ask the youth to think of actions that they are willing to take or not take in order to show others that they are part of God's covenant people. List these on the *Wills* and *Won'ts* posters. Encourage them to relate some of these actions to the content of the lesson *(for example, "I will try to talk with my parents more often and to respect their opinions.").*

Ask:
▼ How will these behaviors help others to understand our faith in and our covenant with God?
▼ In what ways can we help one another to live out the commandments of God?

Ask youth to join hands in a circle to symbolize their commitment to helping one another keep the covenant with God. Close in prayer.

 **CHECK OUT**

God, teach me to count higher than the Ten Commandments.

5. THE SECRET OF LIFE

Philippians 4:4-20

Discovering Paul's secret for joyful living.

✔ CHECK UP!

Had Paul lived an easy, charmed life, the lesson that can be learned from his life would not be nearly so meaningful as it is. However, knowing that Paul experienced pain, hunger, poverty, humiliation, ridicule, imprisonment, and intimidation makes his advice to rejoice always all the more challenging and amazing.

An example of Paul's constant ability to rejoice occurred during his first visit to Philippi. While there Paul and Silas were attacked by the crowds, stripped and beaten, then put in jail. Yet, even there in jail, and in the stocks, Paul and Silas prayed and praised God (Acts 16:19-25).

Paul demonstrated his belief that he could do anything and live through anything with God's help. Paul did not perceive God as a lucky charm to ward off evil or tragedy. Nor was Paul using God as an antidote to pain. Paul simply accepted the strength that God continually offered him. He found great reason to rejoice for that fact alone.

Paul also recommended that every believer be a part of a nurturing Christian environment. Even if a person rejoices in the Lord, prays, shows gentleness and consideration, and is overall a strong Christian, that person still needs to be surrounded by people and opportunities that will help him or her grow even stronger as a Christian.

Paul said that Christians need to keep the following virtues in their hearts and minds: truth, honor, justice, purity, things that are commendable, and things that are worthy of praise.

His letter to the Philippian congregation conveyed his gratitude, encouragement, concern, love, and finally, his thanks for the special gifts that they had sent him. A devoted believer, Epaphroditus, had brought gifts to the imprisoned Paul, all the way from Philippi. Paul is evidently more thankful for the graciousness and love that motivated the gift, than for the gift itself. Almost without exception, Paul did not accept monetary favors throughout his ministry, but the devoted relationship between Paul and the Philippian congregation moved him to accept and appreciate their generosity. Not only does Paul give thanks for the Philippians and their gift, but he also wishes for them the same strength and spiritual power that comes to anyone who trusts in and praises the Lord.

✔ CHECK LIST

STARTING
❏ Enlist an instrumentalist.
❏ Select songs.
❏ Get scorekeeper.
❏ Get a small prize.

EXPLORING
❏ Prepare bag with items.
❏ Make six signs.
❏ Markers.

OPTION 1
❏ Pencils, paper.

OPTION 2
❏ Nice notepaper and envelopes, pens.

OPTION 3
❏ Write statements on poster.

CHECK IN

STARTING

Name That Tune

PREPARATION: Enlist an adult or youth who plays a musical instrument (piano, flute, oboe) to attend the session. Select six to eight songs that have *joy* or *rejoice* in the titles or first lines. Choose songs familiar to youth. Consider Easter or Christmas songs, too.

Divide youth into two teams. Tell them they are going to play "Name That Tune" using songs about joy. The team who thinks they can name a tune by listening to the fewest number of notes gets to try first (10 notes, 9 notes, etc.). If that team fails, the other team tries. Instruct scorekeeper to give 100 points for each tune that is guessed correctly. Begin the team bidding with 10 notes ("I can name that tune in 10 notes"). Declare a winning team and award a small prize. Explain that during this lesson youth will learn the secret of keeping joy in their lives all the time.

EXPLORING

The Secret of Joy

PREPARATION: Place several items in a bag to represent possible circumstances in the lives of youth. For example, include a picture of a family, a set of car keys, a school book, a thermometer or other medical item (representing illness), a newspaper obituary page (representing death), a recent headline, a high school annual. (Feel free to make up your own bag.)

Direct a youth to read Philippians 4:4-7. Explain that Paul encouraged people to rejoice in and through the circumstances in their lives, not under them. Pull out items in your bag one at a time.

Ask:
▼ What circumstance in life could this object represent?
▼ Would it be easy or hard to rejoice during this circumstance? why?

Continue with several items.

Ask:
▼ How does Paul expect us to rejoice when some of those situations are painful?
▼ How could continual rejoicing make a difference in your life?
▼ What are some good things about rejoicing and being happy?
▼ Is it possible to overdo rejoicing and being happy?

OPTION 1

Sing About Joy

Direct youth to name songs about joy or rejoicing.

Ask:
▼ Why did the writers of these songs write about joy?
▼ How is joy an important part of life?

Working either together or in small teams, tell youth to write a song or rap about joy. Provide paper and pencils. Let youth share their efforts. Say: **Today you will learn the secret of keeping joy in your life.**

OPTION 2

Saying Thanks for Real

Hand out nice notepaper, envelopes, and pens. After discussing Paul's words of thanks to the Philippians,

Ask:
▼ Who in your life has been supportive?
▼ Who has encouraged you through tough times?

Direct youth to write a "thank you" note to that person. If possible, urge youth to send that note to the person. If they are people you know, offer to be the deliverer.

The Secret of Virtue

PREPARATION: Post six sheets of poster paper or newsprint in different parts of the room. Write the following words or phrases, one to a sheet: *Truth, Honor, Justice, Purity, Commendable Things, Things Worthy of Praise.* Use permanent ink to write each word or phrase, or an abbreviation, on one of six inflated balloons. Be sure the words are easy to read.

Ask another youth to read Philippians 4:8-9. Pass out markers or crayons to the youth. Have them use the posted sheets as graffiti boards to define each of the words and phrases. When the participants finish their definitions, use the following activity to have the youth indicate which virtues they feel are present in their own life.

Launch each inflated balloon one at a time by batting it gently into the air. If a youth feels that the balloon indicates a virtue present or "under cultivation" in his or her own life, he or she can bat it too. If not, the youth is not to touch that balloon. Read the definition before launching each balloon. Slowly add balloons and see how many the group can keep afloat. Say: **Virtues don't mean much if they hit the ground and stay there! Paul recommends that the only way to have these virtues is to be in an environment that nourishes you.**

Ask:
▼ Do the people, places, and events in your life strengthen you as a Christian? how?
▼ Which people provide the most positive support for you? how?
▼ Which activities provide the most positive support for you? how?
▼ How does media (TV, music, movies) relate to these virtues?
▼ Why is it difficult in modern society to live as Paul suggests that we live? Is it even possible to live the way Paul describes?
▼ What changes would you consider making to make your life conform to Paul's guidelines for living?

CONNECTING

The Secret

Say: **Paul spoke about learning a secret for life.** *(Name a youth),* **please read Philippians 4:11-13 to find out the clues.** After the reading,

Ask:
▼ What is the secret that Paul writes about?
▼ What does this secret mean?
▼ If we followed Paul's advice, would we be free of problems?
▼ Does Paul's secret of contentment protect you from problems? Remember that Paul had his share of pain, hunger, and physical suffering.
▼ How can such a secret help you at your present stage of life?

Say: **There's one more part of this secret Paul can share with you.** Ask a youth to read Philippians 4:18. The gifts from the believers at Philippi served as an expression of their care and concern and love for Paul.

OPTION 3

The Secret Is Out

PREPARATION: Write the following statements on a poster: *Rejoice all the time; Follow strong virtues; Stay in a nourishing environment; Be happy wherever you are; Remember to say thanks.*

Say: **During this session you've looked at several secrets for having a good life.** Point out these statements on the poster. Lead youth to state specific ways they can carry out these activities in everyday life. Write suggestions beside each statement. Challenge youth to pray about living by one of these statements, as you close in prayer.

Ask:
- ▼ Have you ever received a special gift that expressed the love of the one who gave you the gift?
- ▼ How did you show your thanks?
- ▼ What gift have you received from God that expressed the love God has for you?
- ▼ How did you show your thanks?

 **CHECK OUT**

How can you remember to use this secret during the coming week?

6. THE TRUTH DETECTIVE

1 John 4:1-6

Understanding the importance of discernment.

✔ CHECK UP!

We hear frequently that it doesn't matter what we believe, just as long as we believe in something. Many thoughtful youth say this, which makes such movements as New Age so attractive. The Christian church, however, is built on faith in Jesus Christ, who came in the flesh to be our Savior. That is, we are built on faith that God was incarnate in Jesus. Remind youth of this important truth. We do not live on faith in faith, but on faith in Jesus Christ.

There are two sections to this text: verses 1-3, about discerning the spirit of God and the spirit of the antichrist; and verses 4-6, about discerning who belongs to God and who belongs to the world. The two sections are closely related. First, in discerning the spirit of God and the spirit of the antichrist, a healthy skepticism goes hand in hand with faith. Not everyone who uses the name of Christ tells the truth about Christ. It is important that we learn to think critically about what we hear. Youth particularly need to learn how to think critically about the messages that come to them from so many sources. Is the way of life portrayed by the electronic media one they want to embrace? Is violence really a way to solve human problems? Is sex truly the ultimate goal of all relationships? In a world that ignores God, how can we discern what God is doing?

God's action in Jesus is the key to faith. God became human that we might relate to God. So, we're not asked to confess that the baby in Bethlehem was somehow connected to God. We are reminded that incarnation, God coming in the flesh, has to do with the total work of salvation. We're not talking about a heavenly Jesus with a remote connection to the world. We're talking about one who was born in the days of Herod the king, who was caught up in the decree that went out from Caesar Augustus, who was crucified for us under Pontius Pilate. Christian faith is tied to a particular person at a particular place and time, who transcends all times and all places. Antichrist is one who is not of God. This is not a reference to Satan, but persons or ideologies who are from Satan, who are opposed to God. How do we discern true spirits? They are those who insist that Christian faith is specific, not generic. They are the ones who insist on the reality of Incarnation, of the historical action of God in Jesus of Nazareth. They are the ones who insist that there is more to Christmas than sweet sentimentality over a baby in a

✔ CHECK LIST

STARTING
❏ Index cards, markers.

EXPLORING
❏ Paper, pencils.

CONNECTING
❏ Large sheet of paper, marker.

OPTION 1
❏ Prepare index cards.

manger. There is also God's mighty act of salvation that involves the cross and resurrection, blood and pain, as well as joy. The response the disciples are called to make today is the same as the writer of 1 John wanted Jesus' followers to make: Use your heads; learn to think critically about what people say to you in matters of faith; faith is specific, not generic; don't believe in goodness, but believe in a God who became human in Jesus Christ and acted to save the world from sin.

In verses 4-6, the writer moves to the two groups of people who live out these spirits. There are people who are of God and people who are of the world. The writer says that, since you are from God, the one who is in you is greater than the one who is in them. You have conquered them. Those who are faithful to God share God's victory over evil, over the world, over false teaching. You are on God's side, so you don't have to worry about what others say. Note carefully: "You are on God's side," not "God is on your side." All kinds of evil and cruelty have been perpetuated by those who are sure God is on their side. Justice, truth, and compassion are the results of committing ourselves to be on God's side. The significant difference is in those believers who live out their faith in the world, who believe in God's act of salvation, who live as followers of the one who brought salvation. They feed the hungry, clothe the naked, visit those in prison, care for the sick and dying, and work to overcome systems that lead to hunger and homelessness and lack of medical care, injustice, discrimination, war, and on and on.

Those who negate the importance of Christ also live out their faith, usually not so much by doing evil as by not actively doing good. Because there is no commitment to the one who brings salvation, there is no commitment to stand with someone in overcoming pain or evil or suffering. So another way to recognize the spirit of truth or the spirit of error is to examine the way people live their lives. It may not be based on what some believe and others don't, but on how they live and what they do. It may be that all believe, but what they believe is radically different, and that difference is reflected in living.

 CHECK IN

STARTING

Spirit Busters

Give each youth an index card and marker. Have youth write a *T* on one side and an *E* on the other. Tell them the *T* stands for the spirit of truth and the *E*, for the spirit of error. Explain that after you read each of the following Spirit Buster statements, they are to hold up an *E* or *T*. For each statement, ask volunteers holding up each letter to explain how they see the spirit of truth or error evident in the statement.

● God blesses the persons God loves and punishes those who sin against God. Therefore, when you suffer, it is a sign that you have sinned.

OPTION 1

In the Buster Business

PREPARATION: Write the Spirit Busters (see Spirit Busters statements under STARTING) on index cards.

Tell youth to pick a card, read it, and be prepared to convince the others of the statement on the card. (If you have several youth, let them work together.) After youth have tried to defend

- If you have not been "saved" by going to the front of the church during an altar call, you can't get to heaven no matter how good you are.
- It is important to go to church and to give money to the church even if you don't like the pastor. Going to church is the only way a Christian can stay in touch with the community of faith, the body of Christ on earth.
- Christians should believe in miracles like Jesus' resurrection, but they don't have to believe stuff like Jonah's being swallowed by a fish.
- If you have faith, you can do miracles too.
- If it is true that God forgives all our sins, then we can go ahead and do anything we want to do, because it will all be forgiven anyway.
- There are many gods. Just because our God is the main one doesn't mean the others don't have something important to offer.

Say: **You have to be a truth detective, to decide what is true and what is not. During this session, you'll get some tips on being a God-centered truth detective.**

EXPLORING
Basic Christianity
Divide the assembly into groups of three or four youth (if numbers are small, let all the youth work together).

Ask:
▼ **What exactly does a person have to believe in order to be a Christian?**

Give the members of each group five minutes to come up with an answer. Say: **Include in your answer exactly what a Christian has to believe, no more and no less. You should be able to state your answer in no more than one sentence. We're getting down to basics here.** Direct a representative of each group to read the group's answer.

Ask:
▼ **Why is the idea you chose basic to Christianity?**

Read aloud 1 John 4:1-6.

Ask:
▼ **What does the writer of 1 John say is the most crucial belief?**
▼ **Why do you think the writer chose the idea that Christ has come in the flesh?**
▼ **What does it mean to say that Jesus Christ has come in the flesh?**
▼ **Why didn't the writer say that the test of faith was belief in Jesus Christ? belief that Jesus Christ is the Son of God?**
▼ **Would the question, "Has Jesus Christ come in the flesh?" be a good question to ask people when they become members of a church? why? why not?**

OPTION 1 (Continued)

their statements, say: **You have to be a truth detective, to decide what is true and what is not. During this session, you'll get some tips on being a God-centered truth detective.**

OPTION 2
Spirit Study
Ask a youth to read 1 John 4:1-6. Say, **The Bible identifies the spirit of God and other spirits.**

Ask:
▼ **What is the determining factor to being a Christian?**
▼ **What are the other spirits?**
▼ **What power do death, evil, and sin have in the world?**
▼ **How can they be overcome?**

Lead youth in thinking of a specific occasion when someone tried to persuade them to believe something that was untrue or to do something harmful.

Ask:
▼ **How did you respond?**
▼ **When you are confused about what to believe, where do you turn?**

WHEN GOD SCRAMBLES YOUR PLANS

CONNECTING

It's the Truth

Say: **First John 4:4 says that God's Spirit gives us power to make a difference. He says that we are stronger than the world's powers. What do you think? Let's test John's statements using examples from our lives.**

Invite the youth to think of a situation in their school or community in which they are presently involved, where a conflict between right and wrong exists. As they describe the situation, write on the large sheet of paper a summary of the conflict. Be sure all agree with your summary.

Ask:

▼ **What are different groups deciding to do about the situation?** *(This question should help clarify the problem and outline the points of disagreement.)*
▼ **How do you think God would resolve the problem?**
▼ **What would God's solution be?**
▼ **What kind of power would you need in order to act on God's solution?**
▼ **What would be some of the consequences of your actions?**
▼ **What kind of power would you need in order to live with the consequences?**

# CHECK OUT

Is truth flexible? If not, then why are so many people saying that what wasn't O.K. is now O.K.? How do you know what to do?

OPTION 3

Consequences

Pick three or four of the statements listed under STARTING. After each statement,

Ask:

▼ **What would happen if you really believed this and lived your life guided by this belief?**

Encourage youth to be specific as they identify possible consequences of these beliefs. For instance, persons who really believe that sickness is God's way of punishing sin may not only feel ill because of their disease; they may also feel guilty or confused if the cause of illness is not evident, or even be mad at God for being punished while others who do worse things are not. None of these emotions would have a positive effect on the illness. Say: **Significant negative consequences can often result from believing something that comes from a "spirit of error." It is good, and is God's will for us, to live by ideas that we believe are in keeping with the "spirit of truth."**

7. WHAT'S IT WORTH?

Matthew 13:44-46

Deciding what must be given up for the kingdom of heaven.

✔ CHECK UP!

In the United States, we are so used to democratic government, and making choices about who we will and will not support, that we have trouble understanding how different a kingdom is. The kingdom of God is not even a constitutional monarchy, like England's, where the Queen is largely a figurehead. The New Testament kingdom of God is an absolute dictatorship. In this system, the king literally has absolute power, including the power of life and death, over all his subjects. Obedience to the will of the king is not only expected, but demanded. This is radically different from anything we experience in daily life. The real difference between an earthly dictatorship and God's is in God's grace and the way God acts in our lives. The parables in this session deal with the joy of finding the Kingdom, the radical nature of God's grace, the willingness to give up anything that keeps us from the Kingdom, and the importance of being prepared. Matthew 13:44-46 contains two parables about the joy of finding great treasures and giving up all one has for the sake of the treasure.

First, let's look at the treasure hidden in a field. In ancient times people buried their wealth in times of trouble to keep it safe. That practice continued in Europe into the Middle Ages and was revived in Spanish colonies in America because they feared pirates. Even nowadays we hear stories of people who believe their money is safer in a jar buried in a garden than in a bank. So we have a treasure, perhaps hidden centuries before. Perhaps the owner was carried into exile or killed in one of the many invasions that swept over Palestine. Then someone finds the treasure. Perhaps he was a hired man plowing the field and struck the treasure with the plow. Perhaps the frost had heaved it up, and someone taking a shortcut off the beaten path saw it. In any case, the person recognized it as a treasure, hid it again, and went and sold everything he had in order to buy the field. Obviously, his ethics were questionable. He knew more about the worth of the field than the owner did. But Jesus did not tell the parable to make a point about ethics. He told it to make a point about commitment, the willingness to sacrifice everything for the sake of a greater good, in this case, the kingdom of heaven. When we see the Kingdom, Jesus said, and recognize it for the treasure it truly is, we should be willing to give up everything for its

✔ CHECK LIST
STARTING
❑ Play money, dollar bill, gravel, polished stone, basket, shoebox.

CONNECTING
❑ Prepare case studies on cards.
❑ Paper, pencils.

OPTION 1
❑ White poster board, pencils, scissors.

OPTION 2
❑ Bible concordances.

WHEN GOD SCRAMBLES YOUR PLANS

sake. That's a radical idea. The Kingdom is a gift. How else would you describe the treasure you just stumbled across? We give up everything we have in order to receive that gift. Giving up everything is not a way to earn the kingdom of God. To respond to God's grace, we would gladly give up everything we have.

The second parable has a slightly different twist. In the first one, the man accidentally stumbled on the treasure hidden in the field. Here the merchant searches for fine pearls. Pearls were in great demand in the ancient world, and ranked with gold as a symbol of wealth. There were rich pearl fisheries in the Persian Gulf and near the coast of India, so this merchant may have been on a long journey in search of pearls. Or perhaps he was searching among the bazaars in Alexandria or Damascus. In any case, he found one pearl of great value, the pearl equivalent to the Hope diamond. He immediately cashed in all his assets to buy the pearl. Now he had nothing left in all the world except the pearl. And what a prize it was! With it he had everything he had ever wanted. The kingdom of God, Jesus said, is like that. It comes at the end of long searching. To have it, we give up everything, so that all we have is the Kingdom. But, because this is the kingdom of God's grace, that's everything we need.

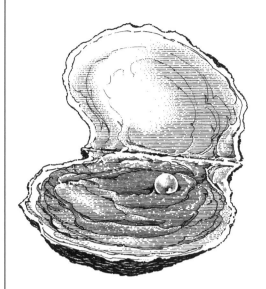

 CHECK IN

STARTING

Treasure Hunt
PREPARATION: Hide a dollar bill in a shoebox filled with play money. Hide a polished piece of agate or quartz in a basket of ordinary gravel. (Look in rock shops or craft stores for polished stones.)

Divide the youth into two groups. In one group, each person should take a bill out of the box and then pass the box to the next person. In the other group, everyone is to take the prettiest rock from the basket and then pass the basket to the next person. When both the real dollar bill and the polished stone have been found, ask a volunteer to read aloud Matthew 13:44-46.

Ask the group with the money box:
▼ Were you expecting to find a hidden treasure?
▼ Was the man in the field looking for hidden treasure?
▼ What was he doing when he found it?

Ask the group with the basket of stones:
▼ You were looking for treasure. Did you expect to find a stone so pretty?
▼ The pearl merchant was looking for treasure too. Did he expect to find so beautiful a pearl? why? why not? (*God wants to give us things more wonderful than we can imagine.*)
▼ In Jesus' parables, the man who found the treasure and the merchant were doing what they normally did; and they were surprised by unexpected good fortune. Jesus said that the kingdom of God is like that. What did he mean?

OPTION 1

Personal Pearls
PREPARATION: Cut "pearls" three inches in diameter from the posterboard.

As the youth arrive, give each of them one of the pearls you have prepared. Ask them to draw or write on the pearls a "treasure" that they have or would like to have. When everyone is finished, have the youth sit in a circle. Ask each one to tell what he or she has drawn or written on the pearl.

Then ask:
▼ If you already possess the treasure you desire, what conditions might cause you to be willing to give it up?
▼ If you do not yet possess this treasure, what would you be willing to give up in order to get it?

EXPLORING

The Search Is On

Form two groups. Have the first group create a modern-day skit based on Matthew 13:44, where God is the one who discovers the treasure in the field. Have the second group create a modern-day skit based on Matthew 13:45-46 in which God is the merchant. Allow five minutes for preparation and planning, then have each group present its skit. Invite everyone to discuss what looking at the Scripture in this way—with God as the seeker—means to them.

Look at the two parables in another way. God is still the seeker; but *you* are now the treasure, the pearl that God has sought and found. Think about how this feels, what this means to you.

Ask:
▼ What does this way of reading the parable teach you about God? about God's kingdom?
▼ What has God given for you?
▼ What can you give for God?

CONNECTING

Ultimate Worth

PREPARATION: Write the following case studies on cards:

- Your dad's car is sitting in the driveway. You and your friends decide to drive by the football field and impress the cheerleaders.
- You have a final exam tomorrow, but your boyfriend wants you to go to a movie.
- You are a cashier in a fast-food restaurant. Near closing time, a man with a gun approaches your register and asks for money.

Say: **Teenagers in some parts of our country have been murdered for their clothes, jewelry, or tennis shoes. Youth need to think about the importance of lasting or ultimate worth.** Hand out the case studies cards. Encourage the participants to discuss their answers.

Ask:
▼ What are our most important values?
▼ What is ultimate worth?
▼ Would a Christian and an unbeliever understand ultimate worth differently? why? why not?

OPTION 2

Kingdom Quotes

Show youth how to use a Bible concordance. (Ask them to look for one in the back of their Bibles.) Let youth work with one another. Tell them to find *kingdom of God* and *kingdom of heaven,* and look for several Scripture references. Direct them to decide what this kingdom is.

Ask:
▼ Who does God want in the Kingdom?
▼ Where is the Kingdom located?
▼ What did God do for you to be in the Kingdom?
▼ What do you give up for God?
▼ How do you feel about this Kingdom that God has prepared for you?

OPTION 3

Fields and Treasures

Say: **It is difficult to describe what it is like to live in the presence of God's grace and love. Jesus understood this kind of life as living in the kingdom of heaven. He used images from everyday life to help people understand what living in God's kingdom could be like. Matthew 13:44 talks about the Kingdom as a treasure discovered in a field.**

Ask:
▼ **What are the "fields" in your life?**

Say: **Think about the different areas of your lives as "fields," the places where you spend time and do things. One field is school. Another is family. You may have other fields.** Encourage youth to name these.

Personal Treasure

Say: **If you are going to find a treasure, you have to know what it is you're looking for.**

Ask the youth to reflect on these questions:
▼ **What is your heart's treasure?**
▼ **What do you want more than anything else in the world?**
▼ **What are the obstacles that prevent you from having the treasure?**
▼ **What would you have to give up?**

Invite each person to draw a treasure map, to mark an X in the place where his or her heart's treasure is, and to use a key to describe the treasure. Then tell participants to add to the map the obstacles that lie between them and their treasure. The obstacles are what must be given up for the treasure. Bring the youth together and invite volunteers to talk about their maps.

 **CHECK OUT**

The kingdom of God is a treasure that God has placed in our path. When we stumble over it we must realize its worth and claim it.

OPTION 3 *(Continued)*

Ask:
▼ **What is the treasure in each of your fields?**
▼ **Why are they treasures to you?**
▼ **Are there other treasures in your life that you value more than these? If so, name them.**
▼ **Would a deeper friendship with God change how you feel about any of these treasures?**
▼ **Would you value any of them more or less? why?**

CHAPTER 2

AT-RISK
BEHAVIOR

8. DON'T TEMPT ME!

Luke 4:1-13

Overcoming temptation in life.

 CHECK UP!

In the temptation story in the Gospel of Luke, Jesus decides how he will win people to God. He can fulfill the people's hopes for a conquering messiah, or he can follow God's will for his life. He rejects earthly power and glory to accept the path that ultimately leads to suffering and the cross.

Temptation involves deciding how to act. During the period of temptation in the wilderness, Jesus was deciding the best way to act so that people could know God. One way would be to turn stones into bread. Jesus could attract numerous followers by providing them food. Jesus could also gain followers by becoming a political messiah. But Jesus knew that God is the only real ruler of the world. Jesus could also use sensational tricks and displays of power to impress people. However, Jesus realized that sensational events, by themselves, would not yield true followers. Jesus met the tests of Satan by quoting passages from Deuteronomy, a book of Jewish law. Jesus' knowledge and understanding of Scripture helped him say no to temptation.

In the wilderness, Satan tempted Jesus with food, a chance to demonstrate God's power, and an opportunity to rule the world in exchange for worship of the tempter. Jesus successfully met these tests.

Finally, Jesus made his choice. He chose to serve God. However, Luke 4:13 indicates that Jesus' temptations and trials were not over. Jesus would continue to struggle with temptations at other times throughout his ministry and even on the cross.

✔ CHECK LIST

STARTING
❏ Large paper, markers.

EXPLORING
❏ Pencils, paper, markers.

CONNECTING
❏ Make and display signs.

OPTION 1
❏ Magazines, newspapers, glue, large sheets of paper.

OPTION 2
❏ Prepare slips of paper with Bible references, chalkboard.

OPTION 3
❏ Paper, pencils.

OPTION 4
❏ Chalkboard, write list.

✔ CHECK IN

STARTING

My So-Called Life

Form two teams (a team can consist of only one person if fewer than four youth are present). Provide a large sheet of paper and a marker for each team captain.

Say: **You are to create a game, similar to an adventure game, that explores a day in the life of a modern Christian teenager. She or he will face three temptations in the space of one day. Select the temptations, the possible responses, and the consequences of each response.** Diagram these items on the paper. If a bad choice is made in response to the first temptation, the game ends (indicate a dire consequence). If a good choice is made, the player is to proceed to the second temptation. If he or she successfully survives all three, create a fantastic reward for the teenager. (Categories of temptations may include immoral sexual behavior, cheating, lying, shoplifting, substance abuse, resorting to violence, and so on.)

After about ten minutes, convene the two groups. Have one team read aloud their script for the first temptation, including possible responses; the other group will decide which choice to make. If the second team gets past this first obstacle, have the first team proceed with their script for the other two temptations. Play another round of the game, during which the second team reads aloud their script of temptations and the first team decides how to respond.

Say: **Being a Christian is a little like participating in an adventure game. Temptations can surprise and confuse you, and you may not know how to react.**

EXPLORING

Real Temptations?—Part One

Hand out pencils and paper. Tell youth to number their papers from one to five. Say: **Write down the first word that comes to mind when I say these words: (1) desert; (2) dangerous; (3) dinner; (4) deserted; (5) desire.** Call on different youth to share their words. Tell youth to read Luke 4:1-4 in their Bible and decide how these words relate to the Scripture. Say: **The purpose of Jesus' temptation was to test his ability to be faithful and obedient to God.**

Ask:
▼ How real was this temptation? why?

OPTION 1

Temptations 'R' Us

Point out the newspaper, magazines, and other supplies. Tell youth to make a group collage that shows people giving in to temptation. As youth work encourage them to talk about why they choose certain pictures and how the pictures show temptation. Display the final collage. Say: **Today you will see how you can handle temptation.**

OPTION 2

Temptation Matchup

Give each youth a slip of paper on which you have written one of the following: *Luke 4:4; Deuteronomy 8:3; Luke 4:8; Deuteronomy 6:13; Luke 4:12; Deuteronomy 6:16.* On the chalkboard write *power, material goods, performance.* Tell each youth to read the Bible passage aloud, and match the New Testament passage to the Old Testament passage. After verses are matched, direct youth to pick the related temptation from the chalkboard. Emphasize that Jesus did not rely on his own cleverness, but used the Scripture to respond to each temptation.

Temptation—Part Two

Ask youth to read Luke 4:5-8 to discover Jesus' second temptation and then to describe the temptation in their own words. Invite someone to tell the answer that Jesus gave to this temptation.

Ask:

▼ **Why do you think Jesus said, "Worship the Lord your God, and serve only him"?** *(When a person worships things other than God, she or he forgets God. One cannot truly serve God while serving Satan or while giving all one's time to other pursuits and pleasures.)*

Give youth sheets of paper and pens or markers. Ask them to draw symbols to represent what some people worship and serve instead of God *(money, a career, fame, possessions).*

Ask:

▼ **How can you tell when you might be worshiping and serving something besides God?** *(You spend all your time or money on it, you think about it a lot, you talk about it instead of about God.)*

Ask:

▼ **How might it hurt both you and God to worship and serve something besides God?** *(You would miss out on some of God's blessings, you might hurt others.)*

Temptation—Part Three

Hold a "spectacular event" contest. Have the youth form pairs to think of a spectacular stunt that would attract the attention of large groups of people. The stunt should be so awesome that it would likely bring the performer fame and perhaps lots of money. Have the youth create TV "spot announcements" as publicity. *(For example: Tickets are now on sale to see the strongest man in the world, who is able to balance an elephant on his hands while standing on a crystal goblet.)*

You can be the judge of the contest, or you can let the youth vote on the ideas by raising their hands and shaking them to tell how "spectacular" they think each event is. A small wave or shake of the hands indicates only "a little" spectacular. Huge shakes indicate "most spectacular." Say: **The tempter tried to tempt Jesus into doing something spectacular.** Then ask someone to read aloud Luke 4:9-13.

Ask:

▼ **Why did Jesus not want to use his special powers to do a terrific stunt? Wouldn't he have gained lots of followers that way?**

▼ **How can spectacular stunts actually harm an understanding of God?**

It Can Happen to You!

After a youth reads Luke 4:1-13 aloud, divide the group into three teams. Assign Luke 4:1-4 to one team; Luke 4:5-8 to a second team; Luke 4:9-13 to the third team. Direct each team to make up a modern-day case study based on Jesus' temptation. For example, the last temptation involves power; youth could write a case study about being tempted to do something destructive to gain power.

CONNECTING

What Tempts You?

PREPARATION: Make two signs that read "No Temptation" and "Great Temptation." Display the signs on opposite walls.

Say: **I will read a list of tempting situations. Decide where you will stand between these two signs.** After stating each situation, allow volunteers to defend their positions. The situations are (you may want to select situations on the basis of the age of your group):

- to drink alcohol
- to cheat
- to lie
- to speed
- to keep the change when the cashier gives you too much
- to take items from the place you work
- to have sex before marriage
- to keep the gold jewelry you find at the mall
- to steal something small from a store

Say: **Many persons can be reliable confidants and helpers for you—a friend, parent, grandparent, guardian, sibling, minister, teacher, or counselor. Some support groups, such as Alateen, provide help in difficult, ongoing situations. A caring listener can help one see beyond the immediate problems to a potential solution.**

Ask:
▼ Who are the people that can help you in a tempting situation?
▼ Why would they be helpful?

Lead youth to make a list of ways to overcome specific temptations. For example,

Ask:
▼ How can you overcome the temptation to drink?
▼ How can you overcome sexual temptation?

 **CHECK OUT**

Ask youth to identify a prayer that Jesus taught the disciples to pray when they were tempted. Pray the Lord's Prayer together.

OPTION 4

A Temptation Role Model

PREPARATION: Write this list on a chalkboard:

Jesus knew the Scriptures.

Jesus relied on the Holy Spirit for guidance and strength.

Jesus put the kingdom of God first in his life. Status, material goods, and worldly power were unimportant to him.

Jesus took time from his busy schedule to be alone with God and pray.

Jesus engaged in spiritual disciplines such as prayer, fasting, and study.

Say: **Jesus was able to overcome temptation because he knew how to walk with God.** Direct youth to substitute their names for Jesus'. Say: **If the statement actually describes you, place a plus sign (+) in front of it. If it does not describe you at all, write a minus sign (-). If the statement describes you at times, write an asterisk (*).**

Call on volunteers to share their responses to different statements.

Ask:
▼ How do you avoid being tempted?
▼ How do you handle a tempting situation?
▼ How do you get out of tempting situations?

9. LIVING LIFE AT RISK

Matthew 5:21-48

Seeing that motive as well as action creates the climate for at-risk behavior.

✔ CHECK UP!

Jesus pointed to a discipleship that was more radical than keeping the rules. For youth to take these verses seriously is to accept an invitation to live by love, rather than by safe codes of conduct. The key is love, the Greek *agape,* which means caring for a person by wanting what is best for him or her as God sees it. This kind of love does not depend on feelings, or whether or not we actually like another person.

In Matthew 5:21-26, Jesus says that intention as well as action comes under the judgment of God. This is why anger is wrong. The mark of a disciple is not anger or revenge, but reconciliation. Jesus cautions followers to forget about how far one can go and still be acceptable to God. The truth is that real discipleship is not about how to avoid judgment while getting even. The real intent is to be reconciled with our enemies.

In Matthew 5:27-30, Jesus again goes beyond act to intention. Adultery is wrong, but lust is also wrong. Why? Because it treats the other person as an object. A disciple cannot say, "It's O.K. to look at pictures," or "No one was ever hurt by what I thought." Both we and the other person are hurt when we treat that person as an object. The true disciple is one who separates himself or herself from whatever causes us to sin.

In Matthew 5:31-32 again, the focus is on the harm done to the neighbor. The divorced woman, in principle, is still the wife of her husband. If she marries again, she becomes an adulteress. This principle also causes the next man who marries her to commit adultery. To prevent harm to the neighbor, the first husband should never divorce her in the first place. Given the prevalence of divorce in our society, almost every group will include at least one youth whose parents are divorced. Usually when we look at Jesus' sayings on divorce, we go to extremes: Either we take the statement literally and condemn everyone who is divorced, which could raise all kinds of negative feelings in our youth; or we explain the saying in such a way that we don't have to deal with it, which youth know is dishonest. Take the text seriously. What does it say about discipleship? In any divorce, no matter how healing it may be to individuals, a relationship is broken. We can acknowledge that brokenness without condemning the persons involved. We can also recognize the per-

✔ CHECK LIST

STARTING
❒ Half-sheets of paper.
❒ Prepare the sayings.

EXPLORING
❒ Paper, pencils, magazines, newspaper, glue, large sheet of paper.

CONNECTING
❒ Paper, pencils, hymnals.

OPTION 1
❒ Half-sheets of paper.
❒ Prepare the game.

OPTION 2
❒ Enlist a person.
❒ Costume.

OPTION 3
❒ Paper, pencils, chalkboard or large sheet of paper.

OPTION 4
❒ Paper, markers.

WHEN GOD SCRAMBLES YOUR PLANS

sonal pain and guilt over divorce for both youth and adults. Claim God's healing power for that pain in those you teach.

In Matthew 5:33-37, Jesus speaks against gradations in oaths. Some believed that a few oaths were more binding than others because of the person or place used in swearing. The disciple, Jesus says, lives on honor and trustworthiness. The word of a disciple is good by itself. This is an important part of discipleship in an age when words are easy to utter and mean so little.

Matthew 5:38-40 relates to our society today. We don't get mad, we get even. The disciple, Jesus says, doesn't get even but endures evil. In the Near East in Jesus' day, the most insulting blow was a backhanded slap to the right cheek. So to say that if we're struck on one cheek, we should turn the other also, means that we accept a deadly insult in silence. The disciple, Jesus says, won't retaliate, but will bear the insult for the sake of Christ.

In the illustrations in Matthew 5:41-48, Jesus calls us to act opposite to what society says. Verse 43, with its reference to hating the enemy, refers to the way it is in the world. The disciple, Jesus says, can't distinguish between friends and enemies; all are neighbors. Live as the Father does, who sends rain—that is, love—on the just and unjust alike. Verses 46-47 have broad humor, based on the way it's done in the world. But disciples don't live on payoffs; they live on love. Love is a gift from the Father, the gift that makes us perfect.

These are hard sayings. In these hard sayings, we admit we can't do that. But God's grace comes to us and makes us perfect to live a life of radical discipleship. Youth can make a choice to be different for the sake of God. The choice is genuine. The choice is heroic. And when we offer youth the chance to make heroic choices, they often choose a more radical form of discipleship than we would anticipate.

 # ✔CHECK IN

STARTING

Say What?

PREPARATION: Write one half of each saying on a half-sheet of paper. The slash (/) shows where to divide the saying. The sayings are: *Take charge / of your life; Everybody's / doing it; Plan / ahead; Greed / is good; Bigger / is better; Respect / yourself; Get outa / my face!; Do what you have / to do to survive; If it feels good / do it; Sexy / sells; Watch out / for number one.* If you have more than 22 youth, prepare more sayings.

Give each youth half a saying and tell them to find their match. Once youth match up, direct them to sit down and decide what their saying means. Call for saying and explanation. Say: **These statements express the values of some people in society. Today we'll see how they stack up to the values of Jesus.**

OPTION 1

If You Say So!

Select ten sayings under STARTING and prepare them as suggested. Turn the half-sheets of paper over, shuffle them, and number the backs from one to twenty. Place the numbered sides up on the floor. Divide youth into two teams to play Concentration: Let one team select two numbers. Turn over these sheets. If they form the correct saying, that team continues to select numbers, two at a time. If there is no match, the other team chooses two numbers. Play until all sayings are shown. The team with the most matches wins.

OPTION 2

Tough Teachings

If you have a small group, use this option. Recruit a youth or worker to play Jesus. Use a costume, if possible. Ask this person to read Matthew 5:21-48 aloud to youth. Following the reading, ask the group to help you list the main points of Jesus' message. Be sure that all the themes are included—murder, adultery, divorce, swearing falsely, getting even, loving one's neighbor.

Ask:
▼ **As you hear this portion of the Sermon on the Mount, which of Jesus' teachings seem harsh to you?**
▼ **Why is it difficult to hear Jesus' words about anger? divorce? lust?**

EXPLORING

A Modern-Day Viewpoint

Divide youth into six groups and assign each group one of the following Scriptures:

Matthew 5:21-26	Matthew 5:27-30
Matthew 5:31-32	Matthew 5:33-37
Matthew 5:38-42	Matthew 5:43-48

Ask each group to read their assigned passages and to rewrite them in current language, the language youth use every day. Bring the groups together to present their rewritten texts.

Then ask:
▼ How did Jesus turn the conventional wisdom upside down?
▼ Why are Jesus' sayings difficult to live by?

The Law of Love

Direct youth to look back through Matthew 5:21-48 and call out words that relate to the unusual love that Jesus taught. After youth have shared their words, say: **Christian love is not dependent on feelings and has nothing to do with whether or not we even like our neighbors.**

Ask:
▼ How can you love someone you don't like?

Give each youth a magazine or newspaper. Ask them to search for a word, phrase, or picture that illustrates Jesus' law of love. Invite each to glue or tape the picture to a large sheet of paper. Ask each of them to explain why he or she chose the picture and how it illustrates Jesus' law of love.

OPTION 2 *(Continued)*
▼ In verses 33-37, what does Jesus mean by swearing? Why is this wrong?
▼ Should we always turn the other cheek (vv. 38-40)?
▼ Can you think of a situation where this response may not be appropriate?
▼ How is it possible to love our enemies (vv. 43-47)?
▼ What do you think Jesus means when he says, "Be perfect . . . as your heavenly Father is perfect"?
▼ What is it that makes Jesus' teachings particularly difficult to hear and accept?

OPTION 3

Before and After

If you have a large group use this option. Divide the group into six groups and assign each group one of the following Scriptures:

Matthew 5:21-26
Matthew 5:27-30
Matthew 5:31-32
Matthew 5:33-37
Matthew 5:38-42
Matthew 5:43-48

Ask each group to prepare a before-and-after skit that demonstrates the difference between the old law and Christ's new way of living. Allow 5-8 minutes for preparation. Invite the groups to present their skits.

Then ask:
▼ What makes Jesus' new commandments radical?
▼ In what ways are Jesus' new commandments more loving or healing than the conventional religious wisdom?
▼ What does Jesus' law of love mean for discipleship?

CONNECTING

Difficult Issues

Ask youth to decide how much they struggle with the difficult issues listed here. Hand out paper and pencils. Direct youth to write these issues on their papers as you list them on a chalkboard or large sheet of paper: *murder; anger; reconciling with someone with whom I have argued; sexual sin; lust; divorce; keeping my word; getting even; loving friends; loving enemies.* Say: **Rank how much you struggle with each issue by writing a number between 1 and 10 beside each issue, with 1 representing "no struggle" and 10 representing "constant struggle."**

Divide the assembly into small groups of two or three youth to talk about how they ranked each issue. Bring the group together. Invite them to consider each issue raised in the Scripture.

Ask:
▼ What behavior is described in the Old Testament laws about murder? adultery?
▼ How difficult is it to obey the Old Testament laws that Jesus described in Scripture?
▼ Is the law a problem for you?
▼ Are any of these issues ones that could cause you harm? how?
▼ Is the new way of love (no anger, no name calling, no lusting) more of a problem for you? why? why not?
▼ How do you feel about Jesus' way?
▼ In what sense would Jesus' way bring love or healing to our world?

Sing of Grace

Direct youth to look through a hymnal for hymns that include the word "grace." Read or sing a few of these hymns.

Ask:
▼ What does grace mean in the context of these hymns?

Say: **We're not perfect! It's hard to live by God's standards. That's where grace comes in. We can't live up to God's standards on our own. We don't deserve God's love, but through Jesus Christ, we are forgiven, accepted, and told to be all we were created to be.**

✔ CHECK OUT

If I live as a disciple of Christ and not a teenager at risk, the world is one person closer to peace.

OPTION 4

Difficult Statements

Hand out paper and markers. Tell youth to write a large *A* on one side of the paper and a large *D* on the other side of the paper. Explain that you will read a statement and they are to hold up the *A* side of the paper if they agree or the *D* side of the paper if they disagree. After each statement use the discussion questions. The statements are:

> The sin of anger is different from the emotion of anger.
>
> It's O.K. to look at magazines picturing nudes because no one is ever hurt by that.
>
> All divorce is wrong.
>
> A Christian does not get even, but endures evil.
>
> You must stand up for yourself.
>
> Living as a Christian is hard to do.

Then ask of each statement:
▼ Why did you agree or disagree with the statement?
▼ Does this statement place you at risk? how?
▼ Would Jesus agree or disagree with the statement? Why do you think so?

10. RUNAWAY!

Genesis 28:10-15

Considering the cost of running away.

✔ CHECK UP!

Jacob and Esau were twins. Esau was firstborn by a few minutes, so he inherited everything. Jacob didn't like that. When they were teenagers, probably, Jacob tricked Esau into giving up his legal rights as firstborn for a dish of lentil stew. Later, when their father was blind and dying, Jacob lied to him to get the blessing. Finally, Esau caught on. Jacob had cheated him out of everything he was to inherit. Being a man of action, Esau swore revenge, threatening to kill that cheating brother of his. So Jacob fled for his life. Jacob chose his destiny and that destiny drove him into a far country. He left behind an angry, vengeful brother.

Then grace enters. First, God appears at a time and place when meeting God was probably the last thing on Jacob's mind. Jacob was just trying to get away from Esau. The story reminds us that God meets us in amazing ways. This meeting happens in a dream. Jacob's waking world is one of fear, loneliness, and lostness. The dream brings him an alternative, a future with God. The dream is about connections between heaven and earth. The physical connection reminds Jacob that there is more to his life than survival. God is relevant to him even in his terror and lostness. The ramp is crowded with angels, the royal messengers of God, who go up and down carrying out God's will. Their coming and going shows that God's will is at work. Terror is being overcome. God is transforming human reality.

Verse 15 goes beyond what God promised Abraham and Isaac. Jacob is a special case, a man of conflict who lives in danger because of his own nature. Verse 15 has three parts to this special promise. First, "I am with you," states God's commitment. Youth in their own loneliness and fear know that if someone goes with them, things will be different. They are not alone. God is willing to go with Jacob. Second, God will protect Jacob wherever he goes, guaranteeing Jacob life. Jacob may be in danger, but God will keep him safe. Finally, there will be a homecoming, the one Jacob thought would never be possible. Humanly speaking, Jacob was right, but with God the impossible can happen. God's grace works to heal interpersonal relationships. For teens, particularly younger teens, this is a powerful word. Broken relationships feel like the end of the world, particularly when the brokenness comes from something a

✔ CHECK LIST

EXPLORING
❏ Bring newspapers, magazines, scissors, glue sticks, markers, large sheets of newsprint.

CONNECTING
❏ Construction paper strips, markers.
❏ Hymnals.

OPTION 1
❏ Construction paper strips, markers.

OPTION 2
❏ Construction paper strips, markers.

OPTION 3
❏ "Footprints" story.

youth has done. We can't forgive ourselves, and we're sure we can never be forgiven. We think we'll never be together again. But God's grace works in those relationships; we can be reconciled. That is new life.

Then, Jacob wakes up and faces an all-too-human dilemma. Jacob realizes that God has broken in on his life. "Surely the LORD is in this place—and I did not know it!" And he was afraid. And if you are like Jacob, with a track record of deceit, fear is not a bad reaction when you come in contact with the holy God.

 CHECK IN

STARTING

I Want to Run Away

Ask:
▼ Have you ever wanted to run away?
▼ What were the circumstances?
▼ Do you know someone who has run away?
▼ What happened?

Encourage youth to listen to each story. After reading each story,

Ask:
▼ Why did this teenager run away?
▼ How can the situation be fixed?

The stories are:

> Robin wanted more freedom. She thought her parents were entirely too strict. They just wouldn't let her do anything. Every time Robin tried to get more freedom it resulted in a fight. Her little brother told his friends that their home had turned into a war zone. One night after a really big fight, Robin sneaked out of the house. She walked a few blocks to a friend's house. Robin's parents weren't sure what to do. They talked to Robin's friend's parents but did not contact Robin directly. They kept track of how Robin was doing but did not try to force her to come home.

OPTION 1

Runaway Bumper Sticker

Ask:
▼ What are some of the bumper stickers you've seen recently?
▼ Do you think people really believe the message they put on their cars?

Hand out wide strips of colored construction paper and markers. Tell youth to write a bumper sticker for someone who wants to run away. After youth have made their bumper stickers, call on each to share. Say: **The runaway we'll study today needed a runaway bumper sticker for his camel!**

> Jeff was getting a lot of pressure from his parents. He fantasized all the time about running away but never did. Instead, Jeff ran away emotionally. Jeff stayed at home, but had no real relationship with his parents. Gradually he became more and more distant and had less and less to do with his parents.

EXPLORING

Jacob's Ladder Skit

Briefly share Jacob's background as told in Genesis 25:23–28:5. Explain why Jacob ran away. Form several small teams of youth. Ask each team to create a skit based on the story in Genesis 28:10-17. Say: **Consider ways that God might communicate with us today. Design a skit to include these modern techniques of communication. Remember, there are many ways to look at the story. Feel free to interpret the text however you wish.**

Give teams time to prepare their skits. Call on each team to perform its skit. Encourage enthusiasm and laughter. After the skits, discuss the different ways that God communicates with people in the Bible and today—through dreams, prayer, other people, Scripture, and worship. Help youth understand that God uses a variety of communication forms to get people's attention.

A Promise Collage

To emphasize the amazing promises God made to Jacob, let youth make a promise collage. Have youth form groups of three. Give each group a piece of newsprint, a glue stick, a pair of scissors, markers and pens, newspapers, and some magazines. Ask each group to reread Genesis 28:10-17 to find all the promises that God gives to Jacob, and to list these on the newsprint.

Ask the groups to reflect on the promises that God gave to Jacob at Bethel. Have them think about how some of these promises may apply to their lives today, and ask them to write these ideas on the newsprint. Then ask each group to create a *Collage of Promises* by looking for words or pictures in the newspapers and magazines that express some of these promises to Jacob and to us. They may also write their own words or draw their own pictures, if they want. Tell volunteers from each group to explain their collages. Hang the collages on a wall in your meeting room to remind youth of the promises that God has given us.

CONNECTING

Promise Bumper Stickers

Ask youth to make a bumper sticker. Suggest they use the promises in the Scripture that relate to a problem that makes them want to run away. For example, if a youth feels deserted because of a family breakup, what promise would be meaningful? After youth share their bumper-sticker promises,

Ask:
▼ How effective is running away from a problem?
▼ In order to get along in life, what do you have to do with difficult relationships or events?
▼ How can you learn to handle these more effectively?
▼ Where does God fit into the process of staying?

Jacob's Ladder Song

Lead your youth in singing "Jacob's Ladder." If youth don't know the song, look it up in a hymnal or chorus book from your church.

OPTION 2

Godly Bumper Stickers

Ask a youth to read Genesis 28:10-17 aloud to the others.

Ask:
▼ On the basis of this story, do you think God's love for us depends on our love for God?
▼ At what times in your life have you felt most alone? most afraid?
▼ At what times in your life have you felt God's presence most strongly?
▼ If you were Jacob, how would you have felt after this experience?

Hand out large strips of colored construction paper and markers. Direct youth to create a bumper sticker slogan that Jacob might need.

OPTION 3

Footprints

Read the following story to youth. Say: **Even when we are not faithful, God remains faithful. Even when it feels that God is not with us, we may trust in God's promise to be with us. Just as God was with Jacob, who certainly was not a stellar example of morality, so God will be with us even when we make mistakes and hurt ourselves, other people, or God. This is God's gift; this is grace. It is something that we do not deserve and cannot earn.**

✔ CHECK OUT

What direction are you running—away from God, away from family, away from circumstances, or toward God and those who want to help?

FOOTPRINTS

One night a man had a dream. He dreamed he was walking along the beach with the Lord. Across the sky flashed scenes from his life. Each scene, he noticed, had two sets of footprints in the sand; one belonging to him, and the other to the Lord.

When the last scene of his life flashed before him, he looked back at the footprints in the sand. He noticed that many times along the path of his life there was only one set of footprints. He also noticed that it happened at the very lowest and saddest times in his life.

This really bothered him and he questioned the Lord about it.

"Lord, you said that once I decided to follow you, you'd walk with me all the way. But I have noticed that during the most troublesome times in my life, there has been only one set of footprints. I don't understand why, when I needed you most, you would leave me."

The Lord replied, "My precious, precious child, I love you and I would never leave you. During your times of trial and suffering, when you see only one set of footprints, it was then that I carried you."

(Author Unknown)

11. SEX—THE GOOD, THE BAD, AND THE UGLY

2 Samuel 12:1-15

Recognizing the consequences and effects of sexual activity outside of marriage.

✔ CHECK UP!

Through the ages, rulers of countries have usually wielded a great deal of power over the inhabitants. Israel was no exception. The prophet Samuel warned Israel that a monarchy would bring with it a lack of freedom and an abuse of power (1 Sam. 8:10-18).

The story of David and Bathsheba, which precedes the scripture for this lesson, is a perfect example of this abuse of power and position. David had it all—power, wealth, respect, God's promise of a glorious future, numerous wives and children, a nice house—everything, except Bathsheba, another man's wife. So David took her too. When Bathsheba found out that she was going to have David's child, he devised a scheme to make it seem as if Bathsheba's husband, Uriah the soldier, might be responsible for the pregnancy. When this plan didn't work, David arranged for Uriah to be killed in battle, after which he took Bathsheba as another wife. The story of David and Bathsheba reveals the depths to which David was capable of sinking.

For all the positive images of David as the shepherd boy or the brave young man who defeats Goliath, this story portrays an unscrupulous, even murderous David, who selfishly destroys a family and a human life to get what he wants.

The ultimate lesson here is that David gets caught and is held accountable, showing that even a king is not above God's laws. The prophet Nathan confronts David with a parable that mirrors David's sin. David's passionate demand for justice in the matter traps him. Once David realizes his guilt, God quickly forgives him, although David must still face the costly consequences. (Second Samuel 12:14 tells us that the baby to be born to Bathsheba will not live.)

Most youth can recognize the need for justice in a given situation. However, they may find it easier to identify with Nathan's role than to examine their own actions that may require confession and forgiveness. Although getting caught or being exposed for who we really are may come as a shock, it usually means that we finally have to face the consequences of our actions. One of the first things we must do in order to try to make amends for the wrongdoing is to admit our mistake or our sin—and to admit it to the One we've sinned against. Our Christian faith tells us that God is always aware of our sins, and yet we are to confess our sin to God, to "come

✔ CHECK LIST

STARTING
❏ Large sheets of paper, markers.

EXPLORING
❏ Prepare the game sheet.
❏ Chalkboard.

CONNECTING
❏ Pencils, paper, chalkboard or butcher paper and markers.

OPTION 2
❏ Prepare two poster-board-sized graffiti sheets.
❏ Markers.

OPTION 3
❏ Enlist a youth.

OPTION 4
❏ Do background check.

clean," and to once again be a truthful and honorable person. The Good News is that just as God forgave David when he admitted his sin, God's forgiveness in Jesus Christ is available for every one of us, as well.

 **CHECK IN**

STARTING

Headline News

Hand out large sheets of paper and markers. Tell youth to use large letters to write the worst possible headline about themselves that they can create. (Be sure youth write imaginary headlines about themselves!) As youth share their headlines,

Ask:
▼ How would you feel if you saw this headline about you in our local newspaper?
▼ How do you suppose your friends would respond to your headline news?
▼ How would your parents or other family members respond?
▼ How would your church respond to the news?

Say: **As we study David today, think about the headlines that David might have seen in the "Jerusalem Journal."**

EXPLORING

King David, This Is Your Life!

PREPARATION: Write each of the following events and Bible references on separate half-sheets of paper: *David anointed by Samuel to be king (1 Sam. 16:10-13); David killed Goliath (1 Sam. 17:41-50); David anointed king of Judah (2 Sam. 5:3-4); David's adultery with Bathsheba (2 Sam. 11:1-26); first son of David and Bathsheba died (2 Sam. 12:13-18a); David and Bathsheba's son Solomon was born (2 Sam. 12:24); David's sons fight one another (2 Sam. 13:30-33); David's son Absalom murdered (2 Sam. 18:9-15); David's son Adonijah rebelled (1 Kings 1:5); Solomon named king of Israel (1 Kings 1:29-30, 38-40).* Take the half-sheets of paper and mix them up. Turn to the blank side of the papers and number them from 1 to 20.

Place the papers, numbered-side up, on the floor. Divide youth into two teams. Play Concentration using these rules:

1. Teams must match the event to the correct Scripture.
2. Each team has 30 seconds to make a match, including looking up the Scripture.
3. If a match is made, the team can play again.
4. If a team does not make a match, turn the sheets over and let the other team try.
5. The team with the most matches wins.

OPTION 1
A New, Old Story
Read the following story aloud.

Once upon a time there were two teenagers—one was well off (we'll call him the rich dude), the other was poor (we'll call him the poor dude). The rich dude had a brand new, red sports car with all the latest equipment. The poor dude drove an older car with an engine that he had rebuilt. One night the two guys decided to double date to a lake party. Because it was down a really dusty back road, the rich dude didn't want to get his car dirty. So, the two couples rode to the lake in the older car with the rebuilt engine. During the evening, the rich dude and his date had a fight. The rich dude asked the poor dude for the keys to the old car, "to just get away and get some fresh air." The poor dude reluctantly gave him the keys. Driving too fast on the dark, dirt roads, the rich dude ran the car into a tree. Although he wasn't hurt, the car was totaled. The rich dude walked to a service station, called his dad, and never went back to tell his date or the poor dude what had happened.

Ask:
▼ How would you feel if you were the poor dude?
▼ Why would the rich dude do something like this?
▼ What do you think should happen?

Say: **Remember this story as you study today's Bible story. It may sound familiar.**

Say: **These are key events in the life of King David. Even though David was king, he sinned. David had an affair with Bathsheba. He ordered her husband killed to cover up his own sin. His sin affected other members of his family. Let's look at what happened.** Direct a youth to read the Scripture, then ask the related questions.

2 Samuel 12:1-6
Was David's sentence on the rich man just?
Why was David angry about what the man had done?

2 Samuel 12:7-12
How did Nathan catch David by surprise?
Why was God angry with David?

2 Samuel 12:13-15
David was the king. What were some other choices he had about how to respond to Nathan?
What did he really do?

Truth and Consequences

Read over 2 Samuel 12:10-15. Come up with a list of consequences of David's actions (examples: *sword in his house, trouble within his house, child dies, wives taken by neighbors, adultery of wives known by everyone*). Write this list on the chalkboard. Talk about what each item on your list might mean (examples: *sword—violence, murder; trouble—rebellion against him*).

Mark your list with a check (✔) beside the consequences that might have arisen from the lack of respect for marriage seen in David's action. Put an asterisk (*) beside those that might occur because the children saw their father break rules. Say: **David was forgiven, but he could not avoid the consequences of his sin.**

Ask:
▼ **What are the consequences of sexual sin today?**

List these as youth call them out. Compare the consequences on the two lists.

Ask:
▼ **Do any of the consequences on David's list occur today?**
▼ **How could the emotional consequences be similar?**

OPTION 2
Alternative Ending

Divide the group into teams of four to five persons. Tell them what happens in 2 Samuel 12:1-6, where Nathan tells David about the rich man and poor man and the lamb, ending with, "You are the man!" Have each team write what they think happened next (an alternative ending for the story in 2 Samuel 12).

After five minutes, have the teams read aloud what they wrote. Then, turn together to 2 Samuel 12:7-12. Read what actually happened.

Ask:
▼ **Was David off the hook?**
▼ **What was different between your endings and what actually happened?**
▼ **Why do you think it happened that way?**

CONNECTING

Dating Do's and Don'ts

Give youth pencils and paper. Tell them to list ten behaviors related to dating. Compile their lists on a chalkboard. Lead the group to decide which behaviors are acceptable on a first date (make these *FD*), a third date (*TD*), a long relationship (*LD*).

Ask:
▼ **Which sexual behaviors are risky?** (Mark these with an R.)
▼ **Which sexual behaviors are wrong outside of marriage?** (Mark these with W.)

If you teach younger youth, you may prefer to ask:

▼ **What dating behavior is risky?**
▼ **What dating behavior is wrong?**

   Say: **God made sex good, but God made it to be shared within the deep commitment of marriage.** Read Genesis 1:27-31; 2:24.

A Prayer for Forgiveness

Say: **Psalm 51 is a prayer of David. It was written after David's confrontation with Nathan. In the prayer, David expressed his guilt and also his desperate need to be forgiven and given a fresh start.** Invite one of the youth to read Psalm 51 as a closing prayer. Then encourage the group to say or shout: **Thanks be to God.**

 # CHECK OUT

Why do we still have to live with the consequences after God has forgiven us?

OPTION 3

Trash the Sin

Distribute pencils and paper. Invite each person to write a note to God about something he or she has done wrong, which has hurt God and other people. Hold the trash bag open. Invite each person to trash his or her sins and to claim a fresh start. After you have collected all the papers, seal the trash bag.
Say: **God is gracious. Just as we have sealed the past into this bag, God has sealed the past off from the rest of our lives. As we have stated our desire to change, God has given us strength and courage to live a new and different way. Know that God loves you and has forgiven you.**

OPTION 4

A Song of Forgiveness

Look for a contemporary Christian song that deals with forgiveness. Play the song as youth listen. Urge them to silently ask for God's forgiveness for any sin they have in their lives.

12. SURVIVING A VIOLENT WORLD

2 Kings 16:1-5; Isaiah 7:1-7, 10-16

Determining who can help youth deal with violence in their lives.

✔ CHECK UP!

During this period of time, Assyria dominated the Middle East, in terms of power and threat. Tribute was demanded from most nations, including Israel and Syria. Isaiah's prophetic warnings were validated when a Syro-Israelite alliance came about in 735 B.C. Hoping for a successful rebellion against the powerful Assyrians, Israel and Syria formed a military coalition made up of the armies of the smaller nations. Judah's King Ahaz refused to join. In retaliation, Israel and Syria besieged Jerusalem from 734 to 732 B.C.

King Ahaz saw danger all around him and little hope of returning to the peaceful world for which he longed. He had come to power at a difficult time in Judah's history. A weak king in the best of times, King Ahaz panicked at the arrival of invading armies on Judah's soil. The Scripture tells us just how frightened Ahaz was: He "shook as the trees of the forest shake before the wind" (Isa. 7:2).

In desperation, Ahaz reverted to an old pagan rite. He burned his son as an offering in the valley of Hinnom, outside the city (2 Kings 16:3; 2 Chron. 28:3). Ahaz hoped that his brutal personal sacrifice would soften God's anger and wrath.

The king could choose to accept defeat at the hands of his enemies or ask other enemies for help. His city was besieged; food and supplies were low. One day, Ahaz went to inspect the city's water supplies, an essential if Jerusalem was to withstand a siege. There he met the prophet Isaiah and Isaiah's son Shear-jashub (meaning "a remnant shall return" or "only a remnant shall return"). This was not chance meeting, for God had sent Isaiah to help Ahaz. The prophet's advice to Ahaz was simple: Isaiah told him not to become dependent on foreign aid, or to remain powerless or hopeless. In a play on words (both in Hebrew and in English), Isaiah affirmed that the greatest source of help in times of trouble is trust in God: "If you do not stand firm in faith, / you shall not stand at all" (Isa. 7:9b). Isaiah insisted that Ahaz must seek divine help to relieve besieged Jerusalem. The prophet used the image of "smoldering stumps" (v. 4) to describe his belief that the destructive power of Israel and Syria was already being extinguished. Isaiah declared that foreign domination was on the way out (vv. 15-16).

Isaiah's advice was clear. He urged King Ahaz to seek God's help. He believed that God was using other nations to punish Judah

✔ CHECK LIST

STARTING
❑ Art supplies like pieces of wire, modeling clay, paper, markers.

EXPLORING
❑ Chalkboard, large sheets of paper, markers, Bible atlas.
❑ Prepare case studies, large index cards.

CONNECTING
❑ Set up three study stops: (Stop 1) Bibles, hymnals, prayers typed on index cards; (Stop 2) Brochures from local help groups; (Stop 3) Make sign pencils, paper.

OPTION 1
❑ Newspapers.

OPTION 2
❑ Invite guest or panel.

OPTION 3
❑ Paper, pencils.

because of its unfaithfulness. The siege of Jerusalem was part of the judgment of Judah. Contrary to what seemed likely, however, Isaiah believed that Assyria's power would ebb, and the prosperity would return to Judah (9:1-7). Why? Although Judah had not faithfully kept the commands of God, and, therefore, deserved God's wrath, God would remain faithful. The days of punishment would eventually end.

Youth experience danger in a variety of ways. In a 1992 Gallup study of youth, 24 percent of the teens reported that they feared for their safety while at school (up from 18 percent in 1977). One has only to watch or read the news to learn of teenagers who experience some form of violent behavior not only in schools, but also within their families, in a dating relationship, or in some other setting.

# CHECK IN

STARTING

Symbols of Violence

As the youth arrive, invite them to use the art supplies to create a symbol of violence. Have the teens work alone or in small groups. When everyone has finished, invite the youth to explain their creations to the whole group.

Ask:
▼ Why did you choose to portray that particular symbol of danger or violence?
▼ What are some other symbols of danger or violence?
▼ How does our society react to or view danger? violence?
▼ How has violence become such a daily part of our society that we assume nothing can be done about it?
▼ Do we thrive on danger or violence?
▼ What are some Christian responses to danger or violence?

Explain that during this study youth will examine violence and look for ways to find help in dealing with violence.

EXPLORING

A Time Line of Fear

Direct one youth to read 2 Kings 16:1-5 aloud. Ask youth to identify the main people in the story (*Ahaz, king of Judah; Rezin, king of Aram; Pekah, king of Israel*). Write these names on a chalkboard. Ask youth to identify the events (*Ahaz became king, Ahaz didn't follow God, Ahaz sacrificed his son by burning him, Rezin and Pekah formed alliance to attack Jerusalem in Judah, Jerusalem was under siege*) as someone writes these on the chalkboard. Use a Bible atlas map to show youth the small size of Judah and the larger Israel.

Direct another youth to read Isaiah 7:1-7 aloud. Ask youth to name any additional people mentioned in this story (*prophet Isaiah, his son Shear-jashub*). Add any other elements to the story (*God told Isaiah to go to Ahaz with a message; Isaiah delivered message*

OPTION 1

Violent News

Hand out recent newspapers. Tell youth to find and tear out an example of violence in the news. Remind them to look on the theater page, too. Call on each youth to share data about the violent news story (or advertisement). Ask the questions under "Symbols of Violence."

OPTION 2

Resource People

Invite a guest (or a panel of people) who can offer practical ideas for getting along in a violent world. For example, call your rape counseling center and ask for a Christian rape counselor. Invite a law officer, a psychologist, your minister, or a perceptive schoolteacher. Prepare a few questions for the person (panel), but encourage youth to ask their questions, too.

at the pool outside Jerusalem; God's message involved assurance of victory if Ahaz followed God).

Ask a third youth to read Isaiah 7:10-16. Add any new names *(Immanuel).* Add other events *(prophecy of Messiah, land taken from Israel and Aram).* Hand out long strips of paper and markers. Working in teams of four or five, tell youth to create a time line of events based on the information on the chalkboard and in the Bible. After several minutes, call on youth to share their time line.

Ask:
▼ **How do you think Ahaz felt being approached by God's prophet Isaiah?**
▼ **Why would Ahaz listen to this prophet if he hadn't been following God?**
▼ **Why did Ahaz not follow Isaiah?**

Study in Danger

PREPARATION: Write or type the following case studies on cards:

● The last day of school had arrived and Thom was leaving the building. As he came around the corner of the parking lot, a speeding car crammed with kids squealed its tires. He recognized the teens; in fact, just the other day he had gotten into an argument with one of them. Suddenly a hand darted out the open window of the car. The hand held a weapon. Before Thom had time to react, he heard a gunshot. Fortunately the bullet missed Thom; but it struck and seriously injured a seventh-grader standing on the corner, waiting for her mom to pick her up.

● Fawn, an attractive teenager of sixteen, was working the night shift at the local coffee shop. She had just waited on two men and was counting the minutes until they would finish their meal and leave. Earlier when Fawn had gone to these customers' table with their food, one of the men had grinned and said, "That looks good enough to eat! But you look even better, Honey!" The man attempted to put his arm around Fawn's waist, but she pulled away.

● Joan had taught English for nearly twenty years. She was a good teacher and most of the kids liked her, even though she was strict. As exam time drew near, there were a couple of students in one of Joan's classes who were in danger of failing the course. If these seniors did not get a passing grade, neither would receive a high school diploma. Exam day rolled around, and Joan proceeded to distribute the tests. As she approached the desk of one of the students who was having difficulty, he grabbed Joan around the collar. "I'd better make it," he snarled. Another student, seeing what had happened, stood up and wedged himself between his classmate and the teacher.

● This wasn't the first time Sean had seen black-and-blue marks on his mother's face and arms. Nor was this the first time he had heard cries in the middle of the night. Sean didn't know what to do. The last time he said something his dad had thrown him against the wall and had threatened to beat him up if he ever interfered again. Sean was afraid to do anything—and afraid that if he didn't someone was going to get killed.

Hand out the case studies. Suggest youth work in four teams. If youth enjoy roleplay, suggest they act out a response. Tell teams to be prepared to share the facts about their studies and to suggest endings. After the enactment or discussion of each case study,

Ask:

▼ *Are situations like this one fairly common in our society? In our community?*

▼ *How might you feel if you were the main character in this particular case study?*

▼ *What is at least one possible Christian response to this situation or a similar one?*

▼ *What tactics or behavior might Christians want to avoid as they respond to situations involving danger or violence?*

▼ *How do these case studies compare to the Scripture we studied?*

CONNECTING
"Sources of Help" Study Stops

PREPARATION: Set up the following three Study Stops:
1) On a table display several Bibles, hymnals, devotional guides, and prayers typed on index cards. Mark references in each print resource that relate to finding help when confronted by danger. Research potential Bible passages using a concordance. Among other helpful passages, consider Psalm 23:1-6; 2 Timothy 4:1-2, 16-18; 1 John 4:18-21. Locate hymns and prayers that relate to peace and healing.
2) Contact a local department of human services, your minister, or a local library to research organizations in the immediate area that can be of service to youth as they encounter violence. Suggestions might include self-help groups such as Alanon (for family members of alcoholics) or Alateen (for teenage alcoholics and teen family members of alcoholics). Place brochures and other handouts on a table.
3) Set up a table with several chairs as an area where the youth can exchange information about sources of help. Put a sign on this table that reads, *Tell Me Where You Turn for Advice.*

Say: **King Ahaz got help from two sources: God and God's messenger Isaiah. Initially, neither source was on his list of possible ways to solve his dilemma. Youth who experience danger often do not know where to go for help.** Tell youth to go to one of the three study stops and find three sources of help when confronting danger or violence.

✔ CHECK OUT

Jesus Christ, whose birth was prophesied in Isaiah 7:14, said, "In the world you have tribulation, but take courage; I have overcome the world" (John 16:33b, NAS).

OPTION 3
My Time Line of Helpers

Give youth paper and pencils. Tell them to draw a line that represents their life. Instead of writing ages or events on the line, urge youth to write the names of people who have been helpful to them throughout their years. Suggest they circle the names of those who can be a source of help in times of violence. Remind youth of the power of God to prevail, even against the violence in this world.

13. THE COST OF REBELLION

2 Kings 17:6-18; Hosea 4:4, 9

Seeing how rebellion often brings consequences and penalties.

✔CHECK UP!

God's expectation for the people of Israel is described here. The rules were clear: Israel could survive and prosper, given one condition. The nation was unconditionally to obey God's commands. Although in later years the Jewish people lived by a strict and lengthy code of laws and regulations, God's primary command at this time was quite simple. Israel had been established as a nation under God. Therefore, Israel was to remain true to the worship of God alone, and to stay away from the worship practices of other faiths. Continuing in the footsteps of some of his predecessors, King Hoshea "did what was evil in the sight of the LORD" (2 Kings 17:2). Clearly, content and faithful leadership were still lacking in Israel. Under Hoshea, Israel continued to stray from God's path, as the people adopted alien religious beliefs and cultic practices.

Superstitious practices, adapted from various cults in the region, were added to Jewish worship. Cultic objects decorated the sites of Jewish worship. Ethical codes, long practiced by the Jews, were abandoned. Kings turned to foreign powers for help and neglected to seek divine guidance. A long line of mediocre leaders led to the eventual overthrow of the nation.

The wayward nation faced severe chastisement. Israel would be conquered and its population exiled. Second Kings 17:3 states that Shalmaneser V (727–722 B.C.) began the siege of Samaria; the conquest was complete under another leader, Sargon II (722–705 B.C.). Sargon deported as many as 27,290 Israelites to Assyria. Why did God allow this to happen? Verses 7-12 give a detailed explanation, beginning with "because the people of Israel had sinned against the LORD their God."

A succession of prophets had warned Israel of God's consuming anger. They had repeatedly emphasized God's primary requirement, namely to keep the covenant that had been made between Abraham and God. How did Israel respond? "They would not listen but were stubborn, as their ancestors had been, who did not believe in the LORD their God" (17:14). Destruction was the price that Israel had to pay for its arrogance and rebellion.

The book of 2 Kings tells how disaster finally came to the Israelite kingdoms through the people's failure to do as God had commanded. The nation of Israel was no more. Thousands of its citizens

WHEN GOD SCRAMBLES YOUR PLANS

became exiles in a foreign land, and many of the leaders were killed. Long years passed before Israel was restored.

Present-day Christians may have difficulty understanding how a loving God can appear to be vindictive. Why, we ask, would God so harshly chastise a beloved, though disobedient, nation? We must keep in mind that Israel was created by God for a purpose: to demonstrate its distinctive faith in God, while rejecting the religions of other cultures. Israel had a special task: to be a model of faithfulness. Successful completion of this task would result in divine blessing. Unfaithfulness would result in uncompromising punishment. From the beginning then, Israel was aware of the requirement to honor its allegiance to only one God.

Youth may find it difficult to digest and accept these concepts. Our culture often equates loyalty to one's nation with loyalty to God. Moreover, teens often resent and resist restrictions.

CHECK IN

STARTING

Ground Rules

PREPARATION: Print in bold letters the following statements (or others that may be relevant for the ages of your youth). Display the posters around the room:

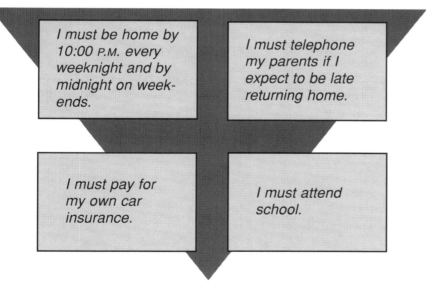

I must be home by 10:00 P.M. every weeknight and by midnight on weekends.

I must telephone my parents if I expect to be late returning home.

I must pay for my own car insurance.

I must attend school.

Read aloud each statement on the posters. Invite the youth briefly to discuss each statement, including the consequences of either adhering to, or breaking, each rule. If the group size is large enough, have the teens form small teams in order to discuss one or more rules and the ramifications. If time permits, discuss rules that the youth would like to live by other than the ones they usually have to follow. Say: **Today we're going to see how breaking the rules brings significant consequences.**

OPTION 1

Color the Rules

PREPARATION: Place the different-colored construction paper on the floor.

Ask:
▼ What rules do you live by?
▼ What rules do you have at home? at school? at church? in a club or sport to which you belong?
▼ Why do we have rules?

Direct youth to select a colored piece of paper that expresses their feelings about rules. After everyone has a color,

Ask:
▼ Why did you pick that color?
▼ How does that relate to your idea of rules?

EXPLORING

Breaking God's Rules

Briefly explain the Bible background under "Check Up!" Remind youth that God tried for many years to get the nation of Israel to return to God. Say: **All God required from these people was that they obey God. Instead, they chose to rebel.** Ask a youth to read 2 Kings 17:6-18. Tell youth to use their Bibles to identify all the ways the people rebelled. As youth name these ways, list them on a chalkboard. Direct youth to Exodus 20:2-17. After you read a broken rule from the list on the chalkboard, tell youth to look for the commandment that was broken. Still using the same list of broken rules, lead youth to name modern-day parallels of ways we rebel.

Ask:

▼ **What rules or restrictions does God place on believers today?**

▼ **How do you feel about these rules?**

God Is Love

PREPARATION: Write one of the following statements on each of nine cards:

- *God loves people no matter how they act.*
- *God punishes only Christians because they have promised to follow God only.*
- *God is not as interested in punishment today.*
- *Everything bad that happens to a Christian is caused by that person's rebellion.*
- *God longs for God's people to return and be faithful.*
- *God loves people so strongly that God's anger at them will eventually disappear.*
- *God is angry enough to punish the people for their disloyalty.*
- *Even though God is powerful enough to destroy the people for being disloyal, God loves them too much to do that.*
- *The people must change their ways or else.*

Make a ticktacktoe board on the floor with masking tape. On sheets of paper, draw 5 X's and 5 O's.

Direct a youth to read Hosea 4:4, 9.

Ask:

▼ **How does Hosea describe God?**

▼ **How does this view of God compare to the previous view?**

Place the nine cards on the floor. Divide youth into two teams. Give one team X's. Give the other team O's. Explain that the youth will play ticktacktoe. Each time a team turns over a card, they have to agree or disagree with the card's statement and give a reason to support their decision. Suggest they use today's Bible study as much as possible to support their decisions. After a winner is declared, read Hosea 4:4 again.

Ask:

▼ **What is God's message to you?**

OPTION 2

A Poem

Direct youth to 2 Kings 17:6-18. Share basic background information to this story. On the basis of these verses, tell youth to compose a haiku (a Japanese form of poetry that expresses one thought or emotion). A haiku poem contains seventeen syllables arranged in the following manner: five syllables in the first line; seven syllables in the second; five syllables in the last line. Here is one example of an appropriate haiku for this lesson:

Many times God speaks

to us in ways loud and clear.

But will we listen?

Have each person work alone or in teams to compose the poems. Invite volunteers to read their poems aloud.

CONNECTING

Rebellious Justin

Tell the following story in your own words.

> Justin began skipping school when he was in the sixth grade. Soon he started drinking and using other drugs. His relationship with his family began to deteriorate. Justin fought more and more often with his parents and his brother and sister. After a while the arguments became violent. One time Justin hit his mother and shoved his father. He also smashed some furniture and the TV. Justin's family began to be afraid of Justin and his outbursts. Then Justin stole money from his parents to pay for drugs. Justin was angry with his family for wanting him to go to school and church instead of hanging out on the streets and doing drugs. So Justin ran away from home.
>
> After he ran away, Justin had to steal to support himself. Justin's parents tried to find him. They still loved him and wanted him to come back.

After telling the story, ask:
- ▼ What do you think people said when Justin's parents kept trying to find him?
- ▼ If you were a parent to a rebellious child like Justin, what might you do?
- ▼ If you were Justin, what would you want to happen between you and your parents?
- ▼ What do you think God would do if God had a rebellious child like Justin?

"I Will Follow Him"

In the movie *Sister Act,* Delores stumbles onto the key of fitting into the convent where she is hiding from her former boyfriend. She teaches the nuns to sing with joy. Play "I Will Follow Him" from either the videotape or the audiotape or CD. Direct youth to listen for how vital it is to follow God.

# ✔ CHECK OUT

How does God's enduring love through Jesus Christ affect the rebellious and those who don't rebel?

OPTION 3

The Stupidest Thing

To help youth see how rebellion brings consequences, ask volunteers to complete this sentence:

The stupidest thing I ever did . . .

Also, ask:

The thing that got me in the most trouble was . . .

As several youth share, ask them also to share the consequences of their actions. (Be prepared for youth to share silly, laughable things, as well as serious events.)

14. THE MYTH OF LIFE WITHOUT BOUNDARIES

Genesis 3:1-7, 22-23

Understanding that living beyond boundaries can result in the loss of freedom.

✔ CHECK UP!

We are created with freedom to choose. Genesis 2 is a discussion of how God intended life to be. Human beings were given freedom and limits, leaving us with many choices within certain perimeters. We were given a vocation, work to do, as part of the human condition. Beginning in chapter 3 the story changes dramatically. We might give a new title to this part of the drama, calling it "Disobedience in the Garden."

Let's dispel several misconceptions right at the beginning. There is a great myth that the woman Eve is a seductive temptress. Eve gave the fruit to her husband who took it and ate it. That is all the narrative says. The myth arises from our culture, not from the Bible. Other myths surround the serpent, a creature that is made more crafty by the Lord than any other wild animal. The serpent enters the story as a foil for asking questions of the human beings. With this new conversation of questioning comes the realization that the human beings are no longer engaged in talking to God or with God, but about God. The relationship that had been obedience and trust in chapter 2 is now ignored for speculation about God. The serpent scrutinizes a prohibition given by God. His comment, "You will not die," turns the prohibition into an option. As the talk continues we realize that it serves to avoid the claims of God rather than to serve the claims of God. The permission given by God to eat of the fruit of all the trees except one, is now changed into a barrier to be overcome.

Thinking of the good-tasting fruit, the beauty of the fruit, and her desire to be wise, Eve acts on her own self-centered thoughts and takes the fruit. The woman and man think only of themselves and break the boundaries set up for them by God. What the couple does is what youth do in similar situations. Number one, they rationalize. Number two, they think they know better than God. And number three, finally, at the end of the story when they get caught, they pass the buck and blame someone else for the problem. The couple stands exposed. They are now beyond previously safe boundaries. They have taken life into their own hands. Their simple act of disobedience results in nothing good. They gain knowledge, but it centers in the loss of innocence. They experience shame at the nakedness of their God-given bodies. They experience estrange-

✔ CHECK LIST

EXPLORING
❏ Bible.

OPTION 1
❏ Paper, markers, colored pencils.

OPTION 2
❏ Instant camera, film.

OPTION 3
❏ Graph paper, pencils.

OPTION 4
❏ Prepare slips of paper, paper bag.

WHEN GOD SCRAMBLES YOUR PLANS

ment from one another, from the world, and from God. They have focused completely on themselves, their new freedom, and the terror that comes with it. Many youth find themselves in this situation. They are confused about their bodies, focused on themselves, and afraid of their freedom. The story reminds us that God gives us freedom to choose, but within certain boundaries. Those boundaries offer protection and liberty to live in faithfulness with God and with one another.

Each new stage in life needs boundaries. God gives us choices within certain prohibitions so that we may be focused on our call to be faithful disciples.

 # CHECK IN

STARTING

Greater Freedom
Invite the youth to dream aloud about what it would be like to enjoy greater freedom in each of the following areas:

freedom to worship or not to worship God
freedom to say what they want to say
freedom to buy what they want to buy
freedom to stay out as late as they want
freedom to drive as fast as they want
freedom to choose their friends
freedom to do what they want when they want.

Have youth consider what it would be like to have less freedom in each area.

Ask:
▼ **Are there areas in which you would prefer less freedom rather than more? why? why not?**
▼ **In what ways is complete freedom good? bad?**
▼ **Which kinds of freedom are of greater value to you?**
▼ **Which are of lesser value?**

EXPLORING

Interesting Perspectives
Divide youth into four groups; give each group at least one Bible. Instruct all the groups to read Genesis 3:1-7. Then, invite one group to retell the story from Adam's perspective, one from Eve's perspective, one from the serpent's perspective, and one from God's perspective.

Ask:
▼ **In what ways were the four perspectives similar? different?**
▼ **Who in the story had the most freedom? the least freedom? why?**

OPTION 1

Imagine Paradise
Invite everyone to use the colored pencils or markers to draw or describe personal images of paradise. As time permits, encourage volunteers to interpret their images for the group.

OPTION 2

Picture This!
Read aloud Genesis 3:1-7. Invite the youth to decide how to tell the story in six to ten scenes in which the action is frozen. The youth should select the scenes to include, the people to play the characters, and the way to set up the scenes. (If your group is large, divide it into small teams and assign one or two scenes to each team.) Using the instant camera, take a picture of each scene. After the pictures are developed, arrange them in order so that they tell the story.

Ask:
▼ **What do the tableaux tell about Eve? about Adam?**
▼ **What about each scene tells you about yourself or the world you live in?**

The Price for Abused Freedom

Direct a youth to read Genesis 3:22-23 aloud.

Ask:

▼ The serpent offered Eve freedom. What kind of freedom did the serpent promise?

▼ What was the price of freedom?

▼ What kind of freedom did Adam and Eve *before* the serpent started talking?

▼ What was the price of exchanging God's freedom for a different kind of freedom?

▼ Why is freedom sometimes scary?

▼ Why is freedom not completely free?

Say: **Let's see how limits work.**

CONNECTING

Set Boundaries

If your group is large, divide it into small teams. Invite each team to discuss what boundaries, if any, they would set in each of the following areas:

the speed limit in their neighborhood
the speed limit in front of their school
the speed limit on an interstate highway
their curfew on weekend nights
the places and the times they can drive the car
their spending limits on a credit card.

Ask:

▼ When are boundaries or limits good?

▼ In what ways do boundaries or limits enhance freedom?

▼ Which of the boundaries or limits in your life would you change if you could?

Break Boundaries

If your group is large, divide it into small teams.

Ask:

▼ Why are there rules?

▼ Are you free to break rules or laws? why? why not?

▼ In what circumstances would you break the rules?

▼ What kind of rules or laws would you break?

OPTION 3

Losing Freedom

Say: **God gave Adam and Eve everything—food, a place to live, creative jobs. But Adam and Eve gave it away. To see how they lost their freedom, let's make a Freedom Graph.** Hand out graph paper and pencils to youth. Tell them to write verse 1, verse 2, verse 3, verse 4, verse 5, verse 6, verse 7 along the horizontal plane of the graph. Then, tell them to write 1 at the bottom left of the vertical plane and go up to 10 at the top (1 stands for no freedom; 10 represents complete freedom). Tell half the group to read Genesis 3:1-7 and graph Adam's freedom. Tell the other half of the group to read Genesis 3:1-7 and graph Eve's freedom. After youth compare their graphs,

Ask:

▼ How did you decide to measure freedoms on the graph?

▼ How did you measure Adam's and Eve's freedom?

▼ What might Adam and Eve have done differently so that they would be more free at the end of the passage?

▼ What kinds of freedom were involved in the story of Adam and Eve?

▼ Did Adam and Eve give up one kind of freedom to seek another kind?

OPTION 4

What Limits?

PREPARATION: Write each of the following situations on a slip of paper and place them in a paper bag.

● *My parents and my date's parents often leave us at home alone, just the two of us.*

● *School is out. I am free until fall.*

 CHECK OUT

How does rationalizing and making excuses get teenagers into trouble when they break the boundaries?

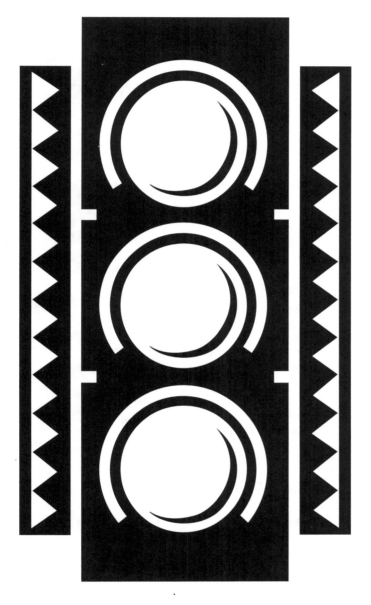

- *I have a driver's license and a car. I can go wherever I want.*
- *God gives me the freedom to make important decisions about my life and my actions.*
- *I'm old enough to stay out as long as I want.*

If your group is small, let youth draw out a slip of paper and discuss the situation as a group. If your group is large, divide into five teams, letting each team draw a slip to discuss. Direct youth to decide what limits come with each freedom. After youth have shared,

Ask:
▼ **Are the limits you've set realistic?**
▼ **In what ways do limits curtail your freedom? In what ways do they enhance your freedom?**

OPTION 5

Freedom Symbolized

Invite each youth to choose an object in the room and to talk about how it symbolizes the freedom given by God.

15. THE TEMPTING AND THE STRONG

Ephesians 6:10-20

Evaluating how well-equipped youth are in God's strength and power to survive worldly temptations.

✔ CHECK UP!

Throughout Paul's letter to the Ephesians, he talked about a new life that is inwardly and outwardly different from the life that Gentiles formerly lived. In 4:24, he calls his readers "to clothe yourselves with the new self, created according to the likeness of God in true righteousness and holiness."

Paul's theme of "putting on" godly virtues appears again in chapter 6. In verses 10-17, Paul writes about the strength that is provided by the armor of God. Such imagery clearly suggests that Paul sees Christians as being at war with the powers of darkness. When wearing the armor of God, we rely on God's power, not our own, to shield us. Isaiah 59:17 shows God wearing "righteousness like a breastplate, and a helmet of salvation on his head" to bring judgment on the enemies of God. In Isaiah 11:5, we read that the Messiah will wear a belt of righteousness around his waist and a belt of faithfulness around his loins. Paul picks up these Old Testament images in his own letter to make his point.

According to Paul, the Lord provides us with truth, righteousness, the ability to proclaim the gospel, faith, salvation, and the Holy Spirit. We may claim these resources for ourselves just as we claim articles of clothing.

Prayer is also an important weapon in the Christian's arsenal. Paul requests intercession on his own behalf so that he might be able to proclaim the gospel boldly. The armor of God supplemented by prayer provides the strength needed to withstand the cosmic forces that are constantly warring with God and God's people. Paul knows these forces only too well, for it is because of them that he is a prisoner for Christ.

✔ CHECK LIST

STARTING
❐ Make popcorn.
❐ Enlist a helper.

EXPLORING
❐ Several books or small dumbbells.
❐ Large sheets of paper, tape, yarn or crepe-paper streamers, scissors.

CONNECTING
❐ Paper, markers.

OPTION 1
❐ Bring sports equipment.

OPTION 2
❐ Prepare half-sheets of paper.

OPTION 3
❐ Slips of paper, markers, paper bag.

 CHECK IN

STARTING

Tempting Popcorn

PREPARATION: Make popcorn and enlist a student to help with this activity.

Place a bowl of popcorn in a central location in the room. After several youth arrive, excuse yourself and leave the room. Tell the youth not to eat any popcorn while you are gone. While you are out of the room, the person you recruited will persuade the others to eat some popcorn. He or she should insist that no one will ever know. When you return, ask who took the popcorn. The youth will look at or point to the person you recruited. Fill the group in on your plan and thank your assistant.

Then ask:
- ▼ **Did you take any popcorn? why? why not?**
- ▼ **If no one had encouraged you to eat the popcorn, would you have eaten it on your own?**
- ▼ **Did having someone encourage you make deciding easier or more difficult? why?**
- ▼ **How tempting was this situation?**
- ▼ **Was it more or less tempting because someone tried to talk you into eating the popcorn?**

Explain that today youth will look at ways to overcome temptations.

EXPLORING

Strength Building

Call for two volunteers. Give each volunteer several heavy books (or small dumbbells) to hold in their hands. Direct them to hold their arms away from their bodies. After thirty seconds, ask the volunteers:

- ▼ **How do you feel?**
- ▼ **Are the books getting heavy?**

Ask everyone:

- ▼ **What is required to hold these books like this for a long period of time?**
- ▼ **How important is physical strength in playing a sport?**
- ▼ **How important is physical strength in everyday life?**
- ▼ **How would you define spiritual strength?**
- ▼ **How important is spiritual strength in the life of a Christian?**

Read Ephesians 6:10. Ask:

- ▼ **What strength is needed here?**

Thank the strained volunteers.

OPTION 1

Equipped for the Game

PREPARATION: Bring a set of equipment used in a sport like football, rollerblading, or baseball. Display the equipment.

Tell youth to explain the purpose for each piece of equipment.

Ask:
- ▼ **What would happen if a player didn't wear this equipment?**
- ▼ **How effective is the equipment by itself?**
- ▼ **How does a new player to the game know what equipment to use?**

Explain that this study will help youth examine the equipment needed to win over temptations.

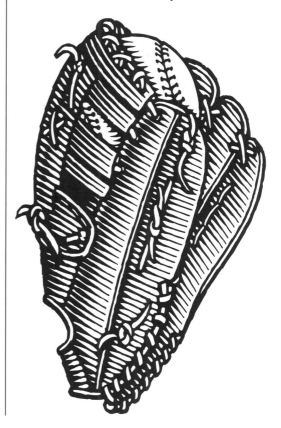

Put on the Armor

Divide youth into teams of five or six. Give each team several large sheets of paper, tape, crepe-paper streamers or yarn, and scissors. Tell each team to read Ephesians 6:11-17 in their Bibles; then dress someone with this armor. Be sure each team identifies how the piece of equipment will help in spiritual warfare. After several minutes, call for a fashion show of each team's model. Instruct a spokesperson from each team to review each piece of equipment and its purpose. Say: **While we had fun putting the armor together for the fashion show, it is not a breastplate or helmet that protects us from temptation, but what that breastplate or helmet or sword represents.** To help youth understand the meaning of each piece of armor,

Ask:

▼ How do you know where to find the truth?

▼ How do you know when you find real truth?

▼ What is righteousness?

▼ How does a person become righteous?

▼ What is the meaning of peace as Paul used it?

▼ How can a Christian find that peace?

▼ Why does the shield need to be faith?

▼ What does salvation have to do with being protected from temptation?

▼ Why are people who are already saved still tempted?

▼ Why is the word of God useful?

Say: **Because Paul had been chained between two Roman guards, he had studied the armor of these soldiers. He compared the armor to Christian requirements to help Christians remember what was needed to fight evil and temptation.**

OPTION 2
Armor Matchups

PREPARATION: Write each of the following on a half-sheet of paper: *gospel of peace, faith, salvation, righteousness, truth, word of God, holiness, Bible, Good News, facts and reality, belief and trust, made right with God through Jesus Christ.*

Give each youth a half-sheet of paper. Tell them to find the person who has the matching word or phrase (i.e., the definition of the key word. The correct matchups are: *gospel of peace/Good News; faith/belief and trust; salvation/made right with God through Jesus Christ; righteousness/holiness; truth/facts and reality; word of God/Bible.*) Next tell each pair of youth to find the reference to their matchup in Ephesians 6:11-17.

Ask:

▼ How can this equipment be used to fight temptation?

CONNECTING

Temptation Variety

Hand out three sheets of paper and a marker to each youth. Tell them to write *N* on one sheet, *S* on another, and *A* on the third. Explain that you will read a situation. Say: **If you can never resist this temptation, hold up the *N*. If you sometimes resist this temptation, hold up the *S*. If you always resist this temptation, hold up the *A*. Different things are tempting to different people. The fact that we are tempted does not mean that we must sin. Instead, God provides us with the spiritual armor to stand against that which we know is wrong. We can resist temptation.** Read each temptation. Allow youth to hold up their sheet. Call on volunteers to share their reactions. Continue with the next temptation.

1. You are walking through a store and see something you like, but you do not have enough money to pay for it. You could sneak the item into your pocket, and no one would notice.

2. You are baby-sitting. The children are asleep. You check the refrigerator for a snack and find a can of beer. No one would miss it.

3. You pay for an item and realize that the cashier has given you too much change. You could keep the extra money. After all, you did not make the mistake.

4. Your parents have left the house for the evening and have told you not to take the car out. No one else is home, and you have the money to refill the gas tank.

5. You arrived thirty minutes late for work, but your immediate supervisor did not notice. If you say you were late, your pay will probably be docked.

Ask:
▼ **Do you feel that your actions in these situations would reflect the moral and ethical standard that you are called to as a Christian? If not, what changes do you need to make?**
▼ **How can putting on the whole armor of God help to strengthen you?**

Point out that situations 1, 3, and 5 relate to money. Situation 2 may represent a chance to try a forbidden product. Situations 4 and 5 involve trust and integrity, which will be compromised by acting on the temptation that is implied.

OPTION 3

Temptation Slips

Hand youth several slips of paper and pencils. Tell them to write on each slip a temptation that youth face every day. Give these examples: *cheating, drinking, lying to parents*. Place slips in a paper bag. Let different youth draw out a slip and decide what piece of armor would help meet that temptation.

Arm Yourself

Say: One of the ways that we grow stronger as Christians is to practice spiritual disciplines. In this case the word *discipline* has nothing to do with punishment. Instead, it means that we are to train ourselves so that we will be responsible and will act according to what we believe. If we have disciplined ourselves, we will resist the temptation to do wrong, even when others try to pressure us.

Ask youth to be honest:
▼ How often do you read and study the Bible?
▼ If study is not one of your spiritual disciplines, would you be willing to begin by reading just one chapter, or story, or parable from the Bible every week?

Read Ephesians 6:17.

Ask:
▼ Do you share what you believe about God with other persons?
▼ Would you be willing to say a few words about your beliefs or what God means in your life to a family member, friend, or stranger?

Read Ephesians 6:15.

Ask:
▼ Do you ever hear gossip and accept it as fact?
▼ Do you believe that any behavior is acceptable as long as you want to do it?
▼ Would you be willing to research a situation to learn the facts before reacting? *(For instance, one may be able to verify facts by checking with reliable sources.)*
▼ How do some people misinterpret the Bible to fit their idea of truth?

Read Ephesians 6:14.

 CHECK OUT

"No temptation has seized you except what is common to man. And God is faithful; he will not let you be tempted beyond what you can bear. But when you are tempted, he will also provide a way out so that you can stand up under it" (1 Cor. 10:13 NIV).

FUTURE—FATAL OR FORTUNATE?

16. CONNECTED TO HOPE

Ezekiel 37:1-14

How God's spirit brings action, power, and hope in times of despair.

✔ CHECK UP!

This text is set against the Babylonian Exile of 596 B.C., followed by the destruction of Jerusalem, and a second exile in 587 B.C. In 596 thousands of the leaders of Judean society were removed forcibly to Babylon. They were not held in prison camps or detention centers. They lived in communities, started their own businesses, lived fairly normal lives, but they could not go home. On top of their personal loss and despair came the destruction of Jerusalem and the Temple, the centers of national and religious life. At this time people believed that gods were tied to the land where they lived. Some did not yet believe in the universal power of God, but assumed that the gods of other nations were all-powerful in the lands where they were worshiped. So, despair was the dominant mood among the exiles.

It was to people filled with despair and hopelessness that Ezekiel sang his song of the valley of dry bones. Youth can identify easily with these feelings. They ask, "Is there any hope? Is there any viable future?"

First, notice that Ezekiel is led into this experience by the spirit of God. The fact that God initiated this event is itself a word of hope. Even in a time of despair and loss of hope, God is at work. The valley of dry bones symbolizes for Israel the hopelessness in personal and national life. Despair was rampant. The question, "Can these bones live?" really asks, "Is there any hope?" Ezekiel's response is, "God knows. I don't."

Ezekiel is a prophet who speaks God's word to the situation. According to Hebrew thought, words had power. Genesis 1 reads: "God said," and it was so. The word of God alone brought creation into being. The word of God brings life to these dry bones. The Hebrew word *ruach* can mean *"wind"* or *"breath"* or *"spirit."* The Bible says the spirit of God came upon these bones and caused them to join together and become human bodies again. So, breath or spirit also symbolizes life.

Finally, verses 11-14 apply the vision to those in Israel who had no hope. As God had done to the dead bones in Ezekiel's vision, so God would do to the dead hopes of God's people. In verse 11, "bones are dried up" is clearly a metaphor for the loss of hope. Verse 14 echoes a familiar theme of Ezekiel: Israel's God is a God who gets things done. You can count on God to keep God's word. And when God's promises are kept, you will know that God is God. The New Testament echoes that idea. God's spirit is a spirit of action and power.

✔ CHECK LIST

STARTING
❏ Gather suggested toys.

EXPLORING
❏ Bible atlas, make signs, balloons.

CONNECTING
❏ Paper, pencils, index cards, masking tape.

OPTION 1
❏ Balloons as suggested, masking tape.

OPTION 3
❏ Make sign or write on chalkboard.

WHEN GOD SCRAMBLES YOUR PLANS

 # CHECK IN

STARTING

Reconnected

PREPARATION: Locate a simple child's toy (snap-together figures, building blocks, etc.) that can be brought to the meeting room in pieces and then assembled by the youth. Distribute to each youth one or more pieces of the toy you have brought.

Ask:
▼ **What do you have?**
▼ **What can you do with it?**

Have the group assemble the pieces with minimal instructions. Then ask them to discuss the same two questions listed above.

Ask:
▼ **What's the difference between a house and a home?**
▼ **What's the difference between a church and a church building?**
▼ **What's the difference between a body and a person?**
▼ **How was this experience like the coming together of the dry bones?**
▼ **How does God's spirit help to connect us together?** *(God can be the center of our lives and hold all the pieces together; the Spirit connects us with God and with other members of Christ's body.)*

Say: **In this study, we're talking about the Holy Spirit in the book of Ezekiel. At an important moment in Ezekiel's life, the Spirit showed him a vision. The Spirit led Ezekiel to a valley filled with dry bones. Ezekiel prophesied to the bones, and they came together to make people; and the people lived. The Holy Spirit brings life and hope to situations of despair and hopelessness.**

EXPLORING

Sound Effect Story

PREPARATION: Write *Boo* on one side of a poster and *Yeah* on the other side.

Use the commentary material and a Bible atlas to explain the background to this event. Say: **The Babylonian Exile was a particularly painful period in the history of Israel. Thousands of the leaders of Judean society were already living in exile when the Temple was destroyed and Jerusalem was overthrown in 587 B.C. With this final blow, many felt that God had abandoned them, that all hope had been cut off. It was a time of "identity crisis," and the Hebrew people had to reformulate their faith in a context of defeat and without a homeland.**

Locate the kingdom of Judah and the city of Jerusalem in the Bible atlas. Then follow the probable route of the Exile from Jerusalem past Damascus to the Euphrates and down the river to the city of Babylon.

OPTION 1

Balloon Buddies

For every four persons, inflate four long balloons and three round balloons. (Or ask youth to inflate the balloons.) Label the balloons as follows:

- *head:* one round balloon
- *body:* two round balloons
- *leg:* two long balloons
- *arm:* two long balloons

Invite youth to tape together the balloons to make balloon buddies.

Ask:
▼ **Did anyone build a balloon buddy that is unconventional? If so, why?**
▼ **What was it like to make a balloon buddy?**

Finish the activity by reading aloud the last paragraph under STARTING.

OPTION 2

A Matter of Mine

Share the background information under "Sound Effects Story." Tell youth that they are going to pantomime the story. Let them read Ezekiel 37:1-14, assign parts, and prepare the pantomime. When they are ready, let them present the mime.

Ask:
▼ **What is the story about?**
▼ **What do the bones stand for?**
▼ **What happens to them? why?**
▼ **What was God's spirit doing in the story?**

Ask:

▼ **How do you think the exiles felt being so far away from their homeland? knowing that their Temple had been destroyed? living in a different culture with different gods?**

Ask one youth to read Ezekiel 37:1-14 aloud. Tell the others to yell "Boo" when there is bad news and "Yeah" when there is good news. Encourage youth to ham it up. Ask a youth to hold up the sign when the group is supposed to respond. After reading the story,

Ask:

▼ **How did you decide what was bad news and what was good news?**
▼ **How do you decide today what is bad or good news?**

Balloon Blow

To help youth understand the power of God's Spirit or breath, play Balloon Blow. Give a deflated balloon to each participant.

Ask:

▼ **How much fun are balloons before you inflate them?**
▼ **What happens when you add a little air?**

Have youth inflate their balloons, and bat them around the room. See how long they can keep the balloons in the air, or play balloon volleyball for a minute or two.

Ask:

▼ **What difference did it make when you added air to your balloons?**
▼ **How does God's spirit or "breath" help bring us to life?**

Say: **The Holy Spirit is God's animating life force. When we open our lives to God's spirit, we truly come alive. We learn what it means to live in good relationships with others, we discover our gifts and abilities, and we find a sense of purpose and direction. In God's spirit, we don't just exist; we live!**

CONNECTING

Up and Downs

Distribute at least thirty index cards. In a large group, give each person one card; in a small group, give each person several cards. Tell the youth to write on each card a word, phrase, or sentence that describes either the ups or downs of teenage life—for example, the youth may write *curfew, chores, friends.* Collect the cards. Give each person a sheet of paper.

Read each card. Then invite the youth to consider whether the word or phrase on the card describes the ups or the downs in a teenager's life. If the description is negative, they should tear off a piece of the paper, a large piece if the description is especially negative, a smaller piece if the life situation is mildly negative. If the statement describes a positive aspect of a teenager's life, the youth should tape a torn piece of paper back onto their sheet of paper. They should choose a large piece of paper for an especially good aspect of life and a smaller piece for situations that are less positive.

▼ **What was the point of the Spirit's actions?**

OPTION 3

Say What?

PREPARATION: Write the following phrase in capital letters on the chalkboard or a large sheet of paper: GODISNOWHERE.

Some will see the message *God is no where;* others will see *God is now here.* Ask youth to explain the difference in the two messages.

Ask:

▼ **How is reading this message like the situation Ezekiel described?**

WHEN GOD SCRAMBLES YOUR PLANS

Ask:

▼ What condition is your paper in now?

▼ When there are too many hard times in our lives, we can feel shredded. What happens if we feel shredded every day?

Say: **The people in exile were depressed about their situation. They felt hopeless. If they'd had a piece of paper to shred, they would have shredded it completely. Ezekiel's words gave them hope. They rebuilt their faith. Part of what we do as a faith community is to build one another up. The Holy Spirit helps to heal us when we feel shredded. Sometimes our worlds get torn up. Ezekiel's certainly did. And sometimes, our worlds are healed, put back together. Ezekiel saw hope in the vision God had given him. Let's bring the brokenness in our lives to God.**

Ask the youth to put the scraps of paper on the floor or a table. Ask them to reflect on what the torn paper represents. Say a prayer: **God, we bring you the scraps and tatters of our lives. We pray for the gift of your Spirit that will bring the scraps and tatters together, the way the breath brought life to the scattered bones. Help us to be whole people. Amen.**

✔ CHECK OUT

Teenagers feel like the exiled people of Israel. How can this story encourage them?

▼ What did God want the people in exile to see that they were unable to see?

▼ Have you ever had the experience of seeing something in a new way?

▼ What made the difference? *(For example, in going back to a place that you knew as a child—even though it may not have changed much, now that you are older it may seem different from how you remember it.)*

▼ What are the possibilities for our lives that God can see but we can't?

17. DREAM ON!

2 Samuel 7:1-17

Examining God's promises and how these can complement youth's personal goals.

✔ CHECK UP!

King David thinks things are under control. The political boundaries of his kingdom are secure. No military threats loom on the horizon. Money pours into the treasury, because his government collects tolls on all trade that moves through the ancient Middle East. David turns his attention to internal affairs. David wants to build a house for God's Ark of the Covenant. David wants to assure God's presence with Israel. David also wants to secure his place on the throne, and one way to do this is to honor God and win the loyalty of the religious elements in society. At first, Nathan the prophet gives David the go-ahead. Nathan says, "God will like that idea." But Nathan has not asked God if God likes the idea. Later, after God speaks to Nathan, there is a different word that Nathan has to give to David.

Why is a permanent house for God not acceptable? Because Yahweh, the name of Israel's God, is a God who moves. A house will limit God's freedom. God will not be limited by David's dynastic ambitions. Space cannot stop God, who is and moves and acts without boundaries.

God will do more for David than build a house. God reminds David through Nathan of all God's acts in the past. God took David from being a shepherd and made him a king over Israel. God has always been with David, defeating David's enemies. God will make David's name great. All that David has is God's doing. What was true in the past will also be true in the future. The climax to God's promise is in verse 11: I "will make you a house." There is a great pun here. David wants to build a house, a temple for God. Instead, God will build a house, a royal dynasty from David. This is a new idea for Israel. David was only Israel's second king. He wanted his rule to be blessed by God in a way that Saul's had not been. That was one reason to build a house for God. But God leaps into the future and promises a dynasty for David.

In political terms, this means a peaceful transition of power to David's son when David dies. God will bless that son and establish his kingdom. This son will build a house for God. God will establish a covenant relationship with David's son that will last forever. David's son Solomon did succeed him to the throne and built the Temple. God makes an unconditional promise. God's steadfast love will never be removed from David's dynasty. "Forever" is a powerful

✔ CHECK LIST

STARTING
❏ Index cards, pencils or markers, masking tape, large newsprint or chalkboard.

CONNECTING
❏ Paper, pencils.

OPTION 1
❏ Playing cards.

OPTION 3
❏ Prepare index cards.

WHEN GOD SCRAMBLES YOUR PLANS

word, and potentially frightening. No longer does Israel have to worry about God's presence. The Ark of the Covenant and the Temple relieve these anxieties.

But now the issue is not God's presence in the community, it is about this one family. God is present in Israel through the house of David. David was not the ideal man for God's promise. David was, in fact, a murderer and an adulterer, one who coveted his neighbor's wife. At a minimum, he violated at least three of the Ten Commandments. Yet David was a man after God's own heart. David's story reminds us that we don't have to be perfect or worthy to experience God's love. God chooses to love us and enters into relationships with us. God continues to improve and to create us in God's image. God never gives up on us. David's dynasty turned out poorly in later generations, but God's steadfast love never changed. Like David, having God on our side does not mean that everything will be great, or that we can do anything we want. Sometimes God says no because of love. God works in our lives to make something new.

✔ CHECK IN

STARTING

Top Ten Promises
PREPARATION: Gather index cards, masking tape, and large newsprint or a chalkboard.

Give each youth four index cards and a pencil. Instruct youth to write an important promise on each card. Suggest that these promises could have been made by friends, family, or others, or they may be promises the youth have made. Tape all promises to a wall.

Review the posted cards with the youth. If any of the promises are duplicates, leave only one copy on the wall. Any of the examples that are similar but not identical may remain in place.

Have the youth indicate which promises should "definitely" or "maybe" be included in the list of top ten promises. Rearrange the cards to reflect these two separate categories. If you end up with more or fewer than ten in the "definitely" group, review the cards again with the youth to see which promises can be eliminated or which ones can be added from the "maybe" list. When all have agreed on the final top ten promises, copy them on newsprint or a chalkboard.

Ask:
▼ Why would anyone want to make a promise to someone else?
▼ What happens when an important promise is kept?

OPTION 1

Build a House
Tell the youth to find partners. Give each pair a deck of cards and tell them to build a house of cards. The house should be as elaborate as possible. After 2 minutes, bring the group together.

Ask:
▼ How hard was it to build a house?

Say: In the Bible, there are several meanings of the word *house*. A house is the place where people live. A house is a dynasty, as in the house of David. And a house is a place of worship, the house of God. Use the Bible background information under Check Up! to help you explain the meanings of the word *house*. You may want to define the words in the context of the story of David's ambition.

EXPLORING

The Promise of a House

Say: **There's a neat reversal in this Bible story. It starts out with David all set to build a house for God; then the tables turn. By the end of the story we learn that it is God who is going to build a house—for David.** Divide the youth into three groups. (In a large assembly, subdivide the groups.) Give the groups the following instructions:

GROUP 1: Read 2 Samuel 7:1-6. Answer these questions:

▼ What do you suppose was David's political agenda?
▼ Why did he want to build a house of worship?
▼ How did the prophet Nathan first respond to David's idea?
▼ What did God say to the prophet to make him change his mind?
▼ What was God's reason for not living in a house?
▼ David thought he could control God if he could confine God to a specific location. What are some ways we try to control God?

GROUP 2: Read 2 Samuel 7:7-11a. Then use a sarcastic or ironic tone to read the verses. Answer these questions:

▼ In what ways does a sarcastic tone of voice change the meaning of the Scripture?
▼ What kind of house is God interested in building?
▼ What has God done for David?
▼ What does God promise to do for David and for Israel in the future?
▼ What has God done for you?
▼ What has God promised to do for you?

GROUP 3: Read 2 Samuel 7:11b-16. Answer these questions:

▼ What kind of house was God going to build for David?
▼ In what ways is God's promise to David a blank-check covenant?
▼ In what ways are God's promises to us like a blank check?

After 6-7 minutes, bring the groups together to report.

God's Steadfast Love

Ask a youth to read verses 14-16. Say: **Let's see what is involved in God's steadfast love.** Read the following list of statements that describe God's love and ask the youth to respond to each statement. If they agree, have them give a "thumbs up" sign. If they disagree, have them register a "thumbs down" vote. If they're not sure, ask them to assume a pose with shoulders shrugged and hands raised, palms up. After each statement, ask volunteers to explain why they responded as they did.

● Being assured of God's love guarantees that I'll be happy. *(God's love brings us joy but doesn't promise perpetual happiness.)*

OPTION 2

Main Players

Recruit three youth to play the parts of David, Nathan, and God as you read the story of David's dream to build God a temple. Assure them that it is O.K. to ham it up a bit.

Read aloud 2 Samuel 7:1-17, pausing for the players to act out each scene. For example: In verse 1, pause and let David "rest from his enemies." Also let the players repeat their lines after you read them.

- If God loves me, then it doesn't matter what other people think about me. *(Yes and no. There is some security in God's love that frees us from constantly seeking the approval of others, but it doesn't give us license to not care about our relationships with others.)*
- God's steadfast love is a model for how we ought to love other people.
- God's love for me means that I can do anything and God will still love me. *(Yes, because even when we blunder, God will forgive us and still love us if we are truly sorry. No, if we use it as an excuse to do whatever we want.)*
- God's steadfast love is something that everyone needs.

Say: **The promise of God's steadfast love—love that never ends, no matter what—does not give us a blank check to do whatever we want. Just the opposite is true. God's steadfast love inspires us to respond in love toward God and other people and strengthens us to avoid anything that would be unloving or unfaithful.**

CONNECTING
House Designs
Give youth paper and pencils. Tell them to draw the basic floor plan for the main floor of their house or apartment. Say: **This house represents the life of a family. Each room contains gifts and promises. In each room of your house write a goal or a promise you have that is related to that room. For example, for the living room, name the goal you have for your life. For the bedroom, name a goal or promise you have for your spouse. In the study, name an education goal you have.** After a few minutes call for volunteers to share their goals and promises for the "rooms" in their houses.

Ask:
- ▼ What's one thing you hope to accomplish in your life that you'll be proud of?
- ▼ What's the most important thing you want people to remember about you after you die?
- ▼ If you have children, what do you want to pass on to them in terms of values, faith, and so on?
- ▼ How does God fit into your long-range plans?
- ▼ How might God help you to accomplish your dreams?
- ▼ Have you considered that God may have different "house plans" for your life?
- ▼ What would it mean for God to build a "house" out of your life?

 **CHECK OUT**

"Unless the LORD builds the house, / those who build it labor in vain" (Ps. 127:1a).

OPTION 3
Finish Your Story
PREPARATION: Write on index cards brief descriptions of future events that could happen to the youth in the group. Include for each person one positive and one negative description. For example, write on one card, *You will be happily married;* write on another, *You will enjoy your chosen career.* Write negative descriptions such as, *You will die young* or *You will be killed in a drive-by shooting.*

Shuffle the cards. Invite each person to draw one card.

Ask:
- ▼ How would you feel if your future were described on the card you selected?
- ▼ Does God decide our futures?
- ▼ Does God decide that for some people, the future will be good and that for others, it will be bad? why? why not?
- ▼ What can you do in your family, neighborhood, or church to change the future?
- ▼ How can you make your future a good one?
- ▼ What can you do to help improve another person's future?

18. IT'S HOPELESS!?

Luke 23:33-46; 24:1-9

Discovering that God is at work even in situations that appear to be hopeless.

✔ CHECK UP!

The place where Jesus was executed was called "The Skull," perhaps because of certain physical characteristics. Those who were crucified were exposed to the hot sun and wind since they were not allowed to wear their outer garments. Nails were driven through their hands or wrists. Their feet were tied together or were also nailed to the post. Death often took more than twenty-four hours.

Jesus seemed to accept his crucifixion as God's will. He lovingly referred to God as "Father." And even in his agony, Jesus requested forgiveness for others.

The Jewish authorities ridiculed Jesus. They urged him to save himself. They thought that if he could not save himself, he surely could not do anything for anyone else. The Roman soldiers also mocked Jesus; and they offered him some sour wine, possibly to revive him and prolong his ordeal.

Jesus was crucified with two criminals. These persons had probably tried to incite the people to revolt against the government. One criminal made fun of Jesus. The second criminal defended Jesus against the criminal who mocked him. This second criminal said that Jesus had done nothing, that Jesus was condemned unjustly. This person saw more in Jesus and seemed to understand more about who he really was than the soldiers or the first criminal had.

The second criminal responded in faith. He recognized that God was about to establish the Kingdom. He even asked Jesus to remember him when Jesus received his kingly powers.

As Jesus died, darkness enveloped the earth and an earthquake shook the Temple so violently that the curtain was torn in two. Jesus' last words let us know that Jesus was obedient to God even to his last breath. He committed himself to God in death even as he had in life.

Jesus' followers were devastated. They evidently did not expect his resurrection. When the women went to the tomb to embalm the body of Jesus, they discovered that the stone had been rolled away and that the body was gone. Their shock and amazement grew as two angels suddenly appeared and began to question them. These messengers wanted to know why the women were seeking Jesus in his tomb; after all, Jesus had told them that he would be crucified but that he would rise again. The implication was that the women

✔ CHECK LIST

STARTING
❏ Yarn or rope with a knot.

EXPLORING
❏ Paper, pencils.

CONNECTING
❏ Construction paper, markers, glue, yarn, sequins.

OPTION 2
❏ Make the signs.

WHEN GOD SCRAMBLES YOUR PLANS

would not have been surprised by the empty tomb if they had truly understood Jesus' teachings.

If the resurrection is *not* true, there is no hope beyond this present existence. The resurrection gives our life on earth a sense of purpose backed by God's power.

✔ CHECK IN

STARTING

A Hopeless Knot

PREPARATION: Tie a secure knot in a piece of string or a rope.

As the youth arrive, struggle to untie the knot. As you struggle with the knot and talk with the group members, say at least once: **"It's hopeless."** Consider allowing one or two of the youth to try to untie the knot. These youth may experience the same feeling of frustration and hopelessness, or they may have faith that the knot will eventually come untied. After a few minutes, either the knot should be untied or everyone may join you in declaring that the situation is hopeless.

Hopeless Definition

Talk briefly about the word *hopeless*. Have the youth tell what hopeless means to them *(being without hope, things will never improve, there is no good solution)*. Encourage youth to share specific situations where everything seemed hopeless. Ask youth to share how they handled these hopeless situations.

EXPLORING

Determine the Questions

Assign the following people at Jesus' crucifixion to different youth: criminal 1; criminal 2; a soldier; a townsperson; a Jewish leader. (Youth can work in pairs if you have more than five.) Hand out paper and pencils. Direct youth to read Luke 23:33-46 in their Bibles. Tell youth to pretend they are reporters who are supposed to interview the person assigned to them. Suggest youth write down two or three questions to ask their assigned person. After a few minutes, read the verses, stopping to let different youth share their questions. If possible, speculate on how the person might have answered the questions.

Ask:
▼ Who thought this was a hopeless situation? why?
▼ What hope did the criminal who spoke to Jesus have?
▼ Why do you think the second criminal had faith in Jesus?
▼ How hopeless or hopeful do you think Jesus felt at this time?

OPTION 1

A Human Knot

Form a human knot by getting youth to make a circle. (If you have more than ten youth, make more than one circle.) Tell youth to put both hands into the circle and grab the hand of another person other than those on either side. Direct youth to untangle their knot without letting go of their hands. Offer comments like: **This looks hopeless. How will you get untangled? I don't think this is going to work.** After youth get untangled (only rarely do they get stuck),

Ask:
▼ How did you feel about being in a tangled knot?
▼ How hopeful were you that it could be undone?
▼ When do you feel tangled in a web of circumstances that seem hopeless?
▼ How do you handle those times?

Too Good to Be True?

Ask:

▼ **What would be an event or situation where you would say, "This is too good to be true"?** *(getting a new car you want; winning lots of money; world peace; perfect grades for the rest of the year).*

Enlist a youth to read Luke 24:1-9.

Ask:

▼ **Is the resurrection an event that is too good to be true? why or why not?**
▼ **How hard would it be for you to believe in the resurrection of Jesus if you had been there?**
▼ **What would have happened if there had been no resurrection?**
▼ **Why is it easy to doubt the resurrection?**
▼ **How would you convince someone who is not a Christian that the resurrection really took place?**

OPTION 2

A Hopeless Situation

PREPARATION: Make a sign of each of these responses:

- *This is so awful that I don't know what to do next.*
- *All we have to do is wait for three days and everything will be great.*
- *Jesus was wrong. He wasn't God's son. He wasn't the Messiah.*
- *Jesus tricked us into believing in him. I was really a fool to think that any of it was true.*
- *I can tell this was really God's plan. No ordinary person would have planned things to be like this.*
- *I believe in Jesus. I know he is the Messiah. But I don't understand why things turned out this way.*

Ask a youth to read Luke 23:33-46 aloud. Say: **For Jesus' followers, the darkest time corresponded to their deepest misery and grief. How could things ever get any better? They had believed that Jesus was the Messiah. They had expected him to bring God's kingdom. They had committed themselves to be his followers. And now he was dead! He had been crucified just like a common criminal.** Place the signs on the floor or on a wall. Ask youth to select a sign that expresses how the disciples might have felt. Tell them to select a sign that says what the people who saw Jesus do miracles might have said.

Ask:

▼ **If you had been present on that fateful day, which sign would state your feelings?**

Invite volunteers to share, each time signs are chosen.

WHEN GOD SCRAMBLES YOUR PLANS

CONNECTING

Dark Before Dawn

Ask:
- ▼ Have you ever heard anyone say, "The darkest hour comes just before dawn"?
- ▼ What does that mean? *(That things seem the worst right before they start to get better).*

Have the youth answer the questions. Invite volunteers to talk briefly about a dark time in their lives. (Be prepared to give an example from your own experience.)

Ask:
- ▼ Can you recall a dark time in your own life?
- ▼ What was that like?
- ▼ How did you feel during that period of time?

No Longer Hopeless

Ask:
- ▼ Who are some people who live in seemingly hopeless situations?
- ▼ Do you have friends who have no hope?
- ▼ How can you meet their hopelessness with your hope?
- ▼ How does knowing Jesus Christ offer hope?

Say: **Let's share that hope with someone you know who needs encouragement.** Point out the art supplies and direct youth to make a greeting card for that person using the ideas of hope discussed in this session. Allow volunteers to share their finished cards. Close with a prayer of hope.

 **CHECK OUT**

How can believing in life after death make a difference to someone's life on earth?

OPTION 3

Celebrate!

Close the session with a moment of celebration for the dawn that follows darkness. Invite the youth to stand in a circle. Or, if the meeting room has a window, have the youth stand near the window and face the light. Recite the words, "The Lord has risen!" Have the youth respond, "The Lord has risen indeed!"

19. LIVING UP TO YOUR FUTURE

Luke 1:67-79

Building a relationship with God from the foundation of covenants in both the Old and New Testaments.

✔ CHECK UP!

This biblical text is often called the Benedictus after the first word in the Latin translation. The priest Zechariah spoke these words at the time of his son's circumcision and naming, a time when a boy child became a member of the people of God. This son is named John, in accordance with the angelic instruction given to Zechariah in Luke 1:5-20. The boy grew up to become John the Baptizer.

Zechariah's inspired speech falls into two parts: verses 68-75 and verses 76-79. Verses 68-75 speak about the fulfillment of Jewish hope for the last days. God will redeem the people by means of a mighty Savior from the line of David. The Greek translation *Savior* literally means "horn of salvation." The literal rendering makes it easier to see that Zechariah's prophecy refers to Psalm 18:1-3. Verse 70 clearly states that the one who is coming will be the fulfillment of holy prophets from of old, such as those in Jeremiah 23:5-6. Verses 72-75 explain that the one who is coming is the fulfillment of the covenant with Abraham established centuries earlier. (See Gen. 22:16-18.)

The second part of Zechariah's speech testifies that his son John will be the forerunner of the Messiah. The term "the Most High" used in verse 76 alludes to the power of God described in 1 Samuel 2:10. John is described as the prophet of the Most High. Luke called Jesus the Son of the Most High in Luke 1:32. Zechariah's pronouncement sounds much like Malachi 3:1-2. "See, I am sending my messenger to prepare the way before me, and the Lord whom you seek will suddenly come to his temple. The messenger of the covenant in whom you delight—indeed, he is coming, says the LORD of hosts. But who can endure the day of his coming, and who can stand when he appears?" John's role will be like the role of Elijah described in Malachi 3:5-6.

The one who comes after John, brings salvation. These verses (78-79) are strongly reminiscent of Isaiah 9:2. It's also easy to understand why the early church saw in Zechariah's prophecy an allusion to Isaiah 42:6-7, from one of the Servant Songs. Those who sit in darkness are those who are lost and separated from God. God's concern for the lost is one of the recurring themes in the Gospel of Luke. For example, Luke includes the parable about the lost sheep, the lost coin, and the lost son. By recording Zechariah's inspired speech, Luke shows

✔ CHECK LIST

STARTING
❐ Prepare the mysteries.

EXPLORING
❐ Write the team assignments on cards, newsprint.
❐ Write the Scripture references on cards.

CONNECTING
❐ Prepare the game cards, pencils.

OPTION 1
❐ Bibles, dictionaries, paper, markers, magazines, glue, wire coat hangers, and string.

OPTION 2
❐ Large sheets of paper, markers.

WHEN GOD SCRAMBLES YOUR PLANS

that Jesus is not a new upstart or some guru who came out of nowhere, but someone in continuity with the covenants of old. To understand Jesus we cannot read the New Testament alone. We need to be familiar with the Old Testament, as the soil in which Jesus' roots were anchored.

✔ CHECK IN

STARTING

Brain Teasers

PREPARATION: Write each of the following "mysteries" on a sheet of paper:

1. *An unconscious and injured man is found in the soft sand of the desert. He is wearing a backpack. There are no tracks around him. When he recovers enough to talk, he cannot remember what happened. Can you figure it out?*
2. *Two girls who have the same birthday (including year) and the same parents, and who look exactly alike walk into a library with their parents. The librarian says, "Oh, you must be twins!" The girls reply, "No, we're not twins." Can you explain?*
3. *In a fishing boat there are two fathers and two sons. Each person in the boat catches one fish and puts it on a stringer. Yet at the end of the day there are only three fish. Why?*
4. *An old man walks out of a building to speak to the crowd waiting for him. He opens his mouth to speak, but nothing comes out. Months later he is able to talk only after he names a baby. Who is the man? What was he doing in the building? Why couldn't he talk? What is the baby's name?*

Bonus Question: Zechariah prophesied about the coming Savior. Five hundred years later, Zechariah prophesied about the coming Savior. How can this be?

Let different youth read a "mystery" aloud. Then, challenge youth to answer the mystery. If they cannot arrive at a solution within a minute or two, tell them the answer and move on to the next mystery.

Solution Number 1: *The backpack contains a parachute. He fell from a plane and is lucky to be alive—let alone remember how he got there.*

Solution Number 2: *The girls aren't twins—they're triplets! Their other sister is shopping with grandparents.*

Solution Number 3: *There are three fish caught because there are only three men in the boat—a grandfather, his son, and his grandson. His son is both a son and a father.*

Solution Number 4: *For the answers, see Luke 1:5-25, 57-66.*

Bonus Question Solution: *The Old Testament prophet named Zechariah prophesied about the coming Savior in about 520 B.C. (see Zech. 9:9-10). Then, five hundred years later, John the Baptist's father, Zechariah, prophesied about the coming Savior.*

OPTION 1

Covenant Collage

PREPARATION: Hand out the Bibles, dictionaries, and art supplies.

Tell youth to make a mobile that explains covenant. They can use phrases from the Bible or definitions from the dictionary. They can use symbols or other words. Urge youth to work in teams of four or five. Let every team share its mobile, explaining the different parts. Say: **We're going to see what the Old Testament covenants meant to the New Testament, and what they mean for youth today.**

EXPLORING

Different Points of View

PREPARATION: Write the following team assignments on cards:

1. *Assume that Zechariah was a poet. What poetic phrases suggest that his song was a hymn of praise and not just a recital of events?*
2. *Assume that Zechariah was a historian. To what events did he refer?*
3. *Assume that Zechariah was a theologian. What did Zechariah say about God?*
4. *Assume that Zechariah was a prophet. What did he say about the future?*
5. *Assume that Zechariah was a father. What did he say about his son?*

Older youth can look at these verses from different points of view. Briefly explain the Bible study background to this passage about Zechariah. Then, hand out cards with these team assignments. Divide the group into five teams. (In a small group, one person can do the work of a team.) Ask each team to read and discuss Luke 1:67-79 from one of these points of view. Bring the teams together to share their findings.

Ask:
▼ **What does the song of Zechariah say from each point of view?**

Then say: **In fact, Zechariah was a poet, a historian, a theologian, a prophet, and a father. Each perspective helps us understand a little more about who he was and what he said.**

Ask:
▼ **How does Zechariah's song connect God's past promises and actions with the future?**

Younger youth may feel more comfortable doing this simpler activity. Ask them to read through Zechariah's prophecy in Luke 1:67-79, underlining in pencil the phrases or sentences in which Zechariah refers to what God has done in the past. After several minutes, ask for volunteers to tell what they have underlined and record these words or phrases on newsprint.

Something Old, Something New

PREPARATION: Write the following Scripture verses on cards:

1. *Luke 1:68-69, Psalm 18:1-3*
2. *Luke 1:70, Jeremiah 23:5-6*
3. *Luke 1:72-75, Genesis 12:1-4*
4. *Luke 1:76, Malachi 3:1-2*
5. *Luke 1:78-79, Isaiah 9:2*

Give every two youth a card containing an Old and New Testament scripture. Tell one person in each pair to look up the Old Testament reference and the other to look up the New Testament reference. Instruct them to decide how the scriptures relate to each other. Present the Old and New Testament verses to the rest of the group.

Ask:
▼ **How does the Old Testament scripture help you understand Luke?**
▼ **What about God's faithfulness in the past helps you believe in God's faithfulness in the present and in the future?**

OPTION 2

A Song About a Song

Consider this activity even if your youth are not musical. Remind them that they can use music from a commercial, a hymn, or any other tune. Say: **The song of Zechariah is an old hymn of the church, based on the theme of God's keeping the covenant in the past, present, and future.** Divide the assembly into groups of three or four youth. Ask the members of each group to read Luke 1:68-79 and to list the kinds of things for which Zechariah praised God. Then ask them to make a list of things for which they would presently praise God. They should begin by answering these questions:

What is God doing in your life? in the life of your family? in the life of the nation? in the life of the church?

What do you hope for from God?

Bring the groups together to read their lists. If the youth are willing, invite them to write a song praising God for what God has done and for what they hope God will do in their lives. If not, display their lists as a reminder of God's activity in their lives.

CONNECTING

Covenant Continuity

PREPARATION: Make one card for each name, description, and scripture:

Abraham • *God made a covenant to give him land, descendants, and blessings in return for faithfulness and obedience* • *Genesis 3:1-2*

Moses • *brought slaves out of Egypt and delivered the Ten Commandments* • *Deuteronomy 6:20-25*

Zechariah • *father of John the Baptist who prepared the way for the Savior* • *Luke 1:76-77*

Jesus • *fulfilled the prophecies of the Old Testament and made a new covenant with God's people* • *Matthew 26:27-28.*

Turn the cards over, mix up the cards, number the backs, and place them face-down on the floor or a table.

Divide youth into two teams. Tell each team to select three numbers, turn over the cards and match the name, covenant promise, and scripture. Encourage teams to use their Bibles. After all the matches have been made, give each youth a card and a pencil. Instruct youth to find a place on the card to write a brief description of their relationship with God. Say: **We will not report or share these descriptions. This is for you only.** After a few minutes, lead youth to pray silently about their relationship with God.

✔ CHECK OUT

Are you living up to all you expect to be, or are you living down to negative expectations? It's your choice!

OPTION 3

This Little Light of Mine

Ask:

▼ How can you "prepare the way of the Lord" at school, at home, and in your everyday lives?

Select two or three of the following to share with your youth.

1. If someone said, "My life is filled with darkness," what would that mean? Name a few of the problems such a person might have.
2. In your opinion, is darkness the absence of light, or is light the absence of darkness?
3. If it is true that darkness is the absence of light and that some people feel like they are "in darkness," how can you bring light into their lives? Give specific examples.
4. When you do the things you listed in the preceding question, how is that preparing the way for the Lord? How is it different?
5. Compare God, Jesus, and John to the battery, the light bulb, and the wires. Which of these are most similar or different, and why?
6. At this time in your life, are you more like the battery, the light bulb, the wires, or the dark room? why?
7. If you feel God bringing light into your life, how do you plan to share it with someone else this week?
8. If you feel more like the dark room, how might the Good News Zechariah was so excited about also make a difference to you?

20. PROMISES WORTH WAITING FOR

Isaiah 55:6-13

Identifying several of God's promises helps youth claim these promises for themselves.

✔ CHECK UP!

When we hear promises, we don't want empty words. We want action. We want people to stand by their words. In today's text, the exiled Isaiah gives us a magnificent poem about God's words and God's actions, about how God keeps God's promises.

These verses are part of a larger poem in which the poet is celebrating God's action. Historically, this is set near the end of the Exile, almost fifty years after the destruction of Jerusalem in Judea and the forced marches of the Jews into captivity in Babylon. For years the prophets had warned about Jerusalem's fall. Because of sin, the people would suffer. God definitely kept God's word on that promise. But more recently, first Ezekiel, and then the prophet who wrote Isaiah 40–55 talked about a new day coming. God would once again set God's people free and lead them back to Jerusalem. A new day of hope was dawning. New world powers appeared. Babylon would be overthrown. Again, God kept God's word.

The first part of Isaiah 55 is about repentance. Repentance changes the direction of our lives in response to God's act or promise. We call upon God because God is near. We return to God because we believe God will have mercy on us and pardon us. God's word of pardon and mercy is true. Unfortunately, we can get in the way of God's keeping that promise. Our wicked conduct and unrighteous thoughts block God's mercy. Repentance radically changes our thoughts and conduct. We repent in response to God's love. Verses 8 and 9 remind us of the vast difference between ourselves and God. Sometimes, it's hard for us to see the wonders of God's grace. But God's vision is greater than ours. God sees all time, all space, all history, all people. It is precisely because of the greatness of God that the invitation to seek God is so important. God draws near and allows God to be found.

Rain brings the gift of life. God's justice rained on us brings life. So, God's word accomplishes its purpose. We say things like, "One's word is one's bond," or "Don't say that. It might come true," or "Don't put those words into the air." We recognize the power of words, just as we also recognize that some words are only empty air. The prophet says that God's word and God's deed are the same. They will happen. God's promise is the word. It does not return empty, but accomplishes that for which it was intended.

✔ CHECK LIST

STARTING
❏ Fortune cookies or fortunes on slips of paper.
❏ Hat or basket.

EXPLORING
❏ Paper, pencils.
❏ Prepare repentance cards, chalkboard.

CONNECTING
❏ Paper, markers.
❏ Prepare Psalm cards, hat or bowl.

OPTION 3
❏ Paper, scissors, markers, stapler.

WHEN GOD SCRAMBLES YOUR PLANS

 # CHECK IN

STARTING

Find a Fortune

PREPARATION: If making your own fortunes, write statements such as: *A new friend will come into your life* on slips of paper.

Hand out fortune cookies or have youth draw a fortune from a hat or basket. After everyone has compared fortunes, ask whether they would like it if their paper fortune could really foretell the future. Say: **You can't trust fortune cookies to tell you what's going to happen. But you can trust God's promises. Today we'll look at several of those promises.**

EXPLORING

Here Comes the Judge!

PREPARATION: Write one of the following on five cards:

Realizing Sin   *Turning From Sin*
Being Sorry for Sin   *Turning Toward God*
Confessing Sin

Hand out paper and pencils. Say: **Each of you is a judge. The following criminals have been found guilty and are brought before you for sentencing. Each expresses deep sorrow for the crime and pleads to be allowed to lead a new life. Write the person's name and your sentence on your paper.** Read the following:

> Ms. Jarrett is a single mother of two. She has been convicted of physically abusing the younger of her children, a six-month-old baby.

> Mr. Smith is twenty-four years old. He is married with no children. He has been convicted of murder. He stabbed his brother-in-law five times in the chest during a drunken brawl in a nearby bar.

> Tony Abbot is a twelve-year-old student at a nearby Junior High School. He comes from a wealthy family but is always looking for a thrill. He has been convicted of selling drugs to his classmates.

> Mr. Hacket is thirty-four years old. He is married and has one daughter. He has been convicted of stealing a loaf of bread and a can of mushroom soup from the local supermarket. He claims it was to feed his family.

Discuss each situation and the sentences the youth pronounced. After reviewing all cases, ask a youth to read Isaiah 55:6-7.

Ask:
▼ **What do you think God's sentence would be in each situation?**

OPTION 1

The Best Promise Ever

Ask:
▼ **What is the best promise anyone ever made to you?**
▼ **What was the outcome of the promise?**
▼ **What is your opinion of the way the promise turned out?**

(Possible examples of the "best promise": a trip, a reward for good grades, one's own room)

Consider revealing your own answers to the questions before asking for volunteers to tell their responses. Discuss some of the feelings that youth had about their best promise.

Ask:
▼ **If the promise was kept, did things turn out exactly as you expected?**
▼ **If not, what was different about the outcome?**

Be sensitive to those people whose past experiences with promises may have been upsetting and disappointing. Say: **Some promises are kept, but some get broken. When things don't turn out the way we expect, we may be unsure whether the promise was kept or broken.**

OPTION 2

Merry Metaphors

Ask:
▼ **What's a metaphor?**
▼ **How many metaphors do you find in Isaiah 55:6-11?**

Say: **O.K., let's begin with an English lesson. A metaphor**

(Although there would still be consequences in each situation, God would be merciful. God would demand repentance, would completely forgive, and would expect a new life.)

Say: **In God's eyes each of these people is a child of God. And if, in fact, each of them is truly sorry for what he or she has done and sincerely intends to lead a new life, God's sentence would be: "Go in peace, my child, your sins are forgiven. Go and sin no more." God's love and forgiveness know no bounds. If we are truly sorry and want to turn our lives around, then God is faithful to forgive us.**

Ask:
▼ How does God's sentence influence us?
▼ What is the promise in these verses?

To help youth understand repentance, hand out five repentance cards. Say: **The word** *repentance* **has gotten a bad rap in our time because of its misuse by televangelists and the like. But Isaiah gives us a pretty good idea of what repentance is all about. Basically repentance is "forsaking wicked ways" and "returning to God." Or, put more simply, it is turning away from sin and turning toward God. Repentance is a process. It is not something that we do once and only once in our lives and then never have to worry about again. Rather, it is something that we do each and every day of our lives—it is a way of life.**

Randomly ask each youth to read aloud what is printed on his or her card. Then ask everyone to arrange themselves in the order in which they think repentance occurs. A proper order is listed under PREPARATION, but in reality most of the steps of repentance occur simultaneously.

When the youth have agreed upon a certain order, ask them to justify their conclusion. Affirm the importance of each step of the process, whatever the order, for those of us who seek to be faithful and to grow in relationship with God.

Promises to Keep

Ask youth to silently read Isaiah 55:8-13 and to underline each promise made by God. Review each verse, calling for the promises youth have found. List these on a chalkboard. Say: **Isaiah used metaphors to express God's promises. These make it easier to understand God's promises.**

Ask:
▼ **Why do you believe God's promises?**

OPTION 2 *(Continued)*
compares one thing to another. Here's the first one to help you get started: In verse 9, God says that God's ways are higher than our ways, as the heavens (skies) are higher than the earth.

Ask:
▼ **What other images in the Scripture make you think of the power of God?**
▼ **What images in the same verses make you feel secure that God fulfills promises?**
▼ **If God fulfills promises, what else can God do?**

CONNECTING

Promise Keeping

Give each youth two sheets of paper and a marker. Tell them to write *1* on one side of a sheet of paper, *2* on the other side, *3* on the second sheet of paper, and *4* on the other side of that second sheet. Say: **I will read a statement. Hold up a 1 if you always believe that statement. Hold up a 4 if you hardly ever believe that statement. You may also choose 2 and 3 as somewhere in between. The statements are:**

- I trust the promises my parents make to me.
- I trust the promises my friends make to me.
- I intend to keep the promises I make to others.
- I trust the promises God makes to me.
- I keep the promises I make to God.

Ask:
▼ How can we become more trusting of God's promises?
▼ How can we become more trustworthy of the promises we make to God?

Pray the Promises

PREPARATION: Select several Bible verses from the book of Psalms that express the promises and the will of God. Some verses you might use are: *Psalm 13:6; Psalm 23:1; Psalm 32:10; Psalm 52:8-9; Psalm 63:3; Psalm 91:15; Psalm 103:1-5, 11-13; or Psalm 119:76.* Write the reference for each passage on an index card and put the cards in a hat or bowl. Write Isaiah 55:10-11 on a card and keep this one for yourself.

Have the youth form a circle and allow each person to draw one card from the hat or bowl. Then ask each person to read prayerfully the Bible passage he or she selected. Say: **We have heard God's promises to love us forever, as well as the praises of people who have experienced that steadfast love and who believe those promises. We, too, have the promise that God will keep God's word, that what God says will be done.** Conclude the prayer circle by reading the passage from Isaiah written on your card and offering a prayer of thanks for God's love and faithfulness.

 CHECK OUT

"Seek the LORD while he may be found" (Isa. 55:6*a*).

OPTION 3

Promise Coupons

Ask the youth to think about God's promises and the way they work out in their lives. Encourage them to consider other promises of God that they have heard about.

Invite everyone to use the paper, scissors, and markers to make coupons or coupon books. Each coupon should name one of God's promises that the youth would like to claim for their lives. Assure the youth that they will not have to report what they write on their coupons. Encourage them to carry the coupons with them or to keep them in a place where they can find them easily and look at them when they need to. One way to use the coupons is to look at a different one each morning (yes, even in the midst of the morning rush) and to claim God's promise for the day.

21. READY OR NOT!

Matthew 25:1-13

Being ready for the return of Jesus Christ.

✔ CHECK UP!

A wedding was one of the greatest times in a Palestinian village. The bride, the groom, and the guests were excused from most religious duties. The groom was excused from military service. Even scholars were excused from studying the Torah, because attending a wedding was more important. The wedding feast lasted from several days up to a week. Jesus enjoyed weddings. In John's Gospel, Jesus performed his first miracle at a wedding. Jesus even said the joy of the wedding is a proper sign for the kingdom of God.

The high point of a wedding came when the bridegroom took the bride from her father's house to their new home. Their friends and guests escorted them. In verse 1, the maidens go out to meet the bridegroom. In the NRSV, a footnote adds, "Other ancient authorities add 'and the bride.'" Other ancient manuscripts support this idea, since maidens were attendants to the bride, never to the bridegroom. Of the ten attendants, five brought extra oil for their lamps, and five did not. The lamps or torches light the procession from the bride's family home to her new home. When the bridegroom was delayed, the attendants slept, and when he finally came their lamps were low on oil.

If these lights were lamps, they were probably clay bowls with a pinched rim to hold the wick. If they were torches, they were probably some kind of bowl on a long pole. Either way, it was time to add oil. Five of the ten attendants had no extra oil, and the others refused to share. "There isn't enough for all of us," they said. "Go out and buy your own." As a teenager, I thought how incredibly selfish this attitude was. Surely, the five attendants could share. But that's not how the story goes. Five of the attendants went off to buy oil. The other five joined the wedding procession. Where do you think the girls got their oil? There were no all-night convenience stores in first-century Palestine. Anyway, they got some, but when they returned to the house the door was shut, the party was going on, and they couldn't get in. Why not let them in? It seems particularly unfair and harsh, even cruel, when they cry out and the bridegroom says, "I don't know you." What's the point to this story? Christians need to be prepared for the coming of the Kingdom. God's gift of the Kingdom is free, but the opportunity to receive it may pass by if we aren't prepared.

✔ CHECK LIST

STARTING
❑ Gather party items, refreshments.

EXPLORING
❑ Long piece of butcher paper, markers.

OPTION 2
❑ Paper, markers, pencils.

OPTION 3
❑ Oil lamp or candle, matches.

CHECK IN

STARTING

Let's Party

Invite the youth to a party. You may want to distribute handwritten invitations as the youth enter the door. In keeping with the wedding theme, light white candles and serve punch, white cupcakes, and mints or nuts. Confetti would be fun, but be sure to sweep it up afterward. Have fun.

Ask:
▼ Jesus said that the Kingdom is like a wedding party. What did he mean?

Explain that in this study youth will evaluate how ready they are for the party that Jesus is throwing.

EXPLORING

A Wedding in Israel

Say: **The wedding story we will read sounds unusual to us because our customs are different from those in Israel.** Share the following information in your own words.

Weddings were such important occasions that bride, groom, and guests were excused from religious duties to attend the wedding. They were also excused from civic duties, and the groom was excused from military service. Even the rabbi was allowed to put aside his study of the Scripture.

The time for the wedding was not set exactly. The bride and her attendants waited at her home until the bridegroom arrived—maybe the same day, maybe two weeks from that day. In fact, the bridegroom would sometimes wait until midnight to show up so that he could catch the girls sleeping.

To play fair, the groom would send runners through the streets ahead of him. The runners would announce the bridegroom's arrival: "The bridegroom is coming! The bridegroom is coming!"

The bride and her friends would get ready in a hurry, and the groom would carry her away to their new home. All their friends would go with them, carrying lamps or torches in a grand procession.

When the couple arrived at their new home, they did not leave on a honeymoon. They held open house. For a week, they entertained their friends; and the merriment of the wedding went on.

OPTION 1

Movie Review

Ask youth to think about movies or television shows they have seen or heard about that deal with the end of the world.

Ask:
▼ What current movies or television shows deal with the idea that the world will end?
▼ What are their plots?
▼ Did they picture the end of the world as violent or frightening?
▼ Did the people in the movie dread the end of the world?
▼ Did a hero or group of heroes intervene to save the earth at the last minute?
▼ Do you ever think about the end of the world?
▼ How do you feel talking about it?

OPTION 2

Comedy Capers

Ask the youth to listen carefully as you read the story of the ten bridesmaids. Tell them to think about how the different characters in the story feel. Read aloud Matthew 25:1-13. Then ask them to talk about what they think the characters in the story must have felt.

Form small groups of two or three and say: **Imagine that you are writers for Christian comedy acts. One of your stars will be invited to appear in a Christian comedy club. The manager has asked each team of writers to create a comedy routine based on Matthew 25:1-13. It should emphasize that life in the Kingdom is fun, that no one should**

Read aloud Matthew 25:1-13.

Ask:
▼ In what ways did knowing about wedding customs help you understand the parable?
▼ Why didn't the foolish bridesmaids bring extra oil? *(They expected the groom to come early; they had not counted on delays. They had not considered all the possibilities.)*
▼ How were the wise bridesmaids realists?

Create a Mural

Divide Matthew 25:1-13 among your group. Unroll a long sheet of butcher paper. Give several youth markers. Tell them to draw the story in panels. The first panel should be based on verses 1-4; the second panel on verse 5; the next panel on verses 6-9; the next panel on verse 10; the last panel on verses 11-13. Let youth share their mural. Lead youth to define the different people in Jesus' parable.

Ask:
▼ Who is the bridegroom? *(Jesus.)*
▼ Who is the bride? *(The church.)*
▼ Who are the bridesmaids with the full lamps? *(Christians who are prepared for Jesus' second coming.)*
▼ Who are the bridesmaids who ran out of oil? *(People who believe they can wait to experience a personal relationship with God. When the groom says he doesn't know them, it's because there is no relationship.)*
▼ Why wouldn't the five prepared bridesmaids share their oil?
▼ What does the wedding feast represent? *(Possibly the feast illustrates the joy of God's kingdom.)*

CONNECTING
Being Ready—Part One

Ask:
▼ When have you felt unprepared?
▼ Why weren't you ready?
▼ What were the consequences of your being unprepared?

Say: What if the minister announced today that Jesus was returning to earth next Tuesday at noon. When Jesus comes he will return to heaven with his believers.

Ask:
▼ How would you feel if:
• you were already a believer?
• you were being persecuted?
• you wanted to get rich?
• you thought the world was about to end?
• you were doubting Jesus because he had not come yet?
• you could not understand why evil persons prospered?
• you knew good people who suffered?

OPTION 2 *(Continued)*
miss the opportunity to be there. But it should also contain a word of caution about the judgment awaiting those who are not ready, for they will not be allowed into the feast. Your task is to come up with the opening dialogue or a few one-liners for the manager to review before deciding upon which guests to invite. Allow several minutes for the teams to work on a comedy routine. Then invite volunteers to present in comedic fashion (or to read if they prefer) the material they have written.

OPTION 3
A Preparation Experience

If you have an oil lamp, light it and explain how the oil provides the energy necessary for the lamp to burn. Or light a candle and explain that the wax provides the fuel for the candle to burn, just as oil does in an oil lamp.

Have a volunteer read aloud Matthew 25:13 and ask the group to suggest ways that they might awaken or open their lives to a deeper relationship with God.

Say: **Being awake means learning how to recognize God's presence and activity in our everyday lives. We are going to practice one way to be open to God's presence. Become very**

Being Ready—Part Two

Say: **There are some things you can't do at the last minute. There are some things you can't borrow.** Ask youth how each of the following can help them be ready for the return of Jesus Christ:

- Pray every day.
- Read the Bible every day.
- Believe that Jesus wants you at his party.
- Seek out people who make you feel closer to God.
- Wear your (emotional) party clothes: Be happy.

 **CHECK OUT**

How can you be sure that you will have oil in your lamp when it is needed?

still and quiet. Invite God's spirit to be with you to help you experience God's kingdom. *(pause)* . . . Focus your eyes on the flame of the oil lamp (or candle) so that you see nothing else. Ask what God wants you to see and note any thoughts or feelings that you have *(pause)* . . . Close your eyes and listen for a few moments. Ask what God is saying to you in the sounds or in the silence you hear and note any thoughts or feelings that you have. *(pause)* . . . Open your eyes and hold your hands close to the flame of the lamp or candle. Feel the warmth and ask what God wants you to feel or touch in your life. Note any thoughts or feelings that you have. *(pause for ten or fifteen seconds)* . . . Now let your eyes shift their focus back to our meeting room and observe all that is around you.

Invite the youth to talk about their experiences of waking up to God's presence through their senses. Explain that this exercise can also include the senses of smell and taste depending on the setting. Encourage youth to sit quietly several times during the coming week as a way to grow more open to God and more awake to the tremendous possibilities of living in the Kingdom.

22. YES! NO? MAYBE!?

2 Corinthians 1:12-22

Realizing that sometimes change is necessary in order to respond to God's great promises.

✔ CHECK UP!

Paul's letters are sometimes difficult to read. He dictated them and kept saying all the things that popped into his head while he was talking. This text is a good example. First it's written about a familiar situation to Paul and the Corinthians; however, we have to guess about part of it. Second, Paul chases several other thoughts while he deals with the main point. In fact, one of these stray thoughts is the most important thing he says.

Corinth was probably the most contentious church Paul ever founded. The members always seemed to be at odds with one another and with Paul. This time the problem involved a change in Paul's travel plans. Originally he was going from Ephesus in modern Turkey, to Macedonia (part of the former Yugoslavia), then to Corinth in modern Greece on his way to Jerusalem. Because of several problems in Corinth, Paul decided to visit Corinth twice, once on his way to Macedonia, and again on his way back. On his return trip he would pick up the offering for Jerusalem. When things improved in Corinth, Paul went back to his original plan. The Corinthians accused Paul of being hypocritical, of saying yes and no in the same breath (v. 17). Since he would pick up the offering on his visit, there were also mutterings about Paul's not caring about the church, only about the money. In these verses, Paul responds to these accusations. Read them as hurt, angry words, as Paul defends himself. In verses 12 and 14, he says he has always been honest and sincere. His conscience is clear about the way he has dealt with the Corinthians. He has been open with them, not trying to hide anything. In fact, Paul has been more open to the Corinthians than to others. Paul makes a good point. This controversy would not have happened if Paul had not been so open about his itinerary. Paul claims his openness is because of God's grace. He does not operate out of the usual human motives. He says what he means and hopes the Corinthians will understand.

While he is talking about saying yes and no at the same time, Paul has another random thought and shares it. This thought is the key to our text. Look at verses 18-22. Paul appeals to the faithfulness of God as a witness to his own faithfulness and integrity. Jesus Christ did not say yes and no, but always yes. We would say, "In

✔ CHECK LIST

EXPLORING
❏ Large sheets of paper, marker.
❏ Hymnal or poster with song, pencils, paper.

CONNECTING
❏ Pencils, paper.
❏ *YES* sign.

OPTION 2
❏ Bibles, paper, pencils.

OPTION 3
❏ Invite a guest.

WHEN GOD SCRAMBLES YOUR PLANS

Christ, every one of God's promises is a YES!" That is, everything that God promised to God's people—God's own love and presence, hope for the future, joy in the present, salvation, community—all find completion in Christ. God keeps God's promises. The reality of our hope is Jesus Christ—YES! This can be a powerful idea for youth who see little hope in their own futures because the structures and rewards of the world can go away so quickly. The world says yes and no to hope, but Christ always says yes. The best response to this idea of hope is praise to God's glory.

Paul's real defense against the charge of fickleness is not how wonderful Paul is, but how God is guiding his life. God established both Paul and the Corinthians in Christ, so they should know that God is involved in every decision, even a change in travel plans. The thing to remember is God keeps God's promises!

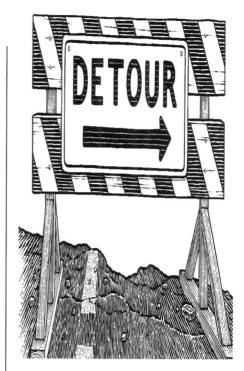

CHECK IN

STARTING

Fortunately, Unfortunately

Invite everyone to sit in a circle. (For a large group, divide into several small groups and ask all the groups to play the game at the same time.) Choose one person to be Player 1. He or she will state a good thing that has happened, for example—"My family went to Florida." The person sitting on his or her left, Player 2, will state something bad that happened. His or her statement should relate to what Player 1 said: "Unfortunately, on the way there, we had a flat tire." Player 3 will then continue the story by stating a good thing that happened, related to Player 2's statement. Encourage the group to add to the story until they run out of ideas.

Then ask:
▼ **Was it hard to think of something good related to something bad? why?**
▼ **How does the game help you understand what Paul wrote to the Corinthians about his change in plans?**
▼ **What has the game taught you about God's working in our lives?**

Say: **Unfortunately Paul had to change his plans to visit the Corinthians. Fortunately, when he wrote a letter defending his changed plans, he shared a great truth about God. Unfortunately, it's hard to understand all of Paul's letter. Fortunately, we understand the part about God's promises.**

OPTION 1

A Change of Plans

Ask:
▼ **When have all your vacation plans been changed at the last minute?**
▼ **Why were they changed?**
▼ **How did you feel?**
▼ **How did the situation turn out?**

Explain that Paul had to change his plans to visit the Corinthians and it caused problems. But while defending himself, Paul shared great truths about God.

EXPLORING

Yes and No

Briefly relate the Bible background in Check Up! Read 2 Corinthians 1:18-19 aloud. To help youth understand the importance of God's yes, ask them to call out the names of people who often say no to them, or people to whom they say no. List these on a large sheet of paper under the heading *NO*. Tell youth to call out people who often say yes to them or people to whom they say yes. List these on a large sheet of paper under the heading *YES*.

Ask:
▼ How important is a positive response?
▼ Why are you more likely to hang around people who respond positively?

To show youth that God is serious about saying yes, read 2 Corinthians 1:20-22, asking youth to identify signs that God is serious about the promises God makes.

"Great Is Thy Faithfulness"

PREPARATION: Bring hymnals that contain the hymn "Great Is Thy Faithfulness," or write the words to the first and third stanzas on a poster.

Ask a youth to read 2 Corinthians 1:19-22 aloud. Direct others to listen for Paul's main concern. After the reading, hand out hymnals and tell youth to turn to "Great Is Thy Faithfulness." Working alone or in pairs, tell youth to find phrases or words in the Scripture that relate or compare to phrases and words in the hymn. After a few minutes call for ideas.

Ask:
▼ How important is faithfulness in a friendship?
▼ How do we know that God is faithful? What promises has God made to us as Christians that we know God has kept?

If youth like to sing, sing the hymn. If not, read the hymn in unison.

CONNECTING

Check Your Fickle Factor

Say: **The Corinthians accused Paul of vacillating, of saying "yes, yes" and "no, no" at the same time. Paul's response was that God does not vacillate; God keeps promises. If God has chosen to change Paul's plans, it doesn't mean that Paul is fickle. It means that Paul doesn't always know what's best; God does.**

Ask (but don't expect answers to each question):
▼ Are you fickle?
▼ Do you say one thing one day and something else the next?
▼ Do you pretend to like someone, but the minute his or her back is turned, you start making fun of him or her?
▼ Do you profess undying love for a guy one day and for his best friend the next? Do you make promises you have no intention of keeping?
▼ Do you know people who are fickle?

OPTION 2

Saying YES to God's YES

Read 2 Corinthians 1:20-22 to youth. Say: **God has said "Yes" to us with God's promises. The way we can respond to that yes is through our action.** Direct youth to read Matthew 25:35-36. Pass out paper and pencils. Encourage youth to discover ways in which they might respond to God's yes by rewriting the passage (or parts of it) in their own words, using experiences that are applicable to their lives. (For example: "I was hungry and you shared your lunch with me. I was a new person at school and you sat with me at lunch. I was sick in the hospital and you came to visit me and brought me a card . . .")

When everyone is finished, allow volunteers to read their paraphrases. Challenge the youth to live out one or more of their responses in the coming week as a way of saying YES! to God.

OPTION 3

A Real, Live Example

PREPARATION: Find and invite someone in your church, either minister or layperson, who planned to do one thing with his or her life, but changed plans because of what he or she thought was God's action.

Ask the guest to talk to the youth about how God changed his or her plans. Allow time for questions from youth.

Challenge youth to identify times when they are fickle.

Ask:
▼ **Why is it difficult to make up your mind?**
▼ **How do you relate to people who keep changing their minds?**
▼ **How can you be less fickle?**

Remind youth that God is not fickle. God keeps God's promises. Hand out paper and pencils. Instruct youth to list three promises they believe God has made to them. (For example, youth might say, "I believe God guides my life if I follow God"; "God has given me eternal life because I believe in Jesus"; "God loves me.") After a few minutes, encourage youth to share their promises.

God's YES

PREPARATION: Make a poster with the word *yes* written in big letters.

Tell youth that you will read (or they can recite with you) "The Apostles' Creed." Explain that when we say the creed, we are saying *yes* to God's *yes*. Hold up the poster at the designated places to emphasize God's *yes*. Use the creed as a closing prayer.

THE APOSTLES' CREED

I believe in God, the Father Almighty,
creator of heaven and earth. YES!

I believe in Jesus Christ, his only Son, our Lord, YES!
who was conceived by the Holy Spirit,
born of the Virgin Mary,
suffered under Pontius Pilate,
was crucified, died, and was buried; YES!
he descended to the dead.
On the third day he rose again; YES!
he ascended into heaven,
is seated at the right hand of the Father,
and will come again to judge the living and the dead. YES!

I believe in the Holy Spirit, YES!
the holy catholic church,
the communion of saints,
the forgiveness of sins,
the resurrection of the body
and the life everlasting. Amen. YES! YES! YES!

(Adapted from The Apostles' Creed, Ecumenical Version,
The United Methodist Hymnal, no. 882)

 **CHECK OUT**

How can you know when to accept change and realize that God is a part of that change?

CHAPTER 4

LIFE ISSUES

23. A WORLD OF RESOURCES AND SINS— THE ENVIRONMENT

Genesis 1:1-19; 3:1-19

Understanding how sin affects God's resources.

✔ CHECK UP!

The creation story found in Genesis 1:1-15 was not designed by the writer to be a scientific document. The main purpose of the author was to make clear that God is the Creator of all that exists. *Who* did the creating was much more important than the specific details of the activity.

The book of Genesis is the product of Jewish editors who, during and after the Exile, compiled written sources that preserved information transmitted by means of oral storytelling. The *P* (Priestly) source, from which the Scripture reading comes, presents an image of God and of God's activity from a priestly point of view: majestic, concerned with order, and magnificently in charge of the essence of life.

How should we view creation today and our place within that creation? Many aspects of nature and the created order can be awesome; some of them are even frightening and overwhelming. Countless people have been inspired by the vastness of the Grand Canyon or the majesty of Niagara Falls. And we all have either seen for ourselves or seen reports of thunderstorms, tornadoes, hurricanes, or other powerful phenomena of nature, yet the Bible tells us that everything God created was considered good.

The story of Adam and Eve explains how sin came about and why life is difficult for us at times. At a deeper level, the story of Adam, Eve, and the serpent points out much about human nature: We are often attracted to what we can't have; and in trying to get those things that are out of our grasp, we often disobey the plan God has for our life.

The serpent was not meant to be a symbol of evil or death, but instead is a device for showing human beings that disobedience to God is an option for them. The "crafty" serpent promised Eve that the knowledge to be gained by eating the fruit of the forbidden tree was most desirable. As Adam and Eve discovered, their new-found knowledge led to fear and guilt instead of wisdom. They learned what it felt like to be ashamed and frightened. They even became frightened of God, their very own Creator, as a result of their expanded knowledge.

The final outcome of Adam and Eve's disobedience was alienation from God and from each other as they tried to blame someone else for the guilt they now felt.

✔ CHECK LIST

STARTING
❏ Make list, butcher paper, paper, pencils.

EXPLORING
❏ Gather props.
❏ Enlist people.

CONNECTING
❏ Enlist three youth.

OPTION 1
❏ Paper, pencils.
❏ Select a route to walk.

Adam and Eve's story is important not only for what it reveals about human nature, but also for what it shows us about the nature of God. God continued to feel the same way toward Adam and Eve. The only feelings that changed were those of the human beings. God's love remained the same even after sin entered the picture.

 # CHECK IN

STARTING

Right or Wrong?
PREPARATION: Write the following list of right and wrong actions on butcher paper:

RIGHT AND WRONG ACTIONS

- *stealing food to feed one's family*
- *cheating on homework*
- *lying to a friend to keep from hurting his or her feelings*
- *going out with friend's girlfriend or boyfriend*
- *tithing the money you earn*
- *getting too much change back from a purchase and keeping it*
- *calling home when you're running late*
- *finding a wallet and not turning it in*
- *taking your little brother or sister to a PG-13-rated movie because he or she begged to go with you*
- *refilling the car's gas tank after using the car*
- *cutting your own Christmas tree*
- *throwing trash out a car window*
- *recycling aluminum cans and plastic cartons*
- *"rolling" a friend's yard*
- *throwing old paint cans and yard debris into a nearby lake*

Divide youth into teams of five or less. Show youth the list of right and wrong actions. Let each team select two right and two wrong actions. Give youth paper and pencils, and tell them to list reasons why the right actions they chose are good. Then tell them to list reasons why the wrong actions might occur so the action appears less wrong. *(For example, a factory pollutes a stream because the factory owner doesn't know it's happening, or the factory has to choose between laying off people and fixing the pollution problem.)* Call for youth responses.

Explain that in this study youth will look at how the right resources created by God are changed by sin.

EXPLORING

Dramatize Creation
Using simple props and devices, have youth act out the Creation story:

OPTION 1

Creation Walk
Take youth outside for a creation walk. Tell half the youth to make notes about the positive things they see in creation and the other half to make notes about the negative things they see. When you return to the meeting room let each group share its findings.

Ask:
▼ **What other positive, powerful examples do we have of creation?** *(Niagara Falls, Grand Canyon, baby's birth)*
▼ **What part of nature or creation confuses or disturbs you?**
▼ **How do you feel about natural disasters like hurricanes or tornadoes?**

Remind youth that what God created, God called *good.*

- Turn the lights on and off to simulate light and darkness or day and night.
- Use an electric fan with streamers attached for the wind that God caused to sweep over the waters.
- Use a globe to represent the earth.
- Use blue poster board cut in half to represent the waters that were separated.
- Make a large poster-board star to represent the heavens, and a tree or flower to represent vegetation.
- Use a calendar "for seasons and for days and years."

Every time youth hear the phrase "And God saw that it was good" (or a variation of it), have them cheer and clap. Select a narrator and an especially alert person to be in charge of turning the lights on and off (there are many references in the Scripture to darkness and light, night and day). As the narrator reads Genesis 1:1-19, have volunteers hold up or operate the props that correspond to the various descriptions in the Creation story.

Ask:
▼ Why is the world God created not so good today?

The Blame Game
After youth read Genesis 3:1-19 aloud,

Ask:
▼ How did Adam and Eve and the snake blame one another?
▼ Why did Adam blame God?

Tell youth to quickly make up other excuses the trio could have used. Then, direct youth to state things each could have said that show he or she accepted personal blame. *(For example, Eve might have said, "I wanted wisdom, but all I got was fear; I'm sorry.")*

Ask:
▼ How did blame help the situation?
▼ How did blame hurt the situation?
▼ What did sin do to the resources God had created?
▼ How was life on this planet changed by the sin of people?

CONNECTING
Showing Appreciation for the Universe
PREPARATION: Find three youth volunteers and ask them to read aloud the following case studies:

- After studying the Creation story, Julie wanted to do something to express appreciation for God's beautiful world. She decided to get up every morning at sunrise for a week and take pictures of the spectacular colors lighting up the sky. She then mounted all the photographs and showed them to the other members of her Bible study class.

- James, who was in the same class with Julie, chose to express his appreciation for God's creative activity in a different way. He decided that the best way to thank God for our unique place in the created order was to take better care of his corner of the

OPTION 2
Silent Play
Form two teams of youth. Assign one team to read and study Genesis 1:1-19 and the other team to look at Genesis 3:1-19. Tell the teams to prepare a silent play based on their Scripture. Remind them that a silent play has no dialogue or sound effects. Suggest that youth share feelings, actions, and reactions in their plays. After a few moments call for each play.

world. James began to monitor his energy consumption at home and to recycle waste products. He also encouraged his class to sponsor a litter-free section of the roadway near their church.

Ask:
▼ How do these stories relate to the resources of our world today?
▼ How do they relate to the world's environment?

● Other class members were prompted by Julie's and James's enthusiasm to take on projects of their own. Russ wrote a song thanking God for the universe and taught it to his classmates. One Sunday Lisa and Paul washed car windshields for the people who attended church and left this note attached to each vehicle: "We hope you will thank God today for all the wonders of the creation that you can see out of your clean window!" Cindy wrote a "creation appreciation" poem that she read during worship, and Phil arranged for the youth group to have a bonfire and hayride so they could all enjoy the outdoors together.

After reading the cases, ask youth to brainstorm answers to these questions:

What are some ways that all of us can try to keep nature in harmony?
What can you do to show appreciation for what God has created?
What can you do within the setting of the church or the community to express your study group's appreciation of God's creation?

Be receptive to any ideas involving the entire group's participation in a church or community project that would honor God's creation. Discuss how to implement a project the group is interested in pursuing.

Action Prayer

Gather youth together in a circle, and give them these directions:
● **Put your arms around one another.**
● **If you have ever failed someone, drop your arms.**
● **If you have ever littered, step back.**
● **If you have ever blamed someone, step back again.**
● **If you have ever damaged something in God's world, turn around.**
● **If you have ever held a grudge, close your eyes.**

Then say:
God seeks us out even when we sin. God wants to love us and to release us from the fear, alienation, and guilt that sin often causes in our life. Continue with these directions:
● **If you have ever supported a person or group of people open your eyes.**
● **If you have ever made someone feel included, turn around.**
● **If you have ever cleaned up a littered place, step forward.**
● **If you have ever thanked God for the universe, step forward again.**
● **If you have ever forgiven someone, rejoin the circle and put your arms around one another.**

Say: **We thank you, God, for your promise of care. In Christ's name we pray. Amen.**

 **CHECK OUT**

How are people a resource for the environment? How are people a detriment to the environment?

24. GANGS—HOME FOR THE OPPRESSED

Ecclesiastes 4:1-8

Understanding how gangs develop out of oppression.

✔CHECK UP!

Vanity here does not mean conceit or preoccupation with oneself. Rather, it means that which is empty of meaning or purpose. In fact, some translations use the word *meaningless* instead of *vanity*. The Hebrew word used, *hebel,* means "vapor"—something fleeting, insubstantial. The core idea is brevity and futility. The search for meaning in life, according to Qoheleth (Hebrew for "teacher"), is elusive and without definite substance. Some understand vanity to mean ascribing ultimate value to goals and objects that, in reality, are not ultimate. Human abilities, achievements, and desires by themselves cannot bear the weight of misplaced trust and hope. Only when our lives are centered on God do human abilities, achievements, hopes, and dreams make ultimate sense. Only when our lives are centered on God are the good things of life ultimately satisfying.

In verses 1-3, we meet the suffering of those who are oppressed. In an uncaring universe, the plight of those who suffer is so bitter that they would be better off dead or never to have been born, says the Teacher. But the consistent testimony of the Old Testament says there is one who cares about the suffering. Remember what the book of Exodus says about the Hebrew people who were slaves in Egypt?

After a long time the king of Egypt died. The Israelites groaned under their slavery, and cried out. Out of the slavery their cry for help rose up to God. God heard their groaning, and God remembered his covenant with Abraham, Isaac, and Jacob. (Exod. 2:23-24)

The Teacher in Ecclesiastes is right about the external evidence. Some people suffer terribly, often without someone to comfort them. Verses 4-6 present an apparent paradox. Neither laziness nor overachievement brings happiness or satisfaction. That confirms what we see in real life. On one hand, without some drive to accomplish something, the life of leisure becomes aimless and frustrating. On the other hand, being a workaholic doesn't guarantee happiness. Instead, overwork frequently leads to health problems and to families who lack the attention they need and deserve. Persons who work hard in order to acquire more things, to keep ahead of the Joneses, seldom know when to be content with what they have. The bumper sticker that says, "The one with the most

✔CHECK LIST

STARTING
❒ A recent news story on gangs.

EXPLORING
❒ Paper, pencils.

OPTION 1
❒ Chairs.

OPTION 2
❒ Newsprint.

OPTION 3
❒ Chalkboard or newsprint, marker, paper, pencils.

WHEN GOD SCRAMBLES YOUR PLANS

toys when he dies, wins," reflects a pathetic outlook on life. The Teacher recognizes the futility of both extremes—idleness and too much work.

Verses 7-8 recognize that life as a loner is unhappy without some larger sense of connectedness. Many youth who feel like loners identify with this description of life. Later, in verses 9-12, the teacher celebrates the benefits of friendship and companionship in a loving relationship. But even friendship and family, as good as they can be, cannot fill the void at the core of our being. Something even deeper is required, something that Augustine had in mind when he wrote, centuries after Ecclesiastes that "our hearts are restless, O Lord, and we find our rest in thee." The relationship to the Lord is the one to hold up to teenagers struggling to become adults. That relationship can bring a profound sense of satisfaction and comfort in life.

✔ CHECK IN

STARTING

Gangs Galore

Say: **Gangs make news. Sometimes the news is bad: gang wars. Sometimes, the news is good: After the riots in 1992, two of the largest gangs in Los Angeles declared a truce in order to work together to help rebuild the city.** Show a recent newspaper or magazine article on gangs in America or your hometown.

Ask:
▼ What is your experience with gangs?
▼ Are there gangs in our community?
▼ Have you been personally threatened by gangs?
▼ What are some positive reasons people join gangs?
▼ What are some negative reasons people join gangs?

OPTION 1

Unfair!

Have youth sit in a circle. In the center of the circle place two chairs facing each other so that participants seated in these chairs will be knee-to-knee. Ask for volunteers to take turns being "the complainer" and "the student." The complainer's job is to complain about the unfairness of life as long as possible without smiling. The student's job is to listen attentively to the complainer and try to get him or her to smile. The student may occasionally say, "Oh, I see," or "Aw, that's too bad," but he or she must listen without argument or discussion. Those around the circle may laugh but must not interfere. Time each session. Stop after one minute if the complainer has not smiled before then.

After you have played the game for a while,

Ask:
▼ What are the complaints in Ecclesiastes 4:1-8?
▼ In your opinion, how significant are these complaints— trivial or very important? Explain your answer.

EXPLORING

The Teacher

Say: **The book of Ecclesiastes is one of four books in the Old Testament labeled Wisdom Literature. These books include reflections on the meaning and purpose of life and on our relationship with God.** Tell youth about the Teacher, the author of Ecclesiastes. Explain what he meant by vanity.

Divide into teams of two or three youth. (If your group is small, invite all the youth to work together.)

Ask each team to complete these questions as if the team is the Teacher after reading the scripture.

Read Ecclesiastes 4:1-3.

▼ What does *oppression* mean?
▼ Was there an experience of oppression in your racial or cultural history?
▼ Have the people in your heritage been the oppressed or the oppressors?
▼ In what ways has historical oppression helped mold who you are?
▼ Ecclesiastes is pretty cynical about oppression: The powerful rule. Being dead might be better than being alive, but never having been born would be best of all. How do you feel about the Scripture?
▼ In all Ecclesiastes' talk of oppression, where is God?

Read Ecclesiastes 4:4-6.

▼ What do you think *vanity* means in the Scripture?
▼ What is the point of verses 4-6?
▼ What does the Scripture say to people who don't live up to their abilities?
▼ What does it say to overachievers and workaholics?

Read Ecclesiastes 4:7-8.

▼ Verses 7 and 8 are about loners. Is life alone a "vanity and an unhappy business"?
▼ Where is God in the midst of loneliness?

Review answers.

CONNECTING

Tombstone Tales

PREPARATION: Draw a large tombstone on the chalkboard.

Say: **Many gang members don't expect to live past twenty years old.** Point out the tombstone. Explain that an epitaph is the words on a tombstone written about that person.

Ask:
▼ What epitaphs might a gang member have?
▼ What epitaph would you want?

OPTION 2

Difficult Feelings

Form four small teams. Ask each team to compare the writer of Ecclesiastes to other biblical figures who had negative feelings and attitudes. Read about their lives in one of the following passages. Jeremiah (Lam. 3:1-20), Jesus (Matt. 26:36-46), Moses (Num. 11:4-15), or Peter (Matt. 26:69-75).

Point out that each of these passages contains negative feelings that these great people of God had. Have each team name the feeling (such as guilt, anger, fear, grief, and so forth) and try to figure out from the text what caused this feeling and how it was resolved, if it was resolved.

Ask a team spokesperson to tell what his or her team learned. Record these ideas on the newsprint. Then ask each group to identify the negative feelings in Ecclesiastes 4:1-8. Record these ideas next to the other list. Remind everyone that these are people of great faith who did tremendous things for God; and yet they too had and expressed negative feelings at times.

Ask:
▼ How does that make you feel about being depressed?

OPTION 3

Animal Symbols

PREPARATION: List on the chalkboard or on a large sheet of paper the following names of animals. (Do not list the information in parentheses):

• ostrich (to deny that oppression exists)
• turtle (to withdraw in order to avoid dealing with oppression)

▼ What would you have to do to be remembered in this way? How would your life have to change?

▼ If this were your purpose in life, what would your life mean to others? to you? to God?

▼ If you feel that your purpose in life will not mean much after death, how could you modify it so that it would?

▼ What would your epitaph mean to those in the world today who are oppressed? What effect does your purpose in life have on them?

▼ What is one thing you can do this week related to your life's purpose that will have a positive impact on someone who is oppressed?

▼ What epitaph do you think the writer of Ecclesiastes would have chosen for himself?

▼ What epitaph do you think the writer of Ecclesiastes would have chosen for a person such as Abraham Lincoln, Mother Teresa, Gandhi, or Martin Luther King, Jr., who spent their lives combatting oppression?

 **CHECK OUT**

What words of wisdom would you say to teenagers who live in oppressed situations today?

● *lemming (to give in and accept another person's point of view)*

● *weasel (to rationalize: Oppression is not important anyway.)*

● *gorilla (to overpower others by forcing them to accept our point of view)*

● *owl (to intellectualize about oppression in order to hide emotions)*

● *sheep (to conform to the norms of the group)*

Say: In Ecclesiastes 4:1-4, the teacher talks about oppression in ways that clearly show sympathy for the oppressed. However, he offers no solutions for their plight. Often, when we talk about what is wrong with our society, we find it easier to complain than to do something about it.

Ask:

▼ We use images to describe our behavior; what does the image of each animal suggest about behavior?

▼ How might a person who is like each animal respond to oppression?

▼ Is insulting another person a form of oppression? why? why not?

▼ Why do people put other people down?

Draw a stick picture of the animal you represent. Call on volunteers to share.

25. LIFE IS UNFAIR

Matthew 20:1-7

Comparing God's fairness with life's fairness.

✔ CHECK UP!

God treats us differently from what we deserve. Which is probably a good thing. This can be seen in this parable told by Jesus.

A landowner hires a crew early in the morning. In Israel, the working day normally lasted from sunrise until the stars could be seen. This made a long, hard day in July or August, with the hot wind blowing off the desert and the sun beating down. The usual daily wage was a denarius, about twenty cents in silver, enough to feed a family for one day. This landowner went out again at nine o'clock and hired more workers. Notice that he agrees to pay the first crew the regular wage of one denarius. With this second group of workers he only says he will pay them what is fair, which probably was understood to be less than a denarius. The landowner again hires more workers at noon and at three, making the same deal. Finally, he goes back at five o'clock and finds men who have not worked all day and hires them. Why hire anyone so late? Since this is the grape harvest, it is important to pick the grapes at the peak of ripeness. After five o'clock in July or August, the men could work two or three hours before the stars came out. So, this was not a foolish gesture on the landowner's part. Up to this point this story makes sense.

Finally, the day is done. It's time for the payoff, both literally and figuratively. It was customary that a worker was paid the day's wages that same day, for two reasons. First, there was no guarantee of work the next day. Second, the worker's family needed those wages for food the next day. The landowner pays those who came to work at five o'clock in the evening a full day's wages, which was certainly an act of grace. If these workers go home with wages for only a couple of hours, their families will not eat. Imagine the surprise when word of the landowner's generosity spread back through the line. Those at the end of the line who had worked all day must have been rubbing their hands anticipating a bonus. Imagine the surprise when everyone was paid exactly the same.

Here's the real payoff. The owner says, "Friend, I am doing you no wrong. Did you not agree with me for the usual daily wage? Take what belongs to you and go. I choose to give to this last the same as I give to you. Am I not allowed to do what I choose with what belongs to me? Or are you envious because I am generous?" In worldly, economic terms, of course, the story makes no sense. No one can do exactly what he wants, even with his own property. Jesus is not teaching that everyone deserves equal wages for unequal labor. Economically, this makes no sense. But remember this is a parable about God as the ultimate owner of all things who can do what God chooses. Grace seems unfair to us, even as it did to those who bore the heat worked all day. Some youth may even ask, "If God is this way, why should I be a disciple now? Why not wait until the last minute since God loves like this? If God is unfair, why not take advantage of that unfairness?" There's only one way to answer that question. If the most wonderful love in the world is offered to you, why wait for years to accept it?

The radical, unfair, undeserved gift of God's love is offered to us. Take it! Rejoice when others accept it later. Don't envy them because God is generous.

 CHECK IN

STARTING

Fair or Unfair?
PREPARATION: Make signs that read *FAIR* and *UNFAIR*. Post the signs on opposite sides of the room.

Read each case study aloud and ask youth to position themselves in the room according to whether they think the case study is fair or unfair. Invite volunteers to explain their positions. The case studies are:

> The teacher orders pizza for a class party. Everyone gets one slice except Janice. The teacher gives her two slices.

> Robert's family is homeless. He has not eaten for two days. At a class party the teacher gives him two slices of pizza while everyone else has one slice.

> You want to stay out all night with your friends. Your parents allowed your older sister to do the same thing two weeks ago. They refuse your request.

> Your youth group is having an all-night bowl-a-thon to raise money for homeless youth. Your parents will not allow you to participate. They say you need your sleep.

> The youth group has been raising money for a trip. Everyone is expected to participate in the workdays in order to go on

OPTION 1

Peanut Payment
Pass around a sheet of paper and ask participants to write their name and the number of years they have been attending church. Visitors should write "zero." Arrange the names so that the people at the top of the list are those who have started attending church most recently and those at the bottom of the list have been attending the longest.

Say: **Today we are going to give awards to people who have been attending church for the longest time. The person who has been attending longest will get one peanut (or pretzel) for each year he or she has been a part of the church. O.K.?** *(Be sure the youth agree; this will be a spoken contract.)* **Everyone else will get what is right.**

Begin awarding peanuts with the person at the top of the list: the visitor or the youth who is new to the church. Give him or her the same number of peanuts as the person who has been in the church for the longest time. Move down the list, giving every the trip. Tom is new in town and in the youth group. He did not work. He is allowed to go on the trip.

One person in class misbehaves. The teacher punishes the entire class.

You promised your parents all week that you would clean up your room. You have plans to go to a movie with a friend. They will not allow you to go until your room is clean.

As youth sit down, ask:
▼ Have you ever felt life was unfair?
▼ What were the circumstances?
▼ Who was responsible for the unfairness?
▼ How did you handle it?

EXPLORING

Parable Rewrite

Ask a volunteer to read Matthew 20:1-16 again.

Ask:
▼ What events of the story seemed unfair to you?
▼ What events seemed fair?
▼ How do you feel about the landowner's response to the disgruntled workers?

Say: If we were to imagine this story happening today, several things might turn out to be different.

Ask:
▼ Who would be the landowner?
▼ What would be the vineyard? (a school, a factory, home).
▼ Who would be the laborers?
▼ What might be the wage and the time of work?

Tell groups of two or three to write a modern version of the parable. Emphasize that they should have an up-to-date plot and that the "boss" in each story should be fair! Invite volunteers to read aloud their versions of the parable. Ask everyone to compare these stories with the biblical story.

Ask:
▼ How is our idea of fairness different from God's idea of grace?

OPTION 1 (Continued)

one the same number of peanuts. You will probably be interrupted by cries of "Unfair!" If you are allowed to finish without protest,

Ask:
▼ Is everybody happy?
▼ Did you all get what you expected to get?

Ask the person who has been coming to the church for the longest time:
▼ Did you get what you were promised?
▼ Should you be upset? why? why not?

Read aloud Matthew 20:1-16.

Ask:
▼ In the game you represented one of the people in the parable. Whom did you represent?
▼ Whom did I represent?

OPTION 2

Complaint Department

Say: **Many stores and businesses have complaint departments in which employees have been trained to listen and respond to complaints.** Divide youth into teams of three. Invite the members of each group to imagine that they are consultants hired by a business to set up a complaint department.

Ask:
▼ How would you train people to work in the complaint department to respond to these situations:

● workers who are paid unfairly, according to them.
● people who own products that don't work properly.
● people who are angry because they don't have what another person has.
● good people who have bad things happen to them.
● people who get exactly what they deserve.

CONNECTING

If Life Were Fair . . .

Say: The point of the parable is that God is not fair. No matter how much we complain, our demands that God be fair don't count for much. God listens instead to the demands of God's own love. And God's love insists that God be more than fair.

Ask:
▼ What would happen to you if God were fair? What if you got no more and no less than you deserve?

Invite the youth to complete these incomplete sentences aloud:

> **If God were fair,**
>
> **then I would . . .**
> **then my family would . . .**
> **then my church would . . .**
> **then my country would . . .**
> **then the world would . . .**

Say: What God gives is not payment, but a gift. God's gift has nothing to do with how hard we work, but everything to do with how much God loves us.

Letter of Thanks

Read aloud Romans 8:28.

Ask:
▼ When has good come out of an unfair situation?
▼ Does the good ever overshadow the difficulty?
▼ How does Romans 8:28 apply to the idea of life being unfair?
▼ If God is still in control, why do we get so upset at life's unfair situations?

Pass out paper and pencils. Invite youth to write a "thank you" letter to God for being God even in unfair situations. They might want to focus on God's grace and love even when they don't deserve it. When everyone is finished, invite volunteers to read their "thank you" letters.

 **CHECK OUT**

How does the parable ultimately offer hope?

Ask:
▼ How do you think God responds to our complaints?

OPTION 3

Exploring Grace

Older youth can deal with the abstract concept of *grace*. Ask youth to define *grace*, being sure they know the undeserved nature of God's grace. Then divide youth into teams of two or three and let them write a case study that ends with the action of grace. Call for the case studies.

OPTION 4

A Song of Grace

Do your youth like to sing? Hand out hymnals or song books and let them choose two or three songs that deal with grace. Lead them in singing these songs.

26. THE WORLD AND ME

Psalm 67; Genesis 11:1-19

Seeing how to be a part of the global community.

✔ CHECK UP!

Psalm 67 is a harvest song, probably sung at the Feast of Tabernacles or another service of public thanksgiving for crops. Because food is universal and because there are frequent references to all nations and all peoples, this psalm reminds us of our part in a global community.

The ancient stories of Yahweh's triumph over chaos give God alone dominion over everything, including control over rainfall and fertility. As a result of God's blessings, all the nations praise God. Verses 3 and 5, "Let the peoples praise you," are the chorus for this hymn. Verse 4 reminds us that all nations rejoice because of God, who judges all people fairly and guides all nations of the earth. God may have a chosen people, Israel, but God is involved in guiding and blessing all people.

There are also some tough questions here. If God's plan is for all nations to live in community, why isn't that happening? What about Bosnia or Haiti or Los Angeles, or wherever headlines of hatred occur? Unfortunately, all God's people are also selfish and sinful and want their own way and their own power without considering the needs of others. Failure in the world happens even with all of God's guidance and blessing. Another tough question is, If the earth has yielded its increase, then why do some people diet to lose weight while others starve to death? Again, the only response has to do with human sin. Our relationship with both God and the human community is damaged. We do not recognize the image of God in the faces of our enemies. We see only enemies, opponents, people who are different from us.

The other text is the story of the building of the tower of Babel in Genesis 11:1-9. There are two parts in the text, verses 3-4 and verses 6-7, both beginning with the words, "Come, let us." One is the action of humanity, sin, and pride; the other is the action of God's judgment on that sin. Humanity wants to build a tower and make a name for itself. Humanity fears being scattered all over the earth and works to prevent it. Instead, God scatters them against their will.

God's will includes unity and scattering. The unity is a reliance on God, to live out God's will and to depend on God's power. The scattering is so that people, wherever they are, will live in God's love

✔ CHECK LIST

STARTING
❑ Nine crackers per person, index cards, eight paper plates, eighty dollars in play money, table.

EXPLORING
❑ Bibles, paper, pencils.

CONNECTING
❑ Paper, pencils.

OPTION 1
❑ Globe or world map.

OPTION 2
❑ Paper, pencils.
❑ Microphone.

WHEN GOD SCRAMBLES YOUR PLANS

and be aware of the needs of all creation. God wills it so that all humanity looks to God and lives in unity despite their differences. In our day, we've accepted our differences of race, class, gender, culture, nation. Where we fail is depending on God.

We define ourselves by a group and look down at others who are different from us. To be secure we emphasize the differences. We insist that we are better than they are. Any hint of the reality that this may not be true is incredibly threatening. In fact, God speaks against that kind of isolation and false security with both judgment and a call to true security.

Another kind of security is the fortress mentality. This mentality shuts out God, as well as the rest of the world. The danger of this kind of unity is that it leads to conformity, and oppression of all those who don't conform. If you don't think this actually happens, watch youth's clothing styles.

Finally, a word about language. Language defines how we care for one another, how we conduct business, how we arrange power. Words hurt, tear, and divide. There are racist, sexist, classist, homophobic words that tear community apart. There are putdown words that destroy self-esteem and create barriers to community. There are also words of openness, healing, and compassion that transcend differences and heal wounds. Language does not have to be oppressive; it can also be liberating. Language can teach us about new worlds and bring about our dreams. In verse 7, look at what God says about the scattering. Part of the judgment is not understanding each other. If this simply means that people will not understand other languages, we have a communications problem. But if language is translated and we don't listen, then we have a deeper problem. Listening that transforms begins with trust, and a willingness to change and to be changed.

 **CHECK IN**

STARTING

Food for All?
PREPARATION: Write each of the following on a separate index card:

- *United States-Canada*
- *Russia*
- *Mexico*
- *China*
- *Europe*
- *Africa*
- *Japan*
- *India*

Invite everyone to sit in a circle. Place a small table in the center of the circle. Divide youth into eight groups, and give each group an index card and a paper plate. (One person can be a group. If you have fewer than eight youth, choose one country for each person present. If you have more than eight youth, ask one person to represent the United States and Canada, one person to represent Europe, and two people to represent Japan. Divide everyone else into five equal groups that will represent the five remaining countries.)

OPTION 1
A Worldview
Invite youth to look at a globe or world map as you read aloud Psalm 67.

Ask:
▼ **What came to mind as you looked at the globe (map) and heard the words of this psalm?**
▼ **What parts of the world are most troubled right now?**

Point to the countries named and ask:
▼ **Do you see God at work here? how?**
▼ **From your knowledge of history, how has God been at work among the nations in the past?**
▼ **How do you understand God's care for the entire world?**

Explain the rules by saying: **The game will be played in three rounds. The same amount of food will be distributed in each round. I will distribute three crackers per person per round. All the food for each round must be distributed and eaten before the next round can begin.**

ROUND 1

Place in the center of the table the food for Round 1. Give each person three crackers.

ROUND 2

At the beginning of Round 2, distribute the money as follows:

United States-Canada $32	China $2
Russia $3	Africa $2
Mexico $3	Japan $20
Europe $16	India $2

Announce that you will distribute the food on the basis of cash payment. One cracker costs $2. Place in the center of the table the food for Round 2 (three crackers per person).

ROUND 3

Distribute the money as in Round 2. Sell the crackers at the same price, $2 per cracker. Place in the center of the table the food for Round 3 (three crackers per person).

Stop the game. Bring the groups together.

Ask:
▼ **What was the difference between Round 1 and the other two rounds?**
▼ **Was the process fair? After we introduced the idea of money, could we have distributed the food evenly?**
▼ **Did you know that food is distributed in much the same way in the world?**
▼ **God provides food and other resources for all of God's people. Why do some people starve to death while others diet to lose weight?**

EXPLORING

To Babel or Not

Distribute Bibles, paper, and pencils. Invite someone to read aloud Genesis 11:1-9. Say: **The biblical account of Babel includes the people's actions and God's actions. Let's see how the story might have changed if God had acted differently.**

Ask youth to write the story of the tower of Babel so that God's actions are the opposite of those in the biblical story. Encourage them to think carefully about how God would act. Would God cooperate? stifle anger? not care? After about 8 minutes, invite volunteers to read their stories.

OPTION 2

News at 11

Form two teams. Tell Team One to write a news story (or to prepare several short interviews) based on Genesis 11:1-9. Tell Team Two to write a news story (or to prepare several short interviews) based on Psalm 67. Suggest they try to tie their stories to events occurring in the world today. After each team has shared its stories,

Ask:
▼ **In what areas are nations most cooperative: space exploration, ecology, politics, prevention of poverty and hunger, arms reduction, conflict resolution?**
▼ **What good things do you think might take place in Africa, Europe, or the Middle East in the next five years?**

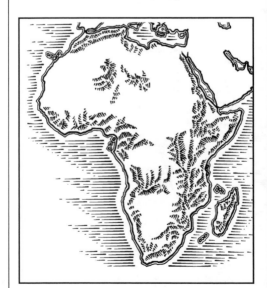

WHEN GOD SCRAMBLES YOUR PLANS

Ask:

▼ What new insights do you have into the biblical story?

▼ How would our relationship with God change if your story accurately described it?

▼ In what ways do we depend on God in your story? in the biblical story?

▼ How could the tower have been a blessing?

Share ideas from Check Up! Read Psalm 67 aloud.

Ask:

▼ What does the story of Babel have to do with the blessings of God in Psalm 67?

Direct youth to debate either of these statements using ideas from both scriptures:

1. God's blessings are distributed the same way the food was distributed in the "Food for All?" game.
2. The differences in language are the basis of all world problems.

CONNECTING

Claim the Dream

Say: **God calls us to global community. But the world seems far from unity and peace. God calls us to live in a world in which all God's children share the harvest of food, but people still don't have enough to eat. And some people starve to death while others diet to lose weight.**

Ask:

▼ Where in this nation or in the world do people need food?

▼ How can we be responsible for those people who don't have food?

Say: **God calls us to global community. God calls us to live in a world in which all God's children join together to give thanks.**

Ask:

▼ What is an example of disunity among people in this nation or in the world?

▼ How can we be responsible for bringing unity to people?

▼ How does that make us thankful?

Say: **God still calls us to be a global community.**

Ask:

▼ What would the world look like if God's dream came true?

▼ How are we responsible for helping God's dream happen on earth?

Pray in conclusion: **God, call us to be a global community of love, joy, and peace. Help us to live by your dream. Amen.**

 CHECK OUT

How can I be a part of the global community when I'm just one person?

OPTION 3

I Believe

Read aloud each statement below. After each statement, ask youth to respond by holding thumbs up if they agree with the statement and thumbs down if they disagree. Then ask youth to defend their decisions.

● I believe that God loves all people, good or bad.
● I believe that God is in charge of the world.
● I believe that God guides the nations of the earth.
● I believe that there can be peace on earth.
● I believe God blesses all people regardless of race or nationality.

Close by asking youth to stand and pray for the country they represented in "Food for All?" or a country of their choice.

27. WAR AND PEACE— THE REALITY

Isaiah 11:1-10; Matthew 2:16-18

Evaluating violence in today's world and identifying ways to encourage peace.

✔ CHECK UP!

Every king was expected to rule with the justice and compassion of God. So the idealistic language in these verses from Isaiah is not so much an expectation of an ideal king in the future, but of this king, this year. The poem is an ancient equivalent of a nominating speech at a political convention. It is full of hopes and dreams for the present and the future. But there is the additional idea that Isaiah believed that God could make this happen only if the king were open to God's leading.

The Lord will anoint the king not only with oil, but also with the spirit of God. The gifts of God's spirit include wisdom and understanding through the fear of the Lord. This fear is an expression of awe, reverence, piety, and an awareness of the proper relationship between God and humanity. In other words, this means, "You may be king in Jerusalem, but remember that God is king of the universe." Armed with these gifts, the king can rule in justice. Through wisdom and understanding he will see reality. He will judge the poor according to what is right, and strike down the unjust tyrants who oppress the poor. One common expectation of the king was that he would champion the cause of the poor. The economic and social reality of Isaiah's time included economic exploitation of the poor by members of the nobility and the merchants. Killing the wicked to bring about justice probably means that the king will have to take action against members of his own class, even members of his own family. The result of a righteous king's bringing justice will be a reign of peace. The idyllic conditions of Eden, where there were no predators or prey among the animals, will be restored. In the new reign of peace, all ancient hatred will be overcome.

In contrast to the righteous king is one of the worst villains in the Bible. Herod the Great ruled Israel as a Roman pawn from 37 B.C. to 4 B.C. His skill as a shrewd administrator and as a builder of magnificent buildings brought notoriety. This man also ordered the execution of one of his wives and three of his sons when he imagined them as threats to his rule. Here was a man who planned to have one member of every family killed when he died so that the nation would truly mourn. The ancient Jewish historian Josephus, who compiled a record of Herod's cruelty, makes no mention of any slaughter of infants, but such a drastic and terrible act was not

✔ CHECK LIST

EXPLORING
❏ Slips of paper, baskets or bowls.
❏ Prepare proverbs, as suggested.
❏ Write questions on index cards.

OPTION 1
❏ Bring newspapers and ads that deal with violence.

OPTION 2
❏ Prepare word puzzle.

WHEN GOD SCRAMBLES YOUR PLANS

inconsistent with Herod's character. In Matthew 2:17-18, the slaughter of the innocents recalls an earlier tragedy in Israel's history, when the Jews were deported to Babylon. Matthew quotes Jeremiah 31:15, where the prophet remembers a picture of Rachel, Jacob's wife, weeping over her exiled children.

The infant Jesus is taken by his parents to Egypt to avoid Herod's slaughter. Matthew 2:16-18 forms the second scene. Herod's massacre of baby boys sounds like Pharaoh's mass murder of the Hebrew baby boys centuries before. Verses 19-23 compose the third scene, the return of Jesus' family to their homeland.

An earlier quotation from Hosea, in Matthew 2:15, is Matthew's way of linking Jesus' return from Egypt with Israel's exodus from Egypt. Clearly, Matthew portrays Jesus as a new Moses, the founder and lawgiver of the true Israel. At the very least, these verses remind us that suffering is not a modern invention, that innocent people have suffered under tyranny and abusive power for centuries. Don't overlook Matthew's more important message. Matthew wants his readers to understand that although Herod wields political and military authority to create terrible havoc, Herod does not have the ability to block God's ultimate will in Jesus. Youth need to remember this message of God's greater will when they are hurt by injustice, or when they feel discouraged by the enormous suffering of others. Despite the tragedy of genuine suffering, God's ultimate redemptive purposes in Jesus Christ cannot be defeated.

✔ CHECK IN

STARTING

War and Peace

Divide the group in half. Instruct the members of one group to whisper the word *peace* over and over again. Tell the youth in the other group to shout the word *war* over and over again. As they shout or whisper, the groups should walk around the room so that their voices mix. Before they begin, remind the group saying "peace" that they are to keep whispering. Arrange for a signal that will let the youth know when it is time to stop. What is likely to happen is that the youth saying "peace" will get louder and louder, trying to drown out the people saying "war." After several minutes, tell the youth to stop and invite them to sit down again.

Ask:
▼ What was it like to call for peace and not be heard?
▼ What did it mean that the people whispering "peace" began to talk louder and louder? In what ways do we try to get things done in the world?
▼ Why do we want peace so much? What would we give for peace on earth?

OPTION 1

Media Violence

Provide copies of newspapers that include movie ads and TV listings (including cable listings if possible). Ask the youth to tear out ads for movies or TV shows that are violent.

Ask:
▼ Why are people so interested in violence?
▼ Do video games increase the amount of violence we're exposed to?
▼ What's the payoff? Why do we want to play games that teach us to be violent?
▼ In a world like ours, is peace possible? why? why not?

Read aloud Isaiah 11:1-10.

Ask:
▼ Do you think there is any chance in today's world of God's keeping God's promise of peace?

EXPLORING

Fractured Proverbs

PREPARATION: Write the following proverbs on separate sheets of paper. Add others so that each youth will have a piece of a proverb. Tear the paper in half so that half the proverb is on each half of the paper. (The slash indicates where the proverb should be separated.)

- *Silence / is golden.*
- *One good turn / deserves another.*
- *The early bird / catches the worm.*
- *Two wrongs / don't make a right.*
- *Every cloud / has a silver lining.*
- *A penny saved / is a penny earned.*
- *An apple a day / keeps the doctor away.*
- *A friend in need / is a friend indeed.*

Put all the papers in a bowl or basket. Invite each youth to take a paper and find the beginning or ending—whichever that youth needs to make a complete sentence—of another proverb that is NOT the original saying. Invite each pair of youth to read their fractured proverbs.

Direct a youth to read Isaiah 1:1-10.

Ask:
- ▼ **Do any of the sayings make sense? Are you surprised?**
- ▼ **How is "A penny saved has a silver lining" like God's promise in Isaiah 11:1-10?**
- ▼ **How could the kingdom Isaiah describes become a reality?**
- ▼ **What is the theme of Isaiah's prediction?**

Say: **Although Isaiah saw a perfect world one day, cruel things were still happening, especially during Jesus' time.**

A Cruel King

PREPARATION: Write the following questions on index cards:

- ▼ *What good reasons could have motivated Herod?*
- ▼ *Does power ever justify murder?*
- ▼ *Is it better for a few children in one town to die or for a whole nation to be caught up in war?*

Read Matthew 2:16-18 aloud. Divide the youth into three teams. Give each team one question on an index card. Call for team reports. Say, **The natural human response to most stressful situations is to fight or flee.**

Ask:
- ▼ **What could have happened if Jesus' parents had stayed to fight Herod?**
- ▼ **How does a person make a choice whether to flee or fight?**
- ▼ **How do suffering and pain change the issue?**
- ▼ **How do you think Mary and Joseph responded to the news they heard out of Bethlehem?**
- ▼ **How do people with horrible diseases, people caught in a violent world, people who live through natural disasters that destroy everything, or people who are addicted keep going?**
- ▼ **How does Isaiah's message relate to these verses in Matthew?**

CONNECTING

Nonviolence Works

Read the following case study aloud.

> Phil was so mad that he could have chewed up railroad spikes and spit out carpet tacks. Three times before he got to his first class, he'd heard that he was being kicked off the baseball team for missing three practices in two weeks. Of course, he'd missed three practices! But he'd asked Coach Stephens, and Coach Stephens had said O.K. Phil's little sister, Sandy, had been sick; and his mom needed Phil to stay home with her. If his mom took time off from work, she would lose her job. The coach had approved all three absences.
>
> Phil stormed into the coach's office. The coach insisted that he hadn't said a word about Phil's being kicked off the team.
>
> Whoa! Reality check! Phil followed the rumor back to a guy named Robby Brown. Robby Brown had a motive: He was an alternate for the team, next in line for an opening. Phil found Robby on the practice field after school, got right in Robby's face, and let him know how angry he was.

Divide the group into two teams. Tell one team to role-play the situation with a violent solution and the other team to role-play the situation with a nonviolent solution.

 CHECK OUT

In what areas of life would you like to be more loving? more peaceful? In what ways could you make Christ's values a part of your life? Write at least one goal for living in a not-so-peaceful world.

OPTION 2

Nonviolent Word Puzzle

PREPARATION: Write the following puzzle on butcher paper.

```
S E L F C O N T R O L K
M N O P A S P C A D D I
G E N E R O S I T Y P N
L F M N O P S T U V E D
A L P A T I E N C E A N
J O Y E F O B C O I C E
B V D F E P D A E U E S
C E G E N T L E N E S S
F A I T H F U L N E S S
```

Ask:
▼ What forms of modern-day violence do you see around you?
▼ What does this violence tell us about ourselves? about God?

Ask youth to brainstorm nonviolent ways to solve problems. List these on a chalkboard. Show the puzzle written on the poster. Instruct youth to find the nonviolent solutions hidden among the letters. Words go across or up and down. If youth have trouble locating the nine words, direct them to read Galatians 5:22-23.

Ask:
▼ What other words describe the type of world God desires?
▼ How can you as a teenager make peace possible?
▼ What can you do this next week (at home, at school, with friends, on the team) to make peace happen in your part of the world?

28. WHY SHOULD I WORRY ABOUT OTHERS' SUFFERING?

John 9

Realizing how physical suffering and spiritual blindness can be helped through the light of Jesus Christ.

✔ CHECK UP!

The healing of the blind man is a perfect symbol for Jesus' claim that he is "the light of the world." As we discover, blindness has a double meaning in this compelling drama.

The account in John 9 is the only recorded miracle in the Gospels in which the person is stated to have been suffering from a disease or disability since birth. Jewish tradition held that sin was the direct cause of any physical impairment, such as blindness. In the case under study today, many persons assumed that the sin of the parents was responsible for the man's being born blind. Jesus doesn't give an exhaustive cause-and-effect explanation of suffering. He does seek to teach that the affliction of the blind man is an opportunity for God's loving intervention. Miracles are ways in which God can express the presence and power of divine love.

After Jesus heals the man, he tells him to go wash in the pool of Siloam. This Greek place-name probably comes from the Hebrew word *Shiloah,* meaning "sending."

The Pharisees are not impressed with Jesus' miraculous healing of the blind man on the Sabbath. They interrogate the man and his parents about the incident. Whereas the man received healing of both his physical and his spiritual blindness, the Pharisees apparently remained stuck in their spiritual blindness.

The blind man was like each of us; his faith in Jesus had to grow. When he first tried to describe what happened to him, he called Jesus "the man" (v. 11). Later, when asked again, he referred to Jesus as "a prophet" (v. 17). And, finally, he came to affirm Jesus as "the Son of Man" (v. 38). The more time he spent with Jesus, the more he realized Jesus' true identity and how Jesus' power had changed his life.

The Pharisees exerted considerable influence in the community. The man's parents refused to say anything that could harm them in the eyes of the leaders of the community. Without judging them harshly, it is still apparent that they had the chance to speak up for what they saw and believed, but they avoided the controversy. The former blind man courageously took on the authorities and stood his ground. What price did he pay? (see v. 34). What might the long-term effect be?

✔ CHECK LIST

STARTING
❏ A blindfold, towelettes or moist wipes.

EXPLORING
❏ Paper and pencils.

CONNECTING
❏ Chalkboard or poster board.

OPTION 1
❏ Newspapers, poster board, glue.

OPTION 3
❏ Newsprint or poster board.

WHEN GOD SCRAMBLES YOUR PLANS

✔ CHECK IN

STARTING

Blinded

Blindfold each person as he or she enters the room. Lead each person into the room, and seat them in a chair or on the floor in a circle. When everyone is seated, have youth imagine that they have been blind since birth and are forced to beg for a living.

Ask the "blind" persons around the circle to imagine what their neighbors say about them behind their back.

Ask:
▼ What tasks and relationships are difficult in their day-to-day life?
▼ How does it feel:
to be in total darkness?
to have someone lead you around the room?

After a brief discussion, distribute individual cleansing towelettes or moist wipes and instruct youth to simulate "washing" their "blind" eyes to restore their vision. Next, have everyone remove their blindfolds.

Ask:
▼ Have you ever known a blind person or talked to a person who was born blind?
▼ What have you learned about being blind?

EXPLORING

Can You Really See?

Say: Today's study is about a blind man and about sighted people who are spiritually blind. Listen carefully as the story is read aloud from John 9:1-12. Ask a youth to read the scripture.

Ask:
▼ How do you think the blind man felt the day he encountered Jesus? What do you suppose he was thinking as he did what Jesus asked him to do?
▼ How was his life different afterward?

Hand out paper and pencils. Say: Pretend that you were an observer at the scene that took place between Jesus and the blind man. As you relax in the evening of that same day, you open your daily diary. Write thoughts and feelings that come to the surface as you reflect on Jesus' act of compassion and healing.

OPTION 1

Refusing to See

Distribute sections of current newspapers to the youth and ask them to tear out articles and pictures that describe suffering in our world. Provide a large piece of poster board or a paper tablecloth, on which everyone can paste or glue pictures and articles to form a collage. Lead a discussion about the possible sins that contributed to, or caused, the suffering in the pictures.

Ask:
▼ How does blindness to the suffering of others cause more suffering and interfere with solutions to suffering?

OPTION 2

Why Suffering?

Ask:
▼ Do you ever wonder why people have to suffer?
▼ Are you sometimes at a loss to understand some personal pain or tragedy?

Say: Jesus refused to say that the blind man's suffering was due to sin. He said instead that the man's condition presented an opportunity to demonstrate what God can do.

Ask:
▼ How did this experience demonstrate how God can respond to our suffering?
▼ Why do we blame suffering on God?

Read John 9:35-41.

CONNECTING
Christ's Example

Ask:
▼ What words and actions communicate Christ's example of caring?

List responses on poster board or chalkboard. Remind youth that we demonstrate caring for others by helping them experience the same sort of healing and love that has come to our own life. Ask each person to silently identify someone whom they can "see" in a new way this week. Ask youth how they can improve their relationships with the people. Have the youth name ways to let people know in a positive way that the source of their love is Jesus Christ. Challenge youth to report one way they help this person next session.

A Prayer
Direct youth to write a prayer about their spiritual vision. Maybe they have been blind to someone's pain or problems, or even to their own. After a few minutes call on youth to reread their prayers as you repeat this one:

O God of light and of spiritual vision, open our eyes to the suffering in our world and remind us of our call to be ministers of love, compassion, and healing. May we never lose sight of your healing power. Amen.

✔ CHECK OUT

What makes us blind to the suffering of others?

OPTION 2 (Continued)

Ask:
▼ How would you describe someone who is spiritually blind?

Say: Spiritual vision is the ability to see what Christ is calling us to be, to do, and to become. Another facet of spiritual vision is the ability to see the connection between our faith and our responsibility to offer Christian compassion and caring to a suffering world.

OPTION 3
Called

On a piece of newsprint or poster board, have youth participate in composing a two- or three-sentence affirmation. The affirmation should express their idea of what Christ is calling them to become and of how they are to express their faith in the world around them.

CHAPTER 5

REAL RELATIONSHIPS

29. ALL IN THE FAMILY

Ephesians 5:21–6:4

Evaluating how youth can contribute to the well-being of their families.

✔ CHECK UP!

This lesson focuses on Paul's rules for Christian households. In the first part of this passage, he talks about husbands and wives; and in the second part he focuses on parents and children. Remember that Paul is writing to a patriarchal society, one in which the male was automatically the head of the household.

Paul does not suggest changing the society as such, but he does suggest a radically new household order for Christians. Instead of seeing the male as having unlimited power, Paul sets boundaries. In verse 21, he writes that we are to be subject to one another.

In Paul's day, there were government rulers who could expect people to be subject to them. However, Paul is not suggesting that one person rule all others in a family, but that each person is to be subject to everyone else. In other words, we are not to dominate other family members but are to consider the needs and desires of others and act accordingly. The needs and feelings of all members of the household are to be taken into account. No longer does the head of the household have absolute authority.

Paul's teachings regarding family relationships were no doubt radical for that era. Women and children were considered the property of the husbands and fathers. The idea of mutual caring, concern, and respect—though not unusual to us—would have been quite novel to people in the Roman Empire during the first century.

In verses 22-33, Paul compares the relationship between husbands and wives to that of Christ and the church. Just as Christ loved the church so much that he was willing to die for it, husbands are to exhibit this same kind of compassionate love for their wives. The model that Paul sets forth is not one of domination but one of mutual care, concern, and love.

Similarly, children are to obey their parents. This relationship is also one of reverence, for parents are charged with the responsibility of teaching their children how to live as God's people. Parents are not to treat their children in ways that cause anger.

In summary, Paul proposes a model for family relationships that is loving and mutually supportive.

✔ CHECK LIST

STARTING
❒ Prepare graffiti sheet, markers.

EXPLORING
❒ Prepare envelopes with verses.
❒ Bring art supplies.

CONNECTING
❒ Index cards, pencils.

OPTION 1
❒ Long sheet of paper, markers.

OPTION 3
❒ Bring art supplies.

✔ CHECK IN

STARTING

Family Struggles

PREPARATION: Tape a large sheet of paper to a wall or table top. In the center of the paper write *Family Struggles*.

Tell youth to write in graffiti style several family struggles they see. These could include *broken homes, setting curfews, brother-sister rivalries,* and *moving.* Note several of these struggles. Say: **Every family has its share of struggles. Sometimes we contribute to those struggles. Sometimes we stand back and can't do a thing about those struggles.**

Ask:

▼ **What position or birth order do you occupy in your family?** *(oldest, middle, youngest, only child)*

▼ **Do you feel that your older or younger siblings get more** *(or fewer, or different)* **privileges than you do? What grounds do you have for this belief?**

▼ **Do you wish you occupied a different position in your family? However you answer, what is the reason for your response?**

▼ **If you are an only child, what kinds of demands does that place on you?**

Say: **Today we're going to see how families can pull together to deal with pressures and struggles.**

EXPLORING

Tips for All Those in the Family

PREPARATION: Write each word of Ephesians 5:21 on a separate slip of paper. Mix up the slips and place them in an envelope. Make two other envelopes with the same verse.

Create three teams of youth. Assign each team a portion of the Bible study—Ephesians 5:22-24, 33 (Wife Team); Ephesians 5:25-33; 6:4 (Husband Team); Ephesians 6:1-4 (Children Team). Tell teams to prepare an infomercial for the perfect wife, husband, or child. Say: **You will have two minutes to present your infomercial. You may use a model, pictures, a slogan, a jingle, or anything else to present the perfect family member. Your infomercial must be based on the Scripture.**

Provide art supplies if youth need these. After youth have worked on their infomercials, call for them to share these with the others. After each team reports, ask the team to briefly state the main characteristics for their assigned family member. After all infomercials,

Ask:

▼ **Why don't family members live up to this ideal?**

▼ **How difficult would it be for your family to adopt some of these positive characteristics?**

OPTION 1

Family Tree

PREPARATION: Hang a long strip of paper on the wall.

Hand out markers and tell youth to draw their family trees. Tell them to go back to their grandparents if they can. Remind them to include aunts and uncles. Be sensitive to the fact that some youth's family trees may be disrupted by divorce and remarriage. Tell youth to circle their names. Without reviewing each family tree, comment about the diversity, the heritage, and the number of people in the family who contribute to who we are today. Continue with the place-in-the-family questions in STARTING.

OPTION 2

Family Scene

After dividing youth into the three teams in EXPLORING, instruct each team to make up a scene with a problem involving the family member of their team. Tell youth to find a solution in Ephesians 5:21–6:4. Let youth share the family problem and the biblical solution.

ALL IN THE FAMILY

▼ What is the key for living in a family?

After several responses, give each team an envelope. Tell them to arrange the words to form the answer. Share what it means to be subject to one another.

CONNECTING

We Are Family

Say: **God has planned for each one of us to be part of a family. Some families enjoy one another and get along well. Other families experience problems with interpersonal relationships. No matter what our family is like, we can usually improve the overall atmosphere by our behavior.**

If youth are open and comfortable, read the following statements, letting youth respond aloud. If youth are quiet, hand out index cards and pencils, letting them write each statement down. Tell youth to grade themselves A to F beside each statement.

> 1. **I respect the privacy of other family members.**
> 2. **I limit my calls to a reasonable amount of time so that others may use the phone.**
> 3. **I treat my family members the way I want them to treat me.**
> 4. **When a problem or argument arises, I try to be a peacemaker.**
> 5. **I apologize when I am wrong.**
> 6. **I try to obey my parents, even when I disagree with them.**

After youth grade themselves, ask:
▼ **How do these actions help the family?**
▼ **How difficult is it to do these things?**
▼ **How can being positive and considerate of others make them positive and considerate of you?**
▼ **What one thing do you wish for your family?**
▼ **What one thing can you do to help your family?**

As you close, direct youth to think of one family member who needs prayer. Lead youth to pray silently for that person as you lead in a closing prayer.

 CHECK OUT

How does being "subject to one another" work in the mixed-up, modern-day family?

For youth who prefer art, let them design a family crest. On the crest suggest they include symbols for each family member and symbols of favorite holidays or special family events. They can add words that are family phrases. After a few minutes let youth share their family crests. Listen carefully to what youth say about their families.

30. MY BROTHER'S KEEPER? NO WAY!

1 Corinthians 8:1-13

Focusing on how actions and attitudes can influence another's relationship with God.

✔ CHECK UP!

Paul addressed a practical problem faced by Christians in Corinth. The meat sold in butcher shops had usually been offered as a temple sacrifice to a heathen idol before being sold. These early Christians wanted to know whether eating such meat amounted to actually participating in the worship of idols. To put their concern another way, they wondered whether they could eat the meat and still be a Christian.

The question about eating meat was more complicated than it seemed, so Paul gave an answer in two parts. To begin with, Paul said that idols represent something that does not exist. If these gods do not exist, then the act of offering a sacrifice to them is empty and without meaning. While Christians don't lose anything by eating the meat, they don't gain anything either. Food has no effect on one's relationship with God. According to this theory, it did not matter whether Christians ate the meat. However, there were other concerns related to the issue of eating meat used in idol worship.

The second part of Paul's answer dealt with aspects of the dilemma that the believers at Corinth probably had not considered. Some Corinthian Christians recognized that idols do not exist. These persons were steadfast in their belief that there is only one God. They were feeling smug and prideful because of this knowledge. They knew they were not participating in idol worship if they ate the meat. These Christians knew that their relationship with God would not be affected by eating the meat. On the other hand, eating the meat sacrificed to idols could have an effect on other Christians.

Many of the Corinthian Christians had formerly believed in the existence of many gods. Such believers might be affected when they saw Christians whom they respected eating the meat that had been offered to idols. They would perhaps think that those who ate the meat were sinners and would consequently lose respect for them. Or they might think that since the others were eating meat, it was right for them to eat the meat also. But after they ate, they would perhaps feel that they had somehow done wrong. Just observing others eat meat could lead to feelings of guilt and to a shaky relationship with God.

The real question became, "Do I give up my personal freedom

✔ CHECK LIST

STARTING
❑ Large sheet of paper, markers.

EXPLORING
❑ Make poster.

CONNECTING
❑ Small pieces of paper, pencils.

OPTION 1
❑ Large sheet of paper, marker, or chalkboard.

OPTION 2
❑ Write statement on chalkboard.

because what I do might mislead someone who does not know as much as I know?" Paul replied, "Yes, that is what you should do. Otherwise you may damage a person's character and her or his relationship with God." A true Christian should never cause another believer to falter.

So Paul suggests a loving, caring solution to Christians who possess knowledge. If an action may cause other Christians to lose respect for you, or if it is likely to affect their behavior and their conscience, you should voluntarily give up your freedom out of respect and concern for Christians who are weaker and less knowledgeable. A responsible Christian asks himself or herself two questions, not just one. First she or he asks, Will this harm me? The second question is equally important: How might my behavior affect others? Paul says that one Christian should never act in such a way that another Christian will fall.

 CHECK IN

STARTING

He Did WHAT?

Direct youth to name people in the following categories: sports star, music headliner, radio personality, movie star, popular person in the community, popular person in the church. List these on a large sheet of paper. Next, ask youth to name actions that would surprise them if these people did them.

Ask:
▼ Why would these actions by these people bother you?
▼ How would you feel about the person doing it?

Say: **Today we're going to look at actions that may not be as bad as the ones we've listed here. We'll see how innocent actions can cause problems for others.**

EXPLORING

Christian Freedom

PREPARATION: Make a poster with this brief letter written on it:

Dear Paul,
Is it O.K. to eat meat that has been sacrificed to idols? Answer quickly.
Your Friends in Corinth

OPTION 1

Freedom for Me

Direct youth to define freedom. Tell them to call out things they are glad to be free to do. Write these on a chalkboard or large piece of paper without making any comments. Next, ask youth to name things they would like to be free to do. Write this list next to the first list. Lead youth to select their top three actions in each list.

Ask:
▼ How will you gain the freedom to do the actions in the second list?
▼ Where does your freedom begin?
▼ Where does your freedom end?

Explain that during this study youth will evaluate how to limit their own freedom for the sake of others.

Point out the poster. Explain how animals sacrificed in the Temple were later sold in local butcher shops. Tell youth to listen to the following responses and decide which would be Paul's best answer:

- Just say no to meat offered to idols.
- Idols are only statues, created by human hands. Since the gods they represent do not exist, sacrifices to idols are meaningless. Food offered as a heathen sacrifice is thus O.K. to eat.
- Some people think that eating food offered to idols is the same as believing in or having something to do with idols. Christians are not to associate themselves in any way with idol worship.

Challenge youth to support their choices.

Christian Choices

Direct a youth to read 1 Corinthians 8:4-6.

Ask:

▼ Do you agree or disagree with Paul's reasoning that eating food probably does not affect a person's relationship with God?

Next, have everyone form a line in the middle of the room. Tell the youth that you are going to list a number of actions. As you call out each item, they are to move toward the wall on their left to indicate their belief that such an action can change a person's relationship with God. If they believe a particular action does *not* change a person's relationship with God, the youth are to move toward the wall on their right. Suggestions for possible actions (add additional ones if you wish): *going to school, taking a walk, hanging out with friends, eating pizza, shopping at a mall, visiting persons at a hospital or a nursing home, going to a movie.*

After naming each action, ask one or more persons to explain their response as to whether it would affect a relationship with God in a positive or a negative way.

Ask:

▼ What are some other things Christians can do that probably would not affect one's relationship with God?
▼ Why would these things not affect a person's relationship with God?

Explain that Paul's answer involved two parts. Direct another youth to read 1 Corinthians 8:7-13. Direct youth to play a quick version of "Simon Says." Invite several youth to take turns being "leaders" (they may choose what they will say and do during this brief period of time). Everyone else is to imitate each "leader" for about fifteen or twenty seconds.

Ask:

▼ How would you feel if you knew that someone was imitating you and might do anything you chose to do?
▼ Would knowing that someone was likely to imitate you make a difference in your words or actions? why, or why not?
▼ What are some possible things you would or would not do if you knew a small child would do what she or he saw you do? Explain.

OPTION 2
Keeping My Brother

PREPARATION: On a chalkboard write *I Am My Brother's Keeper.*

Divide youth into two teams. Tell one team to list the world's argument against this statement. Tell the other team to list Paul's argument for this statement. Urge this team to use Paul's points in 1 Corinthians 8:1-13. Call teams together to share their ideas.

Ask:

▼ What excuses do youth use to support the belief that they are not responsible for others? *("I'm only hurting myself." "No one will ever know.")*
▼ Why would a person give up personal freedom for the good of someone else?

Have youth form another line and repeat the earlier activity, this time using actions that may or may not change a person's relationship with God. Possible actions might be: *going into a liquor store, hanging with the wrong crowd at school, attending church regularly, going to an R-rated movie, praying in public when appropriate, listening to music of a group known for its vulgar language, going to a concert of that musical group.*

Ask:
▼ How willing are you to give up your freedom for another person who might be following your example?
▼ How would that make you feel?
▼ Why does Paul say we should give up personal freedom for others?

CONNECTING
Puffed Up or Built Up

Ask:
▼ What did Paul mean by 1 Corinthians 8:1?
▼ Why should Christians try to build up one another?

Say: **Setting a good example and providing encouragement are probably more effective than telling someone else what to do.**

Ask:
▼ Which of the following ideas seem to you like good ways to build up other people?

- telling other Christians what they should do.
- setting a good example.
- encouraging others to do what you feel God would consider right and appropriate.

Invite youth to name additional ways to build up one another *(praising someone for doing a good job, letting others know you care what happens to them, etc.).* Next, give each person a small piece of paper. Say: **Write the name of one Christian friend who might need your good example and might need to be built up this week. Keep the name confidential. Consider how you can be a good example to your friend this week, as well as two ways to build up him or her.**

✔ CHECK OUT

How can you know when to act "the right way" in case someone else is watching?

OPTION 3
My Keeper
Share a personal story of someone whom you admired who let you down. If you don't have such a story, share one you've read about. Or, invite someone who has such a story to share.

31. THE DAMAGED-RELATIONSHIP DOCTOR

2 Corinthians 5:11-21

Responding to God's reconciliation makes us reconcilers.

✔ CHECK UP!

In this well-known section of 2 Corinthians, Paul once more seems to feel the need to clarify his actions and dampen suspicions that he is boasting, that he may not be in his right mind, and so forth. However, within the space of a few verses, Paul moves from references of possible dissension to one of his most memorable statements—the call to new life and reconciliation in Christ.

The word *reconciliation* refers to restoring harmony and agreement between persons or groups who have been hostile toward one another. In view of the apostle Paul's experiences, it is no wonder that he made the ministry of reconciliation one of the keystones of his thought and his preaching. Paul always seemed to be at odds with someone over something. Since he felt that he could not possibly keep all the laws of the Old Testament, he needed to be reconciled with God. He needed to be reconciled with the Christians whom he had once persecuted. He was often in conflict with the other apostles and church leaders over matters of faith and church leadership. And his beloved church at Corinth, to which he wrote several long letters, was a hotbed of conflict and arguments, often involving Paul.

In the midst of all these experiences of arguing and disharmony, Paul found the solution to conflicts in the love and grace of Jesus Christ. As Paul points out, through the work of Christ, God reconciled us all to God and to one another, so that we can become new people, new creations, and put the old hatreds and conflicts behind us. This brief passage sums up much of Paul's theological thought:

- The source of our faith is the love of Christ, who died and was resurrected for us, so that we might live for him (vv. 14-15).
- The person who accepts Christ becomes a completely new person; the old way of life is a thing of the past (vv. 16-17).
- Through Christ, God reconciles us to one another and to God; our proper response is to participate in a ministry of reconciliation (vv. 18-20).

Today's lesson is particularly relevant to young people, who are in a state of transition as they try to develop their independence while forging meaningful relationships with others. This double focus

✔ CHECK LIST

STARTING
❏ Make tape recording with three youth.
❏ Bring tape and tape player.

EXPLORING
❏ Pencils, paper, chalkboard.

CONNECTING
❏ Duplicate handouts.
❏ Pencils.

OPTION 1
❏ Prepare bags, items for bags.

OPTION 2
❏ Slips of paper, pencils, chalkboard.

OPTION 3
❏ Bring art supplies: construction paper, markers, glitter, yarn, and scissors.

often leads to conflict situations that may involve disagreements with parents, peers, authority figures, institutions, and so forth.

In such situations, teens will find it helpful to use the Christian concept of reconciliation as a frame of reference. The idea of our being called to be reconcilers can provide direction for youth as they deal with conflict and dissension.

 CHECK IN

STARTING

Ask the Doc

PREPARATION: Enlist three youth who are not in your group to read the following situations into a tape recorder.

ROOMMATES

For months Janet and I have been planning to room together on our summer mission trip. The trip is next week. Yesterday I found out that Janet has changed to Maryanne's room and I'm stuck with Diane, the youth group geek. I'm hurt that Janet changed without telling me. What should I do?

FALSELY ACCUSED

After a history test, Mr. Jones found a piece of paper containing dates, places, and other test information. He told us that everyone would have to take the exam over if the cheater was not identified. After class Martha told Mr. Jones that I cheated. She is jealous that I made the basketball team and she didn't. Mr. Jones wants to talk to me in the morning. I can handle that because I know I wasn't cheating. What I need help with is knowing what to say to Martha.

BROKEN TRUST

I have a 12:30 curfew on Friday and Saturday nights. Last night we were having such a great time, we forgot the time. On the way home I slid on the slick pavement and ran over a mailbox. It messed up the person's yard and tore up the front end of the car. The police called my mom, and she came to get me. She was too tired to talk last night, except to say, "The trust is broken. We'll talk about it tomorrow." What can I say or do to restore her trust?

Say: **Today we are listening to the call-in radio program for the Damaged-Relationships Doctor. The doctor is a little late, so you will have to help with these early calls.** Play the first situation on the tape player. Ask youth to share ideas for repairing that relationship. Continue with the other two. Say: **Stay tuned to find out if your advice was on target.**

OPTION 1

Grab Bag Skits

PREPARATION: Determine the number of teams needed and prepare that many paper bags. In each bag put items or pictures of items from the world of youth. *(For example, a picture of a family, a picture of a boy and girl, a textbook, a small telephone, a ring, a movie ad.)*

Divide youth into small teams. Give each team a paper bag with three or four items in it. Tell teams to select one or more objects from their bags and make up a case study about a broken relationship related to that item. *(For example, a crushed flower might be a case study about a guy stood up by a girl, so he couldn't give her the flowers he had bought for her.)* Call for case studies, but don't let them solve these yet. Say, **Today we'll see how broken relationships can be restored.**

WHEN GOD SCRAMBLES YOUR PLANS

EXPLORING

Reconciliation Re-Do's

Ask youth to define *reconciliation*. Explain the background to Paul's letter to the Corinthians using Check Up! Say: **Sometimes it's easier to understand what Paul is saying if you translate the verses into today's language.**

Divide youth into five teams. Assign one team 2 Corinthians 5:11-13; another team, verses 14-15; a third team, verses 16-17; the fourth team verses 18-20; and the final team verse 21. Hand out paper and pencils for youth to use. Let each team share its translation in the correct order. As teams share, identify Paul's suggestions for restoring relationships. List these on a chalkboard as they are named.

Ask:
▼ What does Jesus have to do with reconciliation?
▼ How did Jesus restore our relationship with God?
▼ Now that Jesus has restored that relationship, what is our responsibility?
▼ How can you be a reconciler?

Refer back to the advice youth gave in the first activity.

Ask:
▼ Would you change any of that advice based on this study? If so, what? If not, why not?
(If you used Option 1, ask youth to share some reconciling advice for the situations shared.)

CONNECTING

Rating Relationships

PREPARATION: Duplicate the handout so each youth has one.

RATING MY RELATIONSHIPS

____ with my mother	____ with school classmates
____ with my father	____ with my church
____ with my sister(s)	____ with my school
____ with my brother(s)	____ with my country
____ with my grandparent(s)	____ with people in my clubs
____ with my school teacher(s)	____ with people in general
____ with my pastor	____ with the police
____ with my friend(s)	____ with a neighbor
____ with my other relatives	____ with people I work with
____ _____	____ _____
____ _____	____ _____

From *When God Scrambles Your Plans* by Ann B. Cannon. Copyright © 1997 by Abingdon Press. Reproduced by permission.

OPTION 2

Key Words for Reconcilers

Active youth may prefer to play a game. After youth read 2 Corinthians 5:11-21, let them work in two teams to identify key phrases in these verses. Tell youth to write each key phrase on a slip of paper. Teams will take turns with one person selecting a slip of paper from the other team, then drawing pictures of that phrase to help their team guess the phrase. After the game use the questions in EXPLORING.

Say: Relationships are a central part of our lives. With the exception of hermits and persons in solitary confinement, most of us are involved in personal relationships for most of our waking hours. In addition to relationships with one person at a time, we also have relationships with groups of people and with institutions.

On your handout, rate your relationships by marking each item with a number from 0 to 10. The number 10 indicates a near-perfect, wonderful relationship; use a 0 to indicate a rotten, terrible relationship. Numbers between 0 and 10 indicate relationships somewhere in the mid-range—for example, 3 for not very good, 5 for average, 7 for good, 8 for very good, and so on. Be as honest as you can be in your ratings.

After youth finish, explain that the next part is purely voluntary.

Ask:
▼ How easy or hard was it to evaluate your relationships?
▼ With whom do you have the closest relationship?
▼ With whom do you have the least relationship?
▼ What relationship needs reconciliation?
▼ How can you be a reconciler in one of these relationships?

Thank youth for their open answers.

A Reconciliation Meditation

Say: If you are "on the outs" with someone, whether the conflict is mild or severe, just remember that you are not alone. Having disagreements is a natural part of the human situation. As Christians, however, we are called to follow the example of our Lord, who came to reconcile people to one another and to God, and who "has given us the ministry of reconciliation."

The following exercise in reconciliation is a step-by-step blueprint for helping you to become a reconciler.

1. Think of a relationship with someone that involves a conflict, a disagreement, bad feelings, or some other negative elements.
2. Pray for that other person. Ask God to bless her or him and to grant good things to that person.
3. Pray for yourself. Ask God to help you overcome the difficulties in this relationship.
4. Make plans as to what you will do when you talk to the other person again. Plan on saying and doing something positive and caring.
5. Meditate quietly. Think about God's love. Think loving thoughts. Thank God for all your blessings.
6. Ask for God's guidance and help as you seek to be a reconciler in this one relationship.

 **CHECK OUT**

Sometimes it's hard to know what to do when you have a broken relationship. Who can you trust to help you find a way to reconcile that relationship? Ask that person for help today.

OPTION 3

Reconciling Greetings
PREPARATION: Bring construction paper, markers, glitter, yarn, and scissors. Replace the mediation activity with this idea.

Tell youth to make a reconciliation card for a person with whom they want to renew a relationship. This might be an employer, sibling, a school friend, or a church friend. Let volunteers share their cards. Challenge youth to deliver their cards to this person this week.

WHEN GOD SCRAMBLES YOUR PLANS

32. TO FRIENDS, ENEMIES, AND STRANGERS—WITH LOVE

Romans 12:9-21

Examining ways to show friends, enemies, and strangers Christian love.

✔ CHECK UP!

Let's look at what these practical, common-sense statements in Romans mean for our lives. Verse 9 says that love is not hypocritical. Love is not genuine unless it discriminates between good and evil. Love is not a weak noun, it is a strong verb. Sometimes love expresses itself in hate by naming and opposing evil. Love shows itself in affection and in common courtesy. There's a thought for a culture as competitive as ours. We should compete in showing genuine courtesy and concern for one another. Love is enthusiastic about its devotion to Christ. Love hangs on in tough times and rejoices in the hope of Christ.

In verse 13, Paul suggests more than taking up an offering. His words mean, in the Greek, "to share their needs," "to feel with them, as well as give to them." The church is a community where the hunger of one is felt by all and the wealth of another is shared by all. The Roman church had many believers who were poor, crippled, or unemployed. The church supported these people as a gift of love that comes near to God's gift in Jesus Christ.

The best example of community in the early church was hospitality. Any Christian could go to any large city and find there a church that would welcome him. This welcome included more than "Glad you're here. Hope you'll come back." This welcome included housing, food, help in making business contacts, and finding a job. These verses end with a paragraph on loving enemies with prayer and getting along in the world.

Verse 17 reminds us of Matthew 5:43-44. Don't disparage the convictions of others, no matter how wrong you think they are. Look for the good and the noble in what they say. Live peaceably with all as much as it depends on you. Don't arouse anger or resentment. When someone is angry, don't be angry in return. Never try to get revenge. That's God's role. Paul quotes "Vengeance is mine" from Deuteronomy 32:35 to say that only God has the right to seek vengeance. Who is so good as to be able to take revenge? Deal with evil by repaying it with good. We're not to allow ourselves to hate the enemy. This leads to being consumed by the same evil that has already consumed the enemy. But when we return good for evil, we conquer evil for both of us.

✔ CHECK LIST

EXPLORING
❏ Large sheets of paper, markers.
❏ Prepare case study sheets for each team.
❏ Plastic-foam packing materials or other lightweight material.

OPTION 1
❏ Prepare slips.
❏ Enlist a timekeeper and scorekeeper.
❏ Bring a team reward.

OPTION 3
❏ Magazines, newspapers, long sheet of paper (shelf paper or butcher paper), glue or tape, markers, scissors.

# ✔ CHECK IN

STARTING

"Honey, I Love You . . ."

Move chairs away from the tables or have the youth sit on the floor. Ask for a volunteer to be *It*. Say: **The person who is It must sit in front of one person in the room and ask him or her the question, "Honey, do you love me?" It may ask the question as many times as It likes, as well as make faces and funny gestures; however, It may not touch the other person. Every time It asks the question, Honey must respond by saying, "Honey, I love you; but I just can't smile." And that is Honey's job—not to smile. If Honey does smile, then he or she becomes It. If Honey does not smile after several minutes, It must try to make someone else smile.**

Let the game continue for five or six minutes, allowing several people to play the roles of It and Honey. Say: **Imagine for a moment that this game is the only clue you had to the meaning of love. What would be your understanding of the word *love*?** *(It is something that It wants Honey to do or feel; It believes the only way to know for sure that Honey loves It is if Honey smiles; It feels it is worth spending time to find out if Honey loves It; love may involve trusting Honey if smiling is not possible; etc.).*

Say: **Today you will look at love from three angles to discover what true Christian love involves.**

EXPLORING

Friends, Enemies, Strangers

PREPARATION: Write the following team case studies on separate sheets of paper.

Loving Friends Team
- A close friend begins to hang out with a rough crowd at school.
- If a friend of yours had a problem, would you be able to tell him or her the truth, even if it meant risking your friendship? If you couldn't tell the truth, would your love be genuine?
- Your neighbor peeled out of your yard, leaving a mud slick.
- A friend stole your boyfriend (girlfriend).
- You saw a jealous friend scrape a key along the back of your car.
- Your neighbor's dog bit you.

OPTION 1

Sing-Along

PREPARATION: Write the following on slips of paper: *friend, enemy, stranger, love, evil, revenge, good.*

Divide youth into two teams. Explain that each team will pick a slip of paper and read its topic. Then, the team has two minutes to name (or sing) songs that have the word in the title or lyrics. (You can expand this to include film titles, book titles, and TV programs. Or, direct youth to choose hymns and Bible verses with the word in verse or lyric.) Give ten points for each answer. Give a small reward to the winning team. Say: **Today we're going to see how these words fit together.**

Loving Strangers Team
- A teenager who is new in town comes to Bible study. The teenager looks and talks differently.
- A homeless man stands on the corner holding a sign, *Will Work for Food*. Could you invite him home for dinner?
- Could you tell a friend that you are angry with him or her without waiting for him or her to guess it?
- Could you pray for people you don't know?
- Could you pray with a friend in private?

Loving Enemies Team
- An older woman in church said to the pastor, "You know, I really think you need to talk to the youth about wearing jeans to church. It just doesn't look right."
- A fifth-grader wrote on the wall of the youth fellowship room, but the youth got blamed and were told to clean it off.
- The youth choir used electric guitars for their number in church, and the deacons decided to ban "that rock and roll noise" from worship.
- At the weekend lock-in, three youth had a shaving cream battle. The whole youth group helped clean up the mess. When the adults found out about it, they decided that the youth wouldn't have any more lock-ins.

Divide youth into three teams for the remainder of the session. Name them the "Loving Friends Team," "Loving Strangers Team," and "Loving Enemies Team." Each team will do the same activities, but they will approach the activity with their team's name.

Say: **In Romans 12:9-32 Paul gives rules for getting along with friends, enemies, and strangers. Read these verses and make a list of rules for getting along with people in your category (friends, enemies, or strangers).** Give each team a large sheet of paper and a marker to create their lists. Tell them to title their lists *Rules for Loving _____ (Friends, Strangers, Enemies).*

OPTION 2
Actions of Love
Active youth could select a case study from their set of case studies and act out the problem and the solution. If you have several youth on each team, use more than one case study per team. Urge teams to share a verse or phrase from Romans 12:9-21 that supports their solutions.

Next, direct teams to mark the easiest rules with a *check* and to mark the hardest rules with an *X*.

Give each team their set of case studies. Say: **The case studies on this sheet relate to your team. Decide on a team response to each based on the rules you've prepared.** Call youth together to share briefly. Direct each team to share a case study that was difficult for them to answer.

Ask:

▼ **What is genuine love?**

▼ **If you had genuine love, would the commands in Romans 12 be easier to obey? why? why not?**

▼ **Have you experienced genuine love in your life?** *(Allow volunteers to relate these experiences.)*

▼ **Where do you find examples of genuine love in our world today?** *(Push the youth to be specific.)*

▼ **What difference would it make if genuine love were expressed by every member of this church? your family? our community?**

The Burning Coals Issue

Direct a youth to reread Romans 12:19-21. Ask each person to imagine something extremely evil that he or she could do to another person. Invite a volunteer to play the part of Paul. He or she will stand in front of the group. One by one, the youth will tell him or her the evil they imagined. Paul will say, "I love you anyway," and will pour a handful of plastic-foam coals over the youths' heads.

Ask:

▼ **What does it mean to heap burning coals on the head of an enemy?**

▼ **Is this practical in today's world? why or why not?**

▼ **What would the world be like if people responded to evil with love?**

CONNECTING

Genuine Love Begins with Genuine Prayer

Direct youth to return to their three teams. Tell team members to give the name or initials of someone in their category *(friends, enemies, strangers)* to their team. *(The Stranger team may mention strangers, like "the new neighbor next door" or "the teenager who joined the church last week.")* Then, direct teams to say in unison, **God, we pray for these people. Let us show them your love. Amen.**

 **CHECK OUT**

How can hatred consume the energy needed to love another?

Love Collage

PREPARATION: Hang the long sheet of paper on the wall.

Let youth make a "Love Collage." Tell them to draw or cut out pictures of hatred, evil, and division and to glue or tape them on one end of the paper. Then ask them to cut out or draw pictures of the way people love one another and to glue or tape them on the other end of the paper. Title the collage *Love Is Stronger.*

33. TWO ARE BETTER THAN ONE

Ecclesiastes 4:9-12

Examining the place of friends in life.

✔ CHECK UP!

Ecclesiastes is a part of the Wisdom Literature in the Old Testament, along with Job and Proverbs. The writer is anonymous, but is given the name the Preacher. He is often characterized as a cynic; that's an undeserved reputation. He struggles to find an answer to the question, "What gives life joy and meaning." We struggle with the same question. The Preacher looks at life, and it seems to make no sense. People who do right suffer. Those who act as if there were no God, who have no moral accountability, hold positions of wealth and power. This doesn't fit with the preacher's religious traditions. Something is wrong—either God is far less than the Preacher had been told, because God cannot bring about simple justice, or God is far greater than he had thought and at the heart of the universe is a mystery, a power greater than anyone can begin to understand. In some ways, Ecclesiastes is like a modern teenager trying to make sense out of God, life, and justice.

In verse 9 the Preacher gives some practical ideas for community. He draws his first images from travel and the advantages of having a friend along when traveling. What if you fall? If you're alone and seriously hurt, you die. But if there are two of you, you can help each other. This is sound common sense. National parks warn hikers never to hike alone in the backcountry. In ancient times, there were no motels. You spent the night wherever you could find shelter—from the ground to a crude hut to a palatial home. Bedding was the cloak that you wore during the day. It could get cold and uncomfortable, even wrapped in a warm woolen cloak. But if two sleep together to share the body heat and two cloaks, they can be warm. Why be uncomfortable alone when you can be comfortable with a friend? If you are traveling alone and are attacked by a robber, what chance do you have? Two of you together can drive off a robber and be safe. We're told when we visit certain high-crime parts of cities never to go out alone. Always go, at the very least, in pairs, because there is safety in numbers. Again, sound common sense.

Then, the image changes from travel. The Preacher talks about the difficulty of breaking a threefold cord. A rope of three strands was the strongest rope in use in his day. It's relatively easy to break one of the three strands. But weave the three together to make a

✔ CHECK LIST

STARTING
❏ Building blocks.

EXPLORING
❏ Make the poster.

CONNECTING
❏ Embroidery floss, scissors.

OPTION 1
❏ Large sheets of paper, markers, rewards.

strong rope that's much harder to break. The same is true with sticks. One stick by itself is easily broken. Three or four in a bundle are much harder to break. So there are practical reasons why community and friendship are important. We don't need exaggerated religious reasons for what we do. Practical reality is enough. Two are better than one. Two individuals become a team.

If you fall, it's good to have a friend to help you up. Two can sleep warmer than one. It's hard to break a three-strand rope. In our push for individualism, it's good to stop and hear again the wisdom of Ecclesiastes.

CHECK IN

STARTING

Cooperative Building

Ask youth to work as a team to construct a building using the blocks. (If your group is large, form two building teams.) As youth begin to work, pull one of them aside and *whisper* these instructions: *"During this activity, you are to be completely uncooperative, saying things like, 'No, I don't like that,' or moving blocks around that someone has already positioned."* To a second youth whisper: *"Wait until the building is well underway, then go through and knock all the blocks to the ground, so the building team has to start over. Be sure to do this in a safe manner, so that no one is hit with flying blocks."*

Let the youth begin rebuilding two or three times, depending on how much time you have.

Ask:
▼ **How did it feel to have these two people argue with you and even destroy your efforts?**

After the youth discuss their ideas and feelings, ask everyone to cooperate to complete the building. Then ask your two "unco-operatives":

▼ **How did it feel to be helpful rather than harmful?**

Say: **Today we're going to see how two are better than one. You will also see the advantages of cooperation.**

OPTION 1

All By Myself?

Divide youth into an even number of teams with four persons (or fewer) on each team. Say: **This is a competition to see which team can make the longest list in two minutes.** Hand out large sheets of paper and markers. Tell half the teams to list activities a person can do alone. Direct the other half to list activities that can only be done by two or more persons. Start timing. Stop after two minutes. Let teams share lists. Award the winning team a prize.

Ask:
▼ **What can you do by yourself, but would have more fun doing with someone else?**
▼ **With whom do you most like to do activities?**

Say: **Today we're going to see how two are better than one.**

EXPLORING
Need a Friend?

PREPARATION: Write Sartre's statement on poster board or a chalk-board: *Hell is other people.* Say: **Jean-Paul Sartre said that hell is other people.**

Ask:
▼ Do you agree? why? why not?
▼ Do you need other people? why? why not?
▼ Why do you think God designed human beings to live in a hostile world and to be dependent on the care of others?
▼ Everybody needs to be alone sometimes. What if you had to be alone all the time? What would happen to you?

Direct a youth to read Ecclesiastes 4:7-12 aloud as the others follow in their Bibles.

Ask:
▼ How do these verses relate to Sartre's statement?

To help youth understand these verses, read each verse aloud.

Ask:
▼ What is the main idea in this verse?

Challenge youth not to repeat the verse, but to put it into other words. Be prepared to explain that verse 11 does not deal with sleeping together for sexual pleasure. This idea is comparable to sharing the cost of an apartment in our day. After reviewing each verse,

Ask:
▼ What does this Scripture say about relationships?
▼ Why are relationships one of the most important parts of living?
▼ How can you build strong friendship?

OPTION 2
Friendship Blockers

After reading Ecclesiastes 4:7-12,

Ask:
▼ Why are friends so important?

Continue with this activity. This game should be played in an open space. Choose two persons to be friends, and ask them to leave the room. Invite everyone else to be a friend-blocker. Ask them to list barriers to friendship *(anger, greed, jealousy, and so on)* and to decide who will play the part of each barrier.

Bring the friends back in and tell them to stand at opposite ends of the room. Invite them to walk toward each other. The other youth will take turns trying to block their progress by jumping out in front of one of the friends and shouting the name of a barrier to friendship. When blocked, the friend must say three times "Two are better than one" before the friend-blocker will move out of the way. If the friend forgets to say "Two are better than one," he or she must go back to the beginning. When the friends reach each other, invite everyone to join in a group hug.

Use the last three questions under EXPLORING to discuss the Scripture.

CONNECTING
The Cords of Friendship

PREPARATION: Purchase several skeins of embroidery floss in different colors. Cut the floss into 12-inch pieces so each youth will have at least three pieces.

Read again Ecclesiastes 4:12. Say: **In ancient Israel, the strongest rope available was one made with three strands. A rope made with a single strand was easily broken, but a rope made with three strands woven together was too strong for most people to break.**

Ask:
▼ **How can a friend strengthen you?**

Pair up the members of your group, including yourself. (If you have an uneven number, have one group of three.) Have each person choose three pieces of floss in three different colors and tell everyone to tie their strands together at one end. Then as one partner holds the knotted end, have the other partner braid the three strands together. (Note: Some of your youth may know a fancier braid, perhaps requiring more strands of floss. If there is time, you may let these youth teach everyone else that braid.) When the first person in each pair finishes his or her band, have the partners switch roles and make a band for the second person. As the partners work on their bands, have them talk about why they chose the particular colors they did and what these colors might symbolize in their lives or in their friendships.

When everyone is finished, tell the partners to tie the bands around each other's wrists. Provide scissors in case they need to trim the ends. Bring the youth back together.

Ask:
▼ **Could you have made your wrist band alone? If so, would it have been more difficult? as much fun?**
▼ **What did you learn about your partner as you worked together?**
▼ **What did you learn about cooperation and friendship?**
▼ **What values might wearing this bracelet remind you of in the days ahead?**

 **CHECK OUT**

How does a friend in your life make you a better person?

OPTION 3
Practical Friendships

Tell youth you will read a sentence and let them complete it. Read each statement, allowing time for youth to comment.

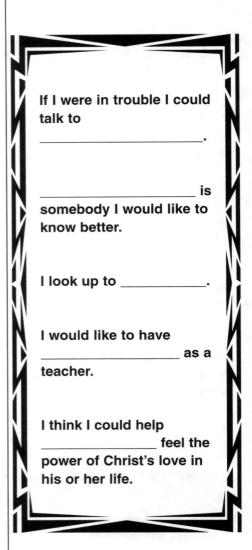

If I were in trouble I could talk to

_____.

_____ is somebody I would like to know better.

I look up to _____.

I would like to have _____ as a teacher.

I think I could help _____ feel the power of Christ's love in his or her life.

Follow up on what youth say. Encourage them to pray for these people who strengthen them.

34. WHEN FAMILY GETS OUT OF CONTROL

Genesis 21:8-21

Helping when families get out of control.

✔ CHECK UP!

God had promised Abraham a son who would inherit the promises of the covenant, but Abraham and Sarah could not have a child. Taking matters into her own hands (Genesis 16), Sarah gave Abraham her slave girl, Hagar, to have a child for her. Today, we would call Hagar a surrogate mother. In ancient times a surrogate would birth a child so that the child was born into the lap of the one who would raise the child, in this case Sarah, and the child would be hers.

This never worked in Abraham's tent. Sarah was cruel to Hagar, and Hagar tended to act superior about being able to have a son. So things were tense. Then Isaac was born to Sarah, and all the problems came boiling out. Isaac was the child of the promise, the one who would inherit the covenant. Isaac was the laughing boy whom God had promised to Sarah in her old age. Abraham believed in the old ways where everything was given to the oldest son, to Ishmael, Hagar's son. Ishmael is now a teenager, strong and healthy and pleasing to his father. But Ishmael gets caught in the terrible jealousy and hatred between his birth mother and his foster mother. Like many teenagers today, he is torn by a divided family in which everyone claims to love and want him, but some only use and abuse him. Sarah wants Ishmael out of the way so he will not threaten Isaac's inheritance. She wants Hagar and Ishmael driven out of Abraham's camp.

Do you wonder how Ishmael felt about Sarah? Was he afraid of her? He surely had to know how Sarah felt about him. The story is clear that Sarah and Hagar made no secret about their feelings about each other. And it was Sarah who had the power. Do you wonder how Ishmael felt when he heard that Sarah was going to have a baby? When Isaac was born, did Ishmael think about running away from home before Sarah caused something to happen to him? Did Ishmael live under a cloud of loneliness and uncertainty knowing he was not the chosen one? Since Isaac was the "laughing boy," was Ishmael the "frowning boy" or the "doomed boy"? The matter distressed Abraham. Ishmael may not be Sarah's son, but he is Abraham's son. And Abraham is not ready to give him up. So Abraham and God have a long talk. God tells him not to worry. Isaac is the child of the promise, but Ishmael will be the founder of a nation, too. God will bless him because he is Abraham's son.

Ishmael is always in God's care, even when he is abused by his family. So Abraham gives Hagar basic provisions and sends her and

✔ CHECK LIST

STARTING
❒ Bring a checkers game.

EXPLORING
❒ Large newsprint, markers, table.

CONNECTING
❒ Pencils, paper.

OPTION 1
❒ Modeling clay or dough, cardboard.

Ishmael away. They wander in the wilderness of Beersheba, a stony desert with long stretches of hills, gullies, and canyons. There is very little that would provide food or shelter for a lonely woman and her teenage son. No wonder Hagar was willing to die when the water ran out. How did Ishmael feel about Abraham when he was sitting under that bush waiting to die? Did he think fondly of the old man? Or did he curse his father? The good part is that God still cares for Ishmael. Sarah wants him dead; Abraham willingly abandons him, although he still loves him. Tradition says that he is the outsider, the unwanted, not the son of the promise. But God still is with him.

The gift of water is literally the gift of life for Hagar and Ishmael. God tenderly directs them to a well in the wilderness. Ishmael still has rights, and God will honor those rights. God loves Ishmael and is active in Ishmael's life to keep him safe. Of course, Ishmael does not receive the full promise given to Isaac, but his promise is a considerable one. God cares about the outsider. God's love is for all his children, even ones cast out by society. God was with the boy as he grew. He lived in the wilderness of Paran and became an expert with the bow and arrow, so he and his mother could live on the results of his hunting. His mother found a wife for him in Egypt, among her own people. And much later, when Abraham died, both Isaac and Ishmael buried him in a cave at Machpelah.

 CHECK IN

STARTING

Out-of-Control Checkers

Choose two volunteers to play "Out-of-Control Checkers" while the rest of the group watches. To explain the rules, say: **This game is played with single checkers, but they are called *kings* and can move in any direction or jump other checkers, like double-checker kings in conventional checkers. Player 1 determines the number of kings each player will have. Player 1 can have as many kings as desired and is required to give only one king to Player 2. Player 1 also decides the placement of these kings anywhere on the board, provided Player 2's king or kings have a buffer of at least two spaces in all directions. Player 2 gets the first move. After that, Player 2 *must* move anytime Player 1 frees up an open square next to Player 2's king. Otherwise, follow the conventional rules for checkers.**

Have the volunteers play one game. Obviously, Player 1 will win quickly since Player 2 is *out of control* from the beginning of the game. When the game is finished,

Ask:
▼ **Player 2, how did it feel to have no choices or advantages in the game?**
▼ **Player 1, how did it feel to have all the choices and advantages in the game?**
▼ **What problems do youth face today that make them feel as if their lives are out of control?** *(feeling disconnected; violence and death; AIDS; pressure to make good grades; competition for college placement or jobs; rising cost of living; lack of time with*

OPTION 1

Out-of-Control Clay

Say: **Some days this world seems out of control. Sometimes we feel out of control. Other times everything around us is out of control. Let's make a sculpture to show what it means to be out of control.**

Put the clay on a sheet of cardboard and invite youth to work on the sculpture. They may choose to work together on one large sculpture, or they may decide to assign different parts of the sculpture to individuals. The sculpture may be an abstract work of art, or it may be lifelike. You may want to participate, but do not offer too much direction. Encourage the youth to work quickly.

As youth work, ask:

▼ **What does it mean to be out of control?**
▼ **How are some families out of control?**

WHEN GOD SCRAMBLES YOUR PLANS

or approval from parents; addiction to drugs, alcohol, or gambling; teen pregnancy; etc.)

▼ Do you think that more youth today would identify with Player 1 or Player 2 in our game of "Out-of-Control Checkers"? why?

Say: **In this lesson we'll look at an out-of-control situation to see who had control and who didn't.**

EXPLORING
The Story in Pictures

Place a large sheet of paper on the top of a table. Provide markers for all youth. Ask a youth to read Genesis 21:8-21 aloud as the others follow in their Bibles. Tell youth to draw a mural telling this story. Lead youth to divide the story into scenes, based on the verses. Suggest they assign scenes to different people. After they finish the drawing, place the mural on a wall.

Ask:
▼ **Which persons in today's Scripture had few options and little control in life? What limited his or her choices and advantages?** (Hagar had few options because she was a slave, a woman, and a foreigner. Abraham and Sarah controlled much of her life.)
▼ **Which persons in the text had more options? What factors gave these persons more choices or advantages?** (Abraham was a man and head of a household. Sarah was a bit more limited as a woman, but she was not a slave or a foreigner.)
▼ **What kind of pain do you think each character in the story might have felt?** (Abraham was distressed about sending Ishmael away; Sarah felt sorrow over being barren and was jealous that Hagar could have children; Hagar felt powerless, outcast, and afraid of death; Ishmael felt thirsty and abandoned.)
▼ **How might the story of Hagar and Ishmael be a source of hope for youth who feel their lives are out of control?**

Focus on Ishmael

Say: **The teenager in this out-of-control family was Ishmael. Think about life from Ishmael's point of view. Sit back, close your eyes, and focus on this youth.** Read Genesis 21:8-21 aloud. Tell youth to open their eyes.

Ask:
▼ **What was Ishmael's deepest pain?**
▼ **How do you think he felt about Abraham? Sarah? Isaac?**
▼ **How did Ishmael feel about himself?**
▼ **How did Ishmael feel toward God?**
▼ **After God rescued them, do you think any of Ishmael's feelings changed?**
▼ **Why might Ishmael have felt that his family was out of control?**

▼ When do you feel like everything in your life is out of control?

OPTION 2
Ishmael's Family Sculpture

Tell youth to read Genesis 21:8-21 silently. Direct them to design several "frozen" sculptures of this family's story. Youth should decide which scenes to sculpture, then arrange themselves to express what happened in each scene. (For example, for verses 8-9, youth might place one person on a table to represent Sarah, another person kneeling on the floor as Hagar, a third youth teasing a shorter youth, representing Ishmael and Isaac.)

CONNECTING
Real Life Out-of-Control

Form two groups. Give each group several minutes to write down two situations, one for a female youth and the other for a male youth. In each case the young person should be in a desperate, out-of-control situation from which there seems to be no way out.

Have the groups switch situations and try to come up with helpful options for the youth in each story. Invite the groups to report. Allow volunteers to suggest additional ideas for resolving each case.

Ask:
▼ **Does our faith in God give us a different perspective on problems that could result in death? how?**

 **CHECK OUT**

How can God use me to deal with an out-of-control situation in my family or my life?

OPTION 3
Out-of-Control Situations

Read each situation one at a time:

A teenager hears his parents fighting. His mom screams at his dad, "Get Out! I want a divorce!"

A teenager's older brother is arrested for drunk driving.

A teenager's single mother denies that she is an alcoholic.

A high school junior considers killing herself because she is failing a class she needs to get a college scholarship.

A teenager's family is moving across the country a week before her senior year begins.

After choosing to live with his dad, a teenager learns that the judge gave custody of his younger brother to his mom.

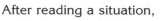

After reading a situation,

Ask:
▼ If this young person turned to you for help, what guidance would you give him or her?
▼ Do you see much hope in this situation? If so, what is the basis for this hope?
▼ Which character in the biblical story might this particular youth identify with? why?

WHEN GOD SCRAMBLES YOUR PLANS

35. WHEN YOU NEED HELP

Exodus 18:13-25

Seeing how youth can turn to others when they need help.

✔ CHECK UP!

God provided for the people of Israel in many ways. One way God provided for their needs was through Jethro's advice. By himself Moses could not continue to meet the needs of all the people. So, based on Jethro's advice, Moses developed a system of shared leadership. That way the needs of more people could be met more quickly.

We cannot be sure of the total number of Israelites at this point in history. Even if only a few thousand people were involved, being responsible for all the civil, criminal, and religious concerns of the community would have been an overwhelming task for only one person.

Moses was trying to function as the judge and probably as the priest for the whole community or all the tribes of Israel. He wanted to do a good job. He took seriously his responsibilities as the leader of the people of Israel. Moses knew God's laws and was the logical person to teach the people about God. He also used what he knew about God's instructions to help the people settle their disputes. Soon Moses was feeling overwhelmed. He was trying to be a priest, a teacher, and a judge all by himself. Trying to juggle all these roles proved to be taxing and frustrating for both Moses and the people.

Fortunately for Moses and the people, Moses' father-in-law, Jethro, recognized what was happening. He knew that Moses would wear himself out if he continued trying to fulfill so many different roles. Jethro told Moses to pick some good, honest, God-fearing people. Train them to do some of the jobs Moses tried to do. The people still needed Moses to make many of the most important decisions, but all of the people would be better off if Moses shared the workload with others.

So Jethro suggested that Moses limit his duties to inquiring of God and making decisions in important or complicated cases. In accordance with Jethro's advice, Moses established a workable administrative structure that would be adequate for the group of people for whom he had responsibility.

Jethro proposed that Moses choose officers or judges who were dedicated to God and who possessed integrity and good moral character. These men were to decide minor cases brought by the people, or those that involved a precedent. Moses would continue to make decisions requiring original instruction. Moses agreed to Jethro's suggestions, recognizing that God was speaking to him through Jethro.

✔ CHECK LIST

STARTING
❑ Make advice posters.
❑ Construction paper, markers to make other advice signs.

EXPLORING
❑ Make poster with summary points.

CONNECTING
❑ Paper, pencils.

OPTION 1
❑ Personal testimony.

OPTION 2
❑ Large newsprint, markers.

OPTION 3
❑ Large newsprint, markers.

# ✔ CHECK IN

STARTING

Getting Good Advice

PREPARATION: Make three or four small posters with familiar advice printed on them. *(For example: Be careful, it's a jungle out there; Wear clean underwear in case you're in an accident; Drive carefully).* Hang these on the wall.

As the youth arrive, ask them to recall examples of good advice they heard this past week or to think about good advice they offered to others. Invite youth to also suggest any good advice they have for you or for one another. Write their advice on construction paper and add these papers to the wall. Review the different pieces of advice. Ask youth to share other examples of advice.

Ask:

▼ **When are you willing to accept someone's advice?** *(Possible reasons: They recognize a way to make life easier for themselves or others; they see their problem in a different light; they see a way to avoid negative or unpleasant consequences.)*

▼ **When are you less willing to accept another's advice?** *(Possible reasons: They want to prove that their way of doing things is best; they don't want anyone else to get credit or recognition for a good idea; they are afraid of what might happen if they follow the advice; they may not realize that it is good advice.)*

Say: **Today we'll see how advice can help us get through tough situations.**

EXPLORING

Overworked!

Ask a youth to read Exodus 18:13-25 aloud.

Ask:

▼ **How many different roles was Moses trying to fulfill in his dealings with the people?**
▼ **Why did Moses accept so much responsibility?**
▼ **What did Jethro advise Moses to do?**
▼ **Do you think Jethro gave Moses good advice? why or why not?**
▼ **Did Moses respond the way you would have expected?**
▼ **Why, do you think, did Moses decide to follow Jethro's advice?**
▼ **Would you call his course of action wise or unwise?**
▼ **What might have happened if Moses had not followed Jethro's advice?**

Instruct youth to prepare a skit of this story that would be relevant to the life of a teenager today. Moses should be a modern teenager. (If you have a large group, divide into smaller teams. If you have a small group, let them work together.) As youth plan the skit, take

OPTION 1

A Helpful Testimony

Recall a time when you tried to do too much and got into trouble or when you were on the verge of failure and someone suggested a way out. Or, share a time when you stepped in and helped a friend who needed help but didn't realize it. After you share your story, encourage youth to relate similar experiences. Ask the questions in STARTING.

OPTION 2

Take My Advice

After reading Exodus 18:13-25, tell youth to analyze Jethro's advice-giving techniques.

Ask:

▼ **How did Jethro go about telling Moses he needed help?** *(Showed concern, pointed out Moses' strengths, provided specific suggestions, was honest.)*

▼ **What would you add to this list of ideas for offering advice?**

List these on a large sheet of newsprint. Label this list *Offering Advice.* Draw a line down the center of the paper. Label the notes about who takes the leadership role in preparing the skit, who offers changes and advice, how that advice is taken, who willingly listens to advice and who doesn't. When youth are ready, let them present their skit. Then, share with them some of the insights you saw about their giving and taking advice.

The Point Is . . .

PREPARATION: On poster board write these points:

- Working hard and doing a good job are important.
- No one can do everything by herself or himself.
- Others can help you do a good job.
- Sometimes you have to ask for help.
- Other people have talents and abilities, too.
- A person can learn how to be a leader.
- God can give you a message through a friend or family members.
- A good leader is trustworthy and honest.

Display the poster.

Ask:

▼ Which statement on this poster best expresses what happened between Moses and Jethro?
▼ Which statement best expresses how you feel about giving advice to others?
▼ Which statement best expresses how you feel about taking advice from others?

second column *Accepting Advice*. Lead youth to list ideas for accepting advice.

Ask:
▼ **What did Moses do with Jethro's advice?** *(Listened carefully, carried out advice immediately.)*
▼ **What would make you want to accept someone else's advice?**

CONNECTING

Help!

Hand out paper and pencils. Tell youth to list all the things they do each day. Tell them to list all the things they do each week. Let volunteers share their lists.

Ask:

▼ Where could you use help?
▼ What kind of help do you need?
▼ Who could help you?
▼ Have you ever thought about asking for help?

Encourage youth to offer to help one another. If you have time, ask:

▼ Who do you know that is carrying a heavy schedule or problem right now?
▼ What could you say to make that person willing to listen to your advice?

Urge youth to be open to God's leadership as they seek help from others and as they offer help to others.

 **CHECK OUT**

How can you turn down someone's advice without turning off the person offering it?

OPTION 3

Who Ya Gonna Call?

Tell youth to measure with their hands how likely they are to take good advice from others. Say: **The farther apart you hold your hands, the more likely you are to take someone's advice.** Call out several people, or groups of people, letting youth measure acceptance of advice with their hands. Say, **Mom, brother, sister, dad, best friend, person who sits behind you in English class, a teacher, the pastor, your next door neighbor.** Then, direct youth to show with their hands how apt they are to take advice if they think it is inspired by God. Compare the two measurements.

Ask:

▼ How do you determine whether advice from others is also what God wants you to do?

WHEN GOD SCRAMBLES YOUR PLANS

THE GODS
OF SOCIETY

36. AND THE WINNER IS . . .

Genesis 25:19-34

Recognizing that competition can have negative effects on family and others.

✔ CHECK UP!

To the Hebrews the importance of family could not be overestimated. Families such as Isaac's considered themselves to be even more special, as they were a direct fulfillment of God's covenant with Abraham. To be barren, or unable to produce children, was a supreme calamity. A reversal of a woman's barrenness was thought to be a blessing from God.

In today's text we read that God answered Isaac's prayers and allowed Rebekah to conceive (Gen. 25:21). Rebekah's pregnancy was considered especially significant due to the fact that she was carrying twins. The children struggling together in her womb came to represent the eventual rivalry between Israel and the desert Edomites, of whom Esau was the first. Jacob and Esau also typify the two rival ways of life during ancient times, that of shepherd and hunter.

Esau was the outdoorsman, a hunter and a man of the field. By contrast, Jacob was gentle and quiet. He was his mother's favorite, while Esau was favored by his father. Esau was hearty and strong, and as Isaac got older he depended more and more on Esau's strength.

The Scripture demonstrates that one of Jacob's strengths was his cleverness and intelligence. Esau evidently relied more on his physical brawn and had a tendency to act without thinking, as was the case when he forfeited his birthright.

In ancient times the firstborn son was the child who received the birthright. A birthright included the privilege of someday being the family's representative, as well as being the family's spiritual adviser, guiding other family members in the ways of God. In biblical times the birthright was a coveted family privilege. Since Esau was the twin who was born first, the birthright was naturally his. Precious metals, jewels, animals, and other material assets, rather than coins, were the typical items of exchange in the ancient Near East. Land was also a precious commodity, and one that was promised to the descendants of Abraham as part of God's blessing.

The eldest son received a double share of his father's assets as his birthright. The promise of a double share meant that Esau anticipated receiving two-thirds of all the material goods and land Isaac owned. Instead, he "despised" his birthright and the portions were reversed. Esau's bowl of soup cost him a third of his father's material estate and the patriarchal leadership of the family as well.

✔ CHECK LIST

STARTING
❑ Gather 15 small items (paper clips, etc.), tray, a cover, pencils, paper.
❑ Bring a prize.

EXPLORING
❑ Gather art supplies: large paper, scissors, markers, construction paper, yarn.
❑ Bible dictionaries, commentaries.

CONNECTING
❑ Bring yearbooks, paper, pencils.

OPTION 1
❑ Enlist youth.

OPTION 2
❑ Several large sheets of paper, markers.

OPTION 3
❑ Sheet of large paper, marker.

✔ CHECK IN

STARTING

Mental Competition

PREPARATION: Place about fifteen small items (paper clips, watch, toys, pencils, and so forth) on a tray and cover it with a cloth so that the items are hidden.

After everyone is assembled, give each person a piece of paper and a pencil. Remove the cover from the tray, and allow the group to observe the items for one minute. After the time limit is up, cover the tray again. Tell the group that they have two minutes to list as many items as they can remember.

When everyone has finished writing, uncover the tray and count how many items they remembered and recorded accurately. Award a small prize *(for example: a new pen, a memo pad, and so on)* to the person who recalled the most items. (Be prepared for a tie.) Issue the prize (or prizes) with great fanfare to give the impression that the youth have just participated in a serious competition.

Ask:
▼ How did this competition make you feel?
▼ How did you feel when you found out you didn't win?
▼ How did you feel if you did win?
▼ Do you generally like competition?
▼ Do you try to avoid competition? if so, why?
▼ Do you consider yourself a competitive person?
▼ Are you more competitive with your friends or with your siblings?

EXPLORING

Competing Brothers

PREPARATION: Provide large sheets of paper, scissors, markers, construction paper, and yarn. Provide Bible dictionaries and commentaries.

Assign half the group to be responsible for finding information about Esau. Assign the other half to be responsible for finding information about Jacob. After youth have discovered traits and actions of each brother, give them several options. Tell them to "dress" one of their teammates in "clothing" that represents their assigned brother. Or, present an "Up-Close and Personal" "TV" study of the person, including interviews with friends, enemies, and family members. Or, draw a large body on a sheet of paper and label parts of the person with traits and actions of Esau or Jacob. Call for each team's presentation. Share information about the birthright from Check Up!

Ask:
▼ How do you consider yourself to be similar to or different from your brothers or sisters?
▼ How do you feel when your parents compare you with your sibling or siblings?
▼ If you don't have brothers or sisters, perhaps you can think of times when you or someone else compared siblings whom you know. How do you think the siblings involved felt?

OPTION 1

Physical Competition

PREPARATION: Enlist a teenager who enjoys arguing. Tell that teenager to aggressively share an opposite point of view during this first activity.

Begin the session by asking:

▼ **What do you think is the most competitive sport? why?** *(At this point if youth say football, the pre-enlisted teenager should name soccer or another sport. This youth should argue with whatever the others say.)*

After a few minutes of argument, explain the set-up situation. Say: **Today we're going to look at competition—its good side and its bad side.** Ask the last four questions in STARTING.

OPTION 2

A Little Competition

Use a competitive approach to Genesis 25:19-34. Divide youth into two teams. Call one the *Esau Team* and the other the *Jacob Team.* Give each team a large sheet of paper and a marker. Direct a youth to read Genesis 25:19-34 aloud. Tell youth they have three minutes to list traits about their person. Encourage them to scan later chapters in Genesis for additional information. At the end of three minutes call for the lists. Name the team with the longest list of traits as the winner.

AND THE WINNER IS . . .

CONNECTING

Most Likely to . . .

PREPARATION: Bring several high school or college annuals (yours or others).

Show youth the sections of the annuals that deal with the "Most Likely to . . ." awards. If you know, share what happened to some of those people.

Ask:
▼ How are most "Most Likely to . . ." titles given?
▼ What "Most Likely to . . ." titles would you give Esau? Jacob?

Invite youth to share short-term goals they have. Then, let them share long-term goals.

Ask:
▼ What "Most Likely to . . ." title would you want to receive? *(Encourage youth to make up a title that expresses a goal they have.)*
▼ How likely are you to achieve that title?
▼ How can setting goals help you compete fairly?
▼ How can being too goal-oriented make you compete unfairly?

Hand out paper and pencils. Ask youth to write down one area where they may be too competitive. Direct them to write a brief prayer about that competitiveness. Lead youth as you conclude with this prayer:

Dear God, give us a spirit of love for all our brothers and sisters, those at home and those around the world. Help us to avoid the jealousy and even hatred that can stem from petty rivalry and competitions. Help us also to remember that taking the easy way out may interfere with our future goals and aspirations. Thank you for your merciful love that continually guides us. Amen.

✔ CHECK OUT

Who or what makes you competitive? How do you feel about that competition?

OPTION 2 *(Continued)*

Ask:
▼ What can you learn about competition from these brothers?
▼ What can you learn about competition from this activity?

OPTION 3

A Competitive Example

Ask:
▼ When is competition healthy?
▼ When does healthy competition change to unhealthy competition?

Brainstorm ways people abuse competition. List youth's comments on a large sheet of paper. *(These might include: use of steroids, drugs, playing unfair, breaking the rules.)* If possible, share a story of a real person who competed unfairly and was forced to leave the game *(Pete Rose for example).*

Ask:
▼ How can you avoid unhealthy competition?

37. FAKE LOVE

1 John 3:11-17

> Comparing the grace-giving love of Christians to the selfish love of this world.

✔ CHECK UP!

"Love one another" was the message John's community had heard from the time the Good News was first preached in Ephesus on the southern coast of modern Turkey. This is the heart of the gospel in Johannine literature. God loved the world so much that God gave his only Son. The interesting twist in this letter is that "one another" refers to the members of the Johannine church. John applies this theme to love within the church that has faced secession, hatred, and alienation. John warns the church, Don't be like Cain, who murdered his brother. Cain and Abel were the first two sons of Adam and Eve (Genesis 4). Each son made an offering to God. Abel's offering was accepted, but Cain's was not. Cain became angry, bitter, and resentful. Acting on these strong feelings, he called Abel out in the field and killed him. When God spoke to Cain, asking about his brother Abel, Cain responded sullenly, "How should I know? Am I my brother's keeper?"

The author of this letter says, Do just the opposite of Cain. Cain belonged to the evil one; all his deeds were evil. These ideas are not found in the Genesis story. But there was a long tradition about the evil nature of Cain in Jewish thought. The author of 1 John warns his people about the dangers of someone like Cain. Cain let his evil desire, anger, and temptation master him, and this led to murder. In Johannine thought evil hates good simply because it is good. So Cain's hatred for Abel comes from the fact that Cain was inclined to evil. The phrase "brothers and sisters" in verse 13 reminds the church again not to be like Cain, who killed his brother, and to remember there's a sense of family within the church. "Don't be surprised that the world hates you" warns Christians not to be caught off guard by that hatred. Christians shouldn't be naive about any form of evil.

Then comes the Good News. The opposite of love is hate and hate leads to death, but love leads to life. Our love for the brothers and sisters of the church is a form of God's love for us. Ultimately God's love leads us from death to life. There is also the reality that we are called to live out that love in practical ways, following the example of Christ. What is the example of love? How do we know love when we see it? Just as Christ laid down his life for us, we ought to lay down our lives for one another. Wow! That's a different

✔ CHECK LIST

STARTING
❏ Enlist youth.
❏ Prepare skit.
❏ Set up meeting room.

EXPLORING
❏ Prepare index cards.

CONNECTING
❏ Large newsprint or chalkboard, markers.

OPTION 1
❏ Large sheets of paper, markers.

OPTION 2
❏ Case studies on index cards.

OPTION 3
❏ Alphabet building blocks, a table, a bag.

vision of love from the one our society teaches us. Contrast that with the message of the world that says, "If you really love me, you'll give me what I want." No, John says, true love is willing to make sacrifices for the sake of the other, even to lay down our lives.

A practical test for love is found in verse 17. How can God's love live in anyone who has the world's goods, sees a brother or sister in need, and refuses to help? How do we make the jump from dying for a brother to giving him the world's goods? The Greek word *biaios* can mean both "life" and "livelihood." So giving up one's *biaios* can mean either. How can we refuse help to the hungry, the naked, the homeless, the lonely and still claim to love? Love is a gift from God. If we do not use that love, how can we hope to have it a part of us?

 **CHECK IN**

STARTING

Cain's Trial
PREPARATION: Ask three youth who enjoy drama to read Genesis 4:1-16 and create a brief skit. Direct them to set up a trial situation for Cain. One youth can play the judge, one, the prosecutor, and one, the defense lawyer for Cain. Set up the meeting room as a courtroom.

Introduce the skit. Let the enlisted youth share their skit.

After the skit, ask:
▼ **What kind of trial do you think Cain would have today?**
▼ **Would he be punished?**

In the story recorded in Genesis, God wouldn't allow anyone to kill Cain, but he was exiled.

Ask:
▼ **What kind of life do you think Cain had?**
▼ **Do you think he ever repented and became obedient to God?** *(If there is time, have one or two persons read the passage from Genesis 4:1-16 to help the group speculate on these questions.)*
▼ **What does Cain's experience tell us about anger and hatred? about our relationship with God? with others?**

EXPLORING

So, This Is Love!
PREPARATION: Write each of the following *love* situations on an index card.

Jeremy borrowed Ryan's sweater and accidentally spilled permanent ink on it. The sweater was ruined, but Jeremy bought Ryan a new one.

OPTION 1

Wanted: Selfish One
Give every three or four youth a large sheet of paper and a marker. Tell them to make a poster entitled *Wanted: A Selfish Person*. On the poster each group of youth should list its criteria for a selfish person. Display the posters.

Ask:
▼ **Is all love the same? What are different kinds of love?**
▼ **How do you know what love is?**
▼ **Does loving other people mean accepting everything they do?**
▼ **Does loving other people mean doing whatever they tell you to do?**
▼ **Is Christian love about feeling, doing, or both? How does a Christian show love?**

WHEN GOD SCRAMBLES YOUR PLANS

Joshua borrowed Dylan's new sweater and tore it playing football. He told Dylan he lost the sweater, and he didn't offer to buy a new one.

Ben asked Maria to go with him. When he gave her his ring, he told her not to talk to any other guys in school.

Mindy told her friend Emily that she loved Emily's new shoes, but she told Sara that Emily's new shoes were ugly.

John followed Jill down the hall and made lewd remarks about what he would like to do to her if he ever got her alone.

Reiko was in church one Sunday when the minister called for a special offering. A widow in the church had broken her hip and needed money to pay for a nurse at home. Reiko looked in her purse, pulled out her lunch money for the week, and dropped it in the offering plate.

The director of the youth choir was getting older, and she couldn't hear well. One day at practice, a group of girls began to whisper so that the director would ask them to speak up.

One morning, Jessamyn missed the bus. Her brother usually took his girlfriend to school, but today he told his girlfriend to take her bus so that he could drive Jessamyn to school.

Say: **Today's lesson is about love. Defining real love can be difficult. Take this simple test.** Hold the cards, letting youth pick a card with a love situation. (If you have more than eight youth, suggest they work in small teams. If you have fewer than eight youth, allow youth who finish early to take another card.) Direct youth to turn to 1 John 3:11-17. Tell them to decide if each situation is real love or fake love and to select a verse or phrase from the Scripture that supports that answer. After a few minutes of work, tell youth to read their love situations and the related verse or verses. Fill in the gaps with ideas from Check Up!

Ask:

▼ **When has doing what you believed was right cost you a friend?**
▼ **In order to be popular, is it necessary to hurt, use, or ignore people? why? why not?**
▼ **How do you respond when somebody makes fun of you because you try to love people everybody else hates?**
▼ **What Christian values or decisions would cost you friends?**
▼ **Where do you go for support when the world hates you?**

Love Laid Down

Direct a youth to read 1 John 3:16.

Ask:

▼ **What does the statement "Jesus laid down his life" mean to you?**
▼ **Cain took a life; Jesus laid down his life. Both are extreme measures. Are there reasons that would lead you to kill another person?** (capital punishment? self-defense?)
▼ **Are there causes for which you would die?** (war? attempts to save another person?)

OPTION 2

Tough Love

PREPARATION: Write the following case studies on index cards.

Your friends pick a fight with a group of people who belong to another race. What do you do?

You are walking down the hall at school when you discover a group of people teasing a student for carrying a Bible. What do you do?

Your friend calls you over to her locker to show you her stash of marijuana. What do you do?

Your friend makes the basketball team, and you don't. You're disappointed, to say the least. What do you do?

You get an A on your math test, but your eyes had "accidentally" strayed to a friend's paper. What do you do?

After reading 1 John 3:11-17, say: **Let's make these verses practical.** Hand out the case studies cards. Tell youth to prepare two quick skits—one that shows the world's way of love and another that shows a Christian's way of love based on 1 John.

After the skits have been presented,

Ask:

▼ **How do Christians make sacrifices?**
▼ **How do Christians lay down their lives for their friends?**

- ▼ Laying down your life is sometimes used as a metaphor for making sacrifices or for helping other people at personal cost. What are some sacrifices youth make for other people?
- ▼ Is helping with routine chores around the house or being especially kind to the other people in your family a way of showing God's love? why? why not?
- ▼ If being a Christian requires you to make sacrifices, then why be a Christian?

CONNECTING

Active Love

Draw a line down the middle of the chalkboard or newsprint. Label one side *Things to Do* and the other side *Things Not to Do*.

Ask:
- ▼ Why do you think loving is so important?
- ▼ How do you show love?
- ▼ What kinds of things do you do for people you love?

Hand out markers or chalk and let the youth list their ideas on the *Things to Do* side of the board.

Ask:
- ▼ What things would you *not* do to someone you love?

Let the youth list these items under *Things Not to Do*. When the lists are complete, ask:

- ▼ How did you learn to love?
- ▼ How did you learn what things to do and not do to people you love?
- ▼ Were you born knowing how?
- ▼ Did you learn to love by being loved?
- ▼ Who in your life has taught you the most about loving?
- ▼ How do you think that person learned to love?

Have youth read through the two lists again and mark the things that God would do or not do to the people God loves.

Ask:
- ▼ If these are God's lists, is anything missing?

Allow youth to add any items they think would describe God's love and then compare how the lists may have changed. Say: **We are able to love because God loved us first. God loved us so much that God came to earth to show us how to love God and one another. How does it feel to know that God loves you so much? Does God's love empower you to love in return? how?**

 **CHECK OUT**

How is fake love like hate?

OPTION 3

Building Love

PREPARATION: Bring a set of alphabet blocks, if possible. Or use blocks from the game Ginga. Write *H* on one Ginga block.

Place the blocks in the bag. Gather youth around the table. Pass the bag to the youth on your right. Ask that youth to take a block out of the bag, to place it on the table, and to name a characteristic or an action of love that begins with the letter on the block. (Or he or she may say the name of a loving person.) Then direct him or her to pass the bag to the person on his or her right, who will name a characteristic or action of love and will place a block on or beside the first block. As the youth continue around the circle, they will use the blocks to create a church building, built on love. The letter *H* stands for hatred; if one of the youth takes out of the bag a block with the letter *H* on it, he or she will knock down the church building.

Ask:
- ▼ How does hatred destroy a church?
- ▼ How can loving fellow Christians be difficult?

Continue with the game. Read John 3:16 as a closing.

38. GOTTA HAVE IT!

Luke 12:22-34

Putting the ownership of things into perspective.

✔ CHECK UP!

Four times in these verses from Luke 12:22-34 we are cautioned not to be anxious. Christians do not need to be fearful, impatient, in suspense, pleasureless, or troubled, all synonyms of anxiety. We are entreated not to be anxious about our lives in any way, neither for the food we eat, nor the clothes we wear. For life is much more than food or clothing, a big house or a hot car. The Evangelist adds that an anxious attitude won't increase the quality or number of years in life. How can Luke write of such assurance? The Evangelist knows that God has already provided and God will continue to provide for us the things essential for life in Christ.

After listing the examples of God's care, Jesus speaks directly to the disciples, and to us, "Your Father knows you need all these things. Instead of your anxious seeking, seek the kingdom of God and all these things will be yours as well." God calls us not to ignore the practical side of life, but to not be anxious about it. This kind of anxiety worries about having friends. To make friends, reach out to help others. This is one way to seek the kingdom of God as commanded in verse 30.

Look for a moment at the word *kingdom* as in "kingdom of God." Maybe you think of Cinderella and Prince Charming when you hear the word. Or maybe you think of a heavenly place where harps play. Hearing the word *kingdom,* we tend to think of a noun, a place. Instead of thinking of God's kingdom as a place, consider it as God's reign or rule. That translates the Greek word better, using verbs of being and action. God's reign can be any place. If we seek the rule or lordship of God, the rest of our lives will be ordered. There is no fear in this seeking. Jesus saves us boldly because God has already decided for us. We are the recipients of God's good pleasure. We can feel free to be confident because we trust in the God of salvation. When our treasure is God, we have no worry or anxiety that a thief might steal it.

The final verse urgently reminds us: "For where your treasure is, there your heart will be also." That which we love is truly our treasure. Our hearts belong to God if God is our number-one priority. These words should not make us feel guilty. Instead, the words keep us from ultimate stupidity—that of confusing the reign of God with material possessions. God as creator seeks to care for us. God as redeemer seeks to prepare a kingdom for us that is not a place but a way of life. Here we can once again know God as a true, present reality.

✔ CHECK LIST

STARTING
❑ Write statement on chalkboard or large sheet of paper.

EXPLORING
❑ Make four signs and display.
❑ Prepare balloons with slips of paper inside them.

OPTION 1
❑ Index cards, pencils.

OPTION 3
❑ Shoe box and construction paper for treasure chests.
❑ Slips of paper, pencils.

 # ✔ CHECK IN

STARTING

A Shrouded Statement

PREPARATION: Write this sentence on the chalkboard or sheet of paper: *There are no pockets in a shroud.*

Tell youth that this is an old Spanish saying.

Ask:
▼ **What does this mean?** *(You may need to explain that a shroud is a burial garment.)*

If no one can explain the saying, write, *You can't take it with you!* on the chalkboard or paper and say that it means the same thing. (Earthly possessions cannot benefit us or make us secure after death.) Say: **Storing up wealth is one thing people do to make themselves feel more secure. Different societies store up wealth in different ways. In Old Testament times people accumulated land, buildings, livestock, grain, gold and silver, and slaves.**

Ask:
▼ **Which of these things do we store up today?**
▼ **Which do we no longer store up?**

Mention that different societies in different parts of the world today measure wealth in different ways. Some African societies measure wealth by how much cattle a family owns. In some countries *(India, for example)* families buy gold jewelry with their extra money. The women of the family wear it, rather than put it in a bank.

Ask:
▼ **How do we in America measure wealth? importance? popularity?**
▼ **What things do you accumulate?**
▼ **Why are labels and certain brand names so important?**
▼ **Does accumulating lots of possessions make you feel better? more secure? more acceptable? If so, how long do you think this security will last?**

Say: **In today's Bible passage Jesus talks about this idea and tells his disciples what provides lasting security.**

OPTION 1

Enough?

Distribute index cards and pencils. Instruct youth to write down their answers to the question, How much is enough of each of these items?

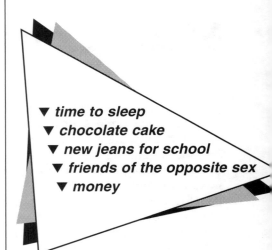

▼ *time to sleep*
▼ *chocolate cake*
▼ *new jeans for school*
▼ *friends of the opposite sex*
▼ *money*

Take up cards, shuffle them, and redistribute. Invite youth to read their cards. Then guess whose card it is as a group.

Ask:
▼ **How would you know if you had enough?**
▼ **If you had enough, would you be completely happy?**

Include in your discussion the questions under STARTING.

WHEN GOD SCRAMBLES YOUR PLANS

EXPLORING

Advice: Don't Worry!

PREPARATION: Prepare four signs. On each sign write one of these reactions:

> Don't worry about life? That's unrealistic. What about drugs and abuse from parents and STDs and college and friends?

> Aw, come on; Jesus didn't live in a real world. The only thing he said that made sense was the part about how we won't live any longer by worrying about it.

> Sure, I know life is more than clothes. Sometimes I feel guilty but I'm just keeping up with the latest styles.

> Do you know what would happen if we all took Jesus seriously? We'd be on the streets, starving to death, just hanging out and trusting God.

Post the signs in four areas of the room. Read Luke 12:22-34 aloud as youth follow in their Bibles. Point out the four signs. Ask youth to move to the area of the room that best represents his or her reaction to the Scripture. Explain that no one has to agree completely with any of the statements; each person should choose the statement that comes closest to his or her response.

Ask:
▼ Why do you agree with this reaction?
▼ With which part of the reaction statements do you disagree?
▼ What statements do you agree with from the Scripture?
▼ What statements do you disagree with in the Scripture?
▼ How practical is the advice Jesus gives?

OPTION 2

Silent Advice

Invite the youth to create a pantomime based on Luke 12:22-34. Every student should be part of the pantomime. (Divide a large group into small groups. In a small group, all the youth should work together.) Let them struggle with how to communicate the meaning of the text without using words. Bring the group together to act out the Scripture.

Ask:
▼ How do you suppose the people felt when they first heard this passage?
▼ How do you think they reacted?
▼ What does the Scripture say about your worries? your life?
▼ Why can't you just forget about school if you believe this Scripture?
▼ Why can't you drive the way you want since you don't have to worry?
▼ How would you explain Jesus' point about possessions?

Advice: Seek God's Kingdom

PREPARATION: Write one word from Luke 12:31 on each of the small slips of paper. Insert one slip of paper into each balloon. Inflate the balloons, tie them off, and mix them up.

Invite each person to select one or more balloons. *(If your group is large, write the words of the Scripture twice and divide the group into two teams.)* Direct youth to pop their balloons and to put the slips of paper in order so that the words form a sentence. Suggest that they check their sentence by reading aloud Luke 12:31.

Ask:
▼ How does the verse you unscramble relate to the meaning of the larger passage?
▼ How does a person seek the kingdom of God? *(Share information from Check Up!)*
▼ How can a teenager put God first?
▼ What happens to that teenager's ideas about possessions? About music and the media? About how to spend free time? About friends and family?

Lead youth to sing "Seek Ye First" if they know this chorus.

CONNECTING

Motto Messages

Say: **There are many mottoes or catchy phrases that deal with possessions and worry. For example, "Shop till you drop" or "The one who dies with the most toys wins."**

Ask:
▼ What mottoes have you seen or heard that are similar to these?

Divide youth into small groups. Ask each group to come up with a new motto that they would live by if they took Luke 12:22-34 seriously. Bring the groups together to compare their mottoes. Conclude the session by offering a prayer. Ask God to help the youth live by their new mottoes.

 CHECK OUT

Why shouldn't we give away our possessions and live off of God's goodwill?

OPTION 3
Treasured Advice

PREPARATION: Create a treasure chest using a shoe box and construction paper.

Pass out a pencil and several slips of paper to each youth. Invite youth to think of things that make us feel rich or make us think someone else is rich. Say, **These will probably be things that persons in our society tend to accumulate in order to feel secure or to appear wealthy.** Ask youth to write their ideas on the slips of paper, using a different slip for each idea. Collect the slips in the treasure chest.

Have youth, one by one, draw out a slip of paper, read aloud what's written there, and say something that could happen to spoil or destroy that thing. Continue until all the slips have been drawn.

Ask:
▼ Why don't earthly possessions help us connect with God?

Direct youth to look again at Luke 12:31-34. Ask them to call out things to put in the treasure chest that would be of lasting value. *(These could include things like healthy relationships, strong family ties, giving to the church.)*

39. MAKE UP YOUR MIND

Joshua 24:14-18; Matthew 6:24

Evaluating whether to choose the gods of society or the one true God.

✔ CHECK UP!

The setting for this text is a time of new beginnings, of choices for life or death. The book of Joshua focuses on Israel crossing the Jordan River into the land of promise. It covers winning the early battles to control the land and beginning a new way of life. The temptation for Israel is to forget Yahweh and to follow the gods of popular culture in their new homeland. Like the original crossing over the Jordan River at the beginning of the Joshua story, a new kind of crossing over is necessary. This crossing over is meant to be a rescue, which brings with it a great sense of urgency. The gods who had tempted the people must be put away. The people must choose to follow only Yahweh once again. They must accept the responsibility and privileges of discipleship, leaving behind the other gods.

In Joshua 24:2-13, the writer recites God's grace throughout the history of Israel. Joshua 24:14-18 emerges with the corollary to divine grace, which is Israel's commitment to serve a covenant Lord. Confessing their sins against the Lord, the Israelites bring contrite hearts seeking renewal. These verses make it clear what is required for renewal, nothing less than to enter into covenant with Yahweh. The covenant isn't any random agreement. It's one of discipleship in which the people choose to serve Yahweh exclusively by proclaiming that Yahweh is God in the heaven above and on the earth below and Lord of all the earth. Serving Yahweh exclusively means having a loving concern for all the people of the earth. This covenant is lived out by putting away old gods, by purification, and through personal renewal.

The gods that must be put away fall into three categories. The gods of ancient religious tradition inherited from past generations may prevent necessary changes for transition. The gods of Egypt tend toward imperialist notions degrading the oppressed. And the gods of the Amorites were a popular religion that exploited human weaknesses. The seductive powers of these gods still attract us today. These gods of culture seem to be a force field that magnetically draws us to places where we get stuck. Joshua points out we must make a conscious effort to cross over into the redemptive power of Yahweh. The word *serve* appears eight times in these few verses. We must pay attention when a word or phrase is repeated so

✔ CHECK LIST

STARTING
❏ Make "Agree-Disagree" signs.

EXPLORING
❏ Make four posters with questions.

CONNECTING
❏ Make "Would You Rather" cards.

OPTION 1
❏ Bring a fist-sized rock.

OPTION 2
❏ Enlist three youth for the skit.

OPTION 3
❏ Bring cake, knife, napkins.

often. "We will serve the Lord" is the central point of Joshua's plea. The problem of serving idols has created alienation. It is time to choose.

This choice creates a change in values and priorities. The change involves serving the Lord in acts of worship and seeking God above all else. The people know of divine grace. What they must do now is choose to make a commitment to serve the covenant Lord.

 CHECK IN

STARTING

Hard Choices

PREPARATION: Make two signs. On one sheet of paper write the word *Agree*. On the other sheet write the word *Disagree*. Post the *Agree* sign on one wall. Post on the opposite wall the sign *Disagree*.

Say: **Sometimes we have to choose from only two options.** Explain that you will make several statements. The youth will decide whether they agree or disagree with each statement and will stand near the sign that indicates their response. They may not stand between the signs.

Read each statement, minus the parenthetical information. Wait for youth to choose. Don't ask youth to explain their decisions until all the statements have been read. The statements are:

(Simple statements that express an opinion)
- I like the color blue.
- Chocolate is my favorite flavor.
- I prefer to be around people who smile.

(Moderately difficult statements)
- The best musical group right now is *(name a popular group)*.
- The best program on TV is *(name a popular program)*.
- The President is doing a good job of running this country.

(Difficult statements)
- It is wrong not to tell the whole truth.
- Cheating is no big deal.
- If a store clerk gives you too much change, you don't have to give it back, because it was the clerk's error.

Ask:
▼ **How did you feel having to choose between agreeing and disagreeing with the statements?**
▼ **What did you do when you did not feel good about either choice?**
▼ **In everyday life, what choices do you face that offer only two options?**

OPTION 1

A Choice Story

Instruct youth to sit in a circle. Explain that they are going to tell a progressive story. They will pass a rock from one person to the next; the person holding the rock will contribute to the story, then pass the rock to the person beside him or her. After the rock has been passed all the way around the circle, you will finish the story. Begin the story by saying: **This rock was once part of a castle.**

After ending the story, ask:
▼ **How did you feel having your choices about the direction of the story limited by the person before you?**
▼ **How did you feel about limiting the next person's choices?**
▼ **In what ways is telling a progressive story like facing choices in real life?**

WHEN GOD SCRAMBLES YOUR PLANS

EXPLORING

No More Choices

PREPARATION: Write the following four questions on separate posters. Hang each poster on a different wall.

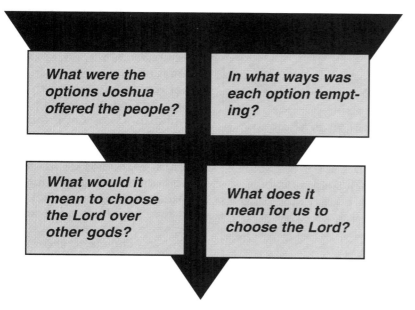

What were the options Joshua offered the people?

In what ways was each option tempting?

What would it mean to choose the Lord over other gods?

What does it mean for us to choose the Lord?

Ask a youth to read Joshua 24:14-18. Briefly share background facts from Check Up! about events leading up to this speech. Tell youth to turn their chairs toward a wall so that their chairs form a square in the middle of the room. Instruct youth to answer the question that is in front of them using Joshua 24:14-18. Tell youth to present their answers in a unique way. They might prepare a monologue for someone to share as Joshua. They might write a rap, prepare an infomercial, or draw a picture on the poster board explaining their answer. After a few minutes call for answers.

The Two Masters Theory

Read aloud Matthew 6:24.

Ask:
▼ In what ways were Jesus' words similar to Joshua's?
▼ What are the consequences of choosing to serve God? mammon *(money)*?
▼ Why did Jesus say that a person cannot serve both God and money?
▼ How do you feel about having to make a choice between God and money?

OPTION 2

Two Masters Skit

Enlist three youth to help with this skit. Two youth should start telling the third youth to do things—get a Bible, pull a chair around, sing a song, rub their feet. As the third youth becomes more frantic in trying to help the other two, the youth who are watching may start laughing. The third youth can then say: **What are you laughing at? You serve two masters, too!** Continue with "The Two Masters Theory."

CONNECTING

"I Choose God—I Think?"

PREPARATION: Write each of the following eleven choices on index cards using the following format—*Would you rather* (first item from first column) *get good grades in school or* (first item from second column) *smoke cigarettes?* Continue with this format with all the statements.

Would you rather . . .		
get good grades in school	*or*	*smoke cigarettes*
have an expensive car	*or*	*be a good athlete*
be a good friend	*or*	*be loved by everyone*
use alcohol or other drugs	*or*	*be attractive*
wear the latest styles	*or*	*date lots of people*
have lots of tapes or CD's	*or*	*go to church*
read the Bible	*or*	*be popular*
go steady	*or*	*save money*
get into a good college	*or*	*be an honest person*
be a good son or daughter	*or*	*have lots of money*
date the most popular person	*or*	*help needy people*

Hand each youth a card. Direct youth to find a buddy and share what they would rather do and why.

Ask:

▼ Which choices were easy to make? why?

▼ Which choices were hard to make? why?

▼ In what ways do people choose, without thinking about it, to serve false gods?

▼ In what ways are rival gods dangerous to us?

 **CHECK OUT**

How committed am I to God alone?

OPTION 3

Cake or Cookies?

Display the cake you brought.

Ask:

▼ What does the saying, "You can't eat your cake and have it, too!" mean?

After several responses say: Most of us don't want to choose between pursuing wealth and serving God. We would prefer to work toward a comfortable lifestyle and to worship God. Both Joshua and Jesus challenge us to choose; we cannot do both at the same time. Whether we like the choice makes no difference. The choice remains. How will you choose? Will you choose to serve God and God alone? After your closing prayer, cut the cake and share it with youth.

40. THE SUPERMAN SYNDROME

Obadiah 1-4; Luke 14:11

Seeing how power gives a false sense of security.

✔ CHECK UP!

Obadiah is the shortest book in the Old Testament. The book is about God's moral judgment on nations, particularly Edom, because of the way it has treated Israel. Edom was a little kingdom just south of the Dead Sea. It was a small country, roughly seventy miles north to south and fifteen miles east to west. Its most prominent geographical feature was the red color in the rocks and cliffs which led to its name, which means "red region" in Hebrew. The people of Edom descended from Esau. The people of Israel descended from his twin brother, Jacob. The tribes acted as if they were enemies. Obadiah's complaint against the Edomites is the way they rejoiced when Jerusalem was destroyed by the Babylonians in 586 B.C.

Obadiah's point is that there's no such thing as national security. Edom thought she was safe behind all the rock cliffs that guarded her, but no country or people are ever safe. Edom's doom is made clear in the voice of God summoning the nations to war. Some may question the morality of that statement. Others may rejoice that it fits their idea of God. The point is not that God is a great warrior who loves war. The point is that in God's plan, nations reap what they sow, and those who try to build systems of false security face ruin and destruction from their neighbors. Notice how the prophet describes both the sense of false security and the sureness of judgment in verse 3. God is in control of the nations. No nation is exempt from God's judgment. No nation lives outside the power of God. What we call the rise and fall of the great powers, the Bible calls God's activity in history. Security, the prophet says, is not in geography, not in military systems, not in power, but in God.

✔ CHECK LIST

STARTING
❑ Bag of candy.

EXPLORING
❑ Prepare learning centers.
❑ Bible commentaries, Bible atlas.
❑ Write questions on paper.

CONNECTING
❑ Make sign.

OPTION 1
❑ Slips of paper, a bowl or basket, large sheet of newsprint, marker, timer.

OPTION 2
❑ Pencils, paper.

OPTION 3
❑ Suggested game.

 # CHECK IN

STARTING

The Power of Ownership

Give a bag of candy bars to one youth, preferably someone with a strong personality who will not feel obligated to share the candy. Invite the others to get the candy by whatever means they choose, except by taking it away or threatening the candy holder.

Be aware of how power affects the person holding the candy. He or she may quickly begin to hoard the candy or to show preference to some of the youth. Notice how the rest of the youth contribute to the candy holder's rising status and increasing power.

After a few minutes, change the rules. Say: **Anyone holding or eating a candy bar thirty seconds from now will have to contribute one dollar per candy bar to the youth fund.** Observe that the person holding the candy bars has a sudden loss of power and is more than willing to relinquish his or her hold on the candy bars. Stop the game. Make sure everyone gets a candy bar.

Ask:
▼ What happened when one person had all the power?
▼ How did you react to him or her?
▼ How did you feel when you held the candy?
▼ How did you feel when other people tried to get on your good side so that you would give them a candy bar?
▼ What happened when the rules changed?
▼ Is it easy to be influenced by power? why? why not?
▼ What does power do to your personality?
▼ What are powerful groups in your school? community?
▼ How is power used?
▼ How much security is in power?

OPTION 1

The Power in Words

PREPARATION: Write each phrase below on a separate slip of paper, then fold the papers and place them in a bowl.

● *power to the people*
● *balance of power*
● *power hungry*
● *the power of the sword*
● *the power of love*
● *power play*
● *power suit*
● *power in the blood*
● *the power behind the throne*
● *Speak softly and carry a big stick.*

Tell youth that the bowl contains phrases that deal with power.

Have one person draw one phrase from the bowl and follow the rules of charades to act it out. Allow two minutes for the group to guess the answer and write it on the newsprint. Then have another person draw a phrase and continue the process until all the phrases have been drawn.

EXPLORING

Powerful Research

PREPARATION: Set up two learning centers. Use signs to identify one as *Obadiah* and the other as *Edom*. Place Bible commentaries at both learning centers. At the *Edom* learning center place a Bible atlas (or use a Bible that has Bible maps). At the *Obadiah* learning center place a sheet with these questions for youth to answer:

1. God shows power in Obadiah's prophecy; where do you see God's power exhibited in today's world?

2. Was Obadiah written before or after the Edomites helped destroy Jerusalem and Judah? What significance does knowing this have?

3. What does the Scripture say to individuals? What does God expect of individuals? In what ways do we seek power?

At the *Edom* learning center place a sheet with these questions for youth to answer:

1. Find Edom, Jerusalem, and Judah on the map. Where are they in relation to each other? Which are cities and which are countries?

2. Were the Edomites friends or enemies of Israel? why?

3. What year did Babylonia, with Edom's help, defeat the city of Jerusalem and the Jewish country of Judah?

4. Did anybody ever defeat Edom's mountain fortress? If so, who?

5. If we act like the Edomites, what can we expect from God?

Let youth work together to find answers and share information. After a period of study, call everyone together. Have them discuss the information they discovered about Edom. Basically, they should uncover the fact that in 586 B.C., the Edomites, ancient enemies of the Jewish people, helped the Babylonians defeat Judah (the last remaining part of the Jewish kingdom) and Jerusalem (the location of the Temple). The Edomites felt proud and haughty because they had built atop rocky cliffs a fortress that seemed impossible to conquer. The prophet Obadiah, however, said that they would someday be brought low; and he was right! Direct a youth to read Luke 14:11.

Ask:
▼ How does this New Testament verse relate to this Old Testament history?
▼ What does this New Testament verse mean for us today?

Encourage youth to state the verse in their own words.

OPTION 2

Power Parable

Have a volunteer read aloud Luke 14:7-11.

Then ask:
▼ **Which verse from this passage could be added as verse 5 to Obadiah's message?** *(v. 11)*

Have a volunteer read aloud Obadiah 1-4, followed by Luke 14:11. Allow volunteers to comment on this combination of Scripture. Form small groups of two or three and ask each group to write a parable to replace the one Jesus uses in Luke 14:8-10. The new stories should still fit the larger context of Luke 14:7-11; but they should be about the Edomites, their sinful pride, and God's vow to humble them. When everyone is finished, ask representatives from each group to read Luke 14:7-11, replacing verses 8-10 with their new stories.

CONNECTING

Society's Power

PREPARATION: Make a sign that says *In order to be successful in life, you must have power and influence.*

Divide youth into two teams. Ask one team to list reasons for believing the statement. Ask the other team to list reasons for not believing the statement. (This team can use arguments from today's Bible study.) After a few minutes, let each team take turns sharing its points. Point out that this is what society believes about power.

Ask:
▼ **How is this statement a false sense of security?**
▼ **How can the search for power become a destructive lifestyle?**
▼ **How can someone be powerful and not be damaged by that power or damage others?**

Urge youth to observe how power occurs in their lives during the next week—who has power, how that person uses or abuses it. Close by praying for the leaders in power.

 **CHECK OUT**

"If I don't have some power, others will walk all over me." How would you respond?

OPTION 3

Power Play

PREPARATION: Locate a game of Sorry, backgammon, or some other game in which one player can make another player start over.

Have a few volunteers play the game for a few minutes while the rest of the youth watch. To save time and to increase the chances that players will bump each other back home, you might let everyone begin with their playing pieces spread out around the game board rather than gathered at their home bases.

After the game, ask:
▼ **In the game, it is when you move ahead of someone else that you are most likely to get bumped and have to start all over. How is this similar to Obadiah's message?**
▼ **Which words or phrases from Obadiah 1-4 might also apply to the game we just played?** *(v. 4)*
▼ **What are God's "rules of the game"? Why is Edom likely to get bumped?**

CHAPTER 7

TRANSITIONS

41. BEING ADOPTED— BY GOD

Galatians 3:23–4:7; Ephesians 1:4-8

Discovering what it means to be a chosen child of God.

✔ CHECK UP!

Paul explains a Christian's relationship to God in several different ways. In Galatians 3:23-26 he compares the law to a "disciplinarian," a word that is also translated as "schoolmaster." In ancient Greece, a schoolmaster's task was to attend boys under the age of sixteen. These custodians escorted children to and from school and served as their chief disciplinarians. Thus these guardians readied the youth for the eventual freedom of adulthood.

In a similar fashion, the law disciplines us and readies us to receive the freedom that is available through Christ's grace. Just as the Greek schoolmasters delivered their charges to school and to a higher level of maturity, the law serves as a delivery agent to bring persons to the maturity of being in Christ.

In verses 26-29, Paul describes what it means to live "in Christ Jesus." Our baptism in Christ unites us with other believers. As a result of this new relationship, external differences no longer matter; we are all inheritors of God's promise to Abraham.

In Galatians 4:1-7, Paul compares being under the law with being a minor (a person who is not ready for adult responsibility). Jewish tradition held that a father was responsible for his son until the age of thirteen. At that point the boy became a bar mitzvah, literally "a son of the commandment." For the Greeks and Romans also, a child became an adult at a precise time and in a definite way. Similarly, the law has prepared us for responsibility. With the coming of Christ, we are able to move from being like a slave to being like a son or a daughter.

The Ephesians passage is an extended benediction or prayerful blessing to God for what the Father of our Lord Jesus Christ has done in Christ for all Christians. God chose us in Christ before the foundation of the world to be holy and blameless before God in love. God destined us for adoption as children through Jesus Christ. In Christ we have redemption through his blood, the forgiveness of our sin, because God lavishes the riches of grace on us with all wisdom and insight.

The first clue that this passage transports us beyond the earthly and mundane occurs in verse 3. This identifies us with every spiritual blessing in the heavenly places. This is characteristic of the author of Ephesians, who tends to see Christians as already seated

✔ CHECK LIST

STARTING
❒ Magazines, newspapers.

EXPLORING
❒ Invite a guest.
❒ Chalkboard, paper cut into fourths, pencils.

CONNECTING
❒ Gift-wrapped box with separate top with stones, candies or shells.

OPTION 1
❒ Prepare sacks and mirrors.

OPTION 2
❒ Prepare wall signs.

OPTION 3
❒ Prepare fortune cookies.
❒ Pencils, paper.

WHEN GOD SCRAMBLES YOUR PLANS

with God in the heavenly places with Christ Jesus. If your youth take this as a wishful attempt to escape this world's struggles, remind them that Ephesians does not evade conflict, but sees the world's conflict with Christians from heaven's perspective. As the author of this letter says later, our struggle is not against enemies of blood and flesh, but against the cosmic powers of this present darkness, against the spiritual forces of evil in the heavenly places.

Spiritual blessings are not private goodies stashed away for us in a heavenly trust fund, to be inherited upon our death. In Ephesians, spiritual blessings appear most dramatically manifest in the community of Christian believers. These are available to us right now as an inheritance that we have already obtained in Christ. From this exalted cosmic standpoint the writer of Ephesians unfurls and repeatedly brandishes a handful of banner themes. One such theme is God's blessing displayed through Christ and lavished upon us. The author of Ephesians uses a variety of metaphors to convey this idea. For example, in verse 5 we are adopted as God's children through Jesus Christ. This refers to a legal stipulation during the time of the Roman Empire whereby a wealthy, childless adult could adopt a boy, sometimes even a slave, to be his legal heir. What a wonderful gesture of love!

CHECK IN

STARTING

Costly Collage

Using several magazines and newspapers, invite youth to locate and tear out examples of the things they consider most costly and valuable. Direct youth to make a collage of these items, taping them on newsprint or poster board.

Ask:
▼ What makes an item valuable?
▼ How can something be valuable to one person and not valuable to another? Give an example.

Say: **Even though there are many costly and valuable items in this world, none is more valuable than living as God's child. In this study you will discover what being God's child involves.**

OPTION 1

God's Gift

PREPARATION: Place a mirror in a sack so that when persons look down into it they can see their own reflections. (If you have a large number of youth, prepare several sacks.)

Tell youth that you want to show them a very special gift that God has given them. Let everybody look into the bag one at a time. Tell them to take a few moments and seriously consider what they see as a gift from God, but to tell no one else what they see.

Ask:
▼ How did you feel about what you saw?
▼ How do you know you are valuable to God?
▼ How are you a gift from God?

EXPLORING

Adopted

PREPARATION: If possible, invite someone you know who is adopted to come and talk with the youth about what being adopted means. Allow time for youth to ask questions about adoption. If you choose not to invite someone who is adopted, read the following story about Ann.

When Ann was a baby, her mother could not take care of her. Her mother had no home or resources, and she already had an older baby to take care of. Ann was passed from friend to friend and moved from shelter to shelter. When Ann was two years old, her mother made the painful decision to take her to a home operated by a church from which Ann could be placed in foster care with someone who would take care of her. Later Ann's mother disappeared, and no one knew how to find her.

Ann needed parents and to be a part of a family. When Ann was four the church found a home and foster parents for her. She had a new mother and father she never had before. After six months Ann and her foster parents went to court for her formal adoption. In the court the judge asked if she wanted her foster parents to be her adopted parents. The judge also asked if the foster parents were willing to take care of Ann and be her parents forever. Through this pledge Ann was adopted into her new family and received a new last name. Ann now lives with her new family in her new home. She now belongs to someone.

After reading the story, ask a youth to read Galatians 3:23–4:7 aloud.

Ask:
▼ How are the two stories similar?
▼ How are they different?
▼ What does it mean to be adopted by a family?
▼ What does it mean to be adopted by God?
▼ What privileges does a child gain once adopted by a family?
▼ What privileges does a Christian gain once that person is adopted by God?

Count Your Blessings!

PREPARATION: On a chalkboard write *life, family, health, friends, church family.* Cut several sheets of paper into fourths.

Direct youth to look at Ephesians 1:4-8 and find a verse that tells that God has given us the blessings listed on the chalkboard. Hand out the paper. Tell youth to look for other blessings in the passage and write one blessing on each sheet of paper. Tell youth to put tape on the backs of their papers and stick them to their clothing. (They may need to put several pieces of tape on each piece of paper so that it will stick quickly and securely.)

Play a fast session of "Blessings Tag," where each person takes a piece of paper off of his or her own clothing and tries to stick it onto someone else. Read these simple rules:

OPTION 2

Gift Shopping

PREPARATION: Make two signs that read: *1—nope, wouldn't want it* and *10—gotta have it!* Hang the signs on walls that are directly opposite each other.

Call out a few items that youth think are important *(brand name clothing, the latest CD, faddish tennis shoes, favorite sports team's jacket, an expensive piece of jewelry, the latest computer game, etc.).* As each item is named have youth place themselves according to how much they would like to have each item. As you mention each item, let several persons tell why they are standing where they are. If possible, have youth who are standing far apart discuss briefly why they are at opposing places.

Next mention a couple of the gifts from today's study in Ephesians. Have youth use the same scale to place themselves. Discuss the difference between these gifts from God and the gifts we might get at the mall.

1. You can only stick one piece of paper on a person at a time.

2. If your paper does not stick and falls off the other person, you must pick it up and try again.

3. You can take papers that others stick on you and stick them on other people.

Let youth play the game for a few minutes, then bring everyone together and ask them how many papers they have. Get volunteers to pick up any papers that fell on the floor. Ask each person to read his or her blessings out loud. As each blessing is read, briefly discuss why it is a blessing. Repeat the procedure until all of the biblical blessings have been mentioned. To close, stress that even though you are adopted into God's family, a Christian receives the same blessings and inheritance as Jesus did. Christians are important to God; they are part of God's family.

CONNECTING

The Gift

PREPARATION: Gift wrap a box and its top separately. Inside put brightly colored stones (like the ones used in the bottoms of fish tanks—available from any pet store), hard candies, or some other objects that youth can take with them. (If you have a large group, you may need more than one box. You'll need a box for every 10 to 12 persons.)

Have youth form circles of no more than 10 to 12 individuals. Pass the box around the circle and have each person receiving the box tell what God's greatest gift is to him or her personally. After everyone has had a turn, open the box and let each person take an object to represent the gift God has given them. Close with a "build-a-prayer." You begin by saying:

Dear God, we thank you for . . . The person on your left continues the prayer by completing your sentence and beginning a new one. The next person builds on that statement and so forth so that the prayer may take many new directions. When the prayer has gone around the circle once, end it yourself.

 CHECK OUT

If you gain so many benefits from being in God's family, how can you get adopted? (If you have youth who have never accepted Jesus Christ as a personal Savior, challenge them to stay and talk with you about this decision.)

OPTION 3

Fortune Cookie

PREPARATION: Bring a bag of fortune cookies. (These can be purchased in most stores or at a restaurant specializing in Asian cuisine.) Give out pencils and paper.

Say: **On the basis of what you know about God, write a "fortune" that you think God would give you.** Give each person a cookie. Say: **You have been adopted by God. God has given you many gifts. God has given you a future. As we go around the circle, break your fortune cookie, then read the blessing.**

42. DIGGING OUT OF DOUBT

John 20:24-29

Talking about doubt as a means to growth.

✔ CHECK UP!

In approaching basic Christian confession, young people, like adults, exhibit a spectrum of faith and disbelief. In grappling with this reality, teachers and interpreters are helped by the Fourth Evangelist's unique presentation of Easter and the shades of belief and doubt that colored Jesus' survivors.

We might also recall Jesus' pronouncement in John 6:44: "No one can come to me unless drawn by the Father who sent me." In this Gospel, and indeed throughout the Bible, faith is not something you create for yourself or for your youth. Though we can nurture the faith planted in us and others, faith is a gift from God.

Thomas represents a complex array of attitudes in the Fourth Gospel. On the one hand, Thomas seems to lack faith. He calls for a set of empirical conditions of faith, a form of unbelief that Jesus has rejected earlier in this Gospel in chapter 4. Thomas says that unless he sees signs and wonders he will not believe. On the other hand, in the Fourth Gospel faith often follows these signs. Thomas is basically confirming that the risen Christ is the same Jesus of Nazareth that he and the others have known, not a ghost or a hallucination. Whether Thomas actually touches the risen Jesus is not clear. The text climaxes with Thomas' acknowledgment of the risen Jesus as "My Lord and my God," the most explicit confession of Jesus' divinity in all of John's Gospel, and perhaps in all of the New Testament. At the end of the day skeptical Thomas becomes the one who receives a blessing for all generations of Christians. The blessing is for John's own readers and we who have not seen Jesus, yet rely on faith in the preaching of the gospel itself. Our distance in time and space from Jesus does not make us second-class Christians, nor must we scramble for a miracle to prop up our faith. The church believes that Jesus is Christ through the word of those who have preached that belief, and that, John assures us, is blessing aplenty.

✔ CHECK LIST

STARTING
❏ Prepare signs.

EXPLORING
❏ Paper, pencils.

CONNECTING
❏ Prepare index cards, copies of the litany.

OPTION 1
❏ Prepare signs.

OPTION 3
❏ Prepare bag or box, index cards, pencils.

✔ CHECK IN

STARTING

Believe–Not Believe

PREPARATION: Make and display the *Believe* and *Not Believe* signs. Designate one wall as "believe" and the opposite wall as "not believe."

Name one of the following topics: *flying saucers, angels, ghosts, life on another planet, a real and personal devil, the resurrection of Jesus from the dead.* Tell youth to stand in a place between the two walls that represents where they are on a continuum of belief and doubt about the topic. Ask them to defend their positions. Repeat the process with each topic.

EXPLORING

A Letter from Thomas

Say: **We will use the story of Thomas to explore issues of faith and doubt in our lives.** Instruct a youth to read John 20:24-29 aloud. Tell the others to listen for Thomas' feelings at each event. After reading the Scripture, ask:

▼ **What makes something believable?**
▼ **What makes something difficult to believe?**

Hand out paper and pencils. Say: **Imagine that you are Thomas. You have just discovered that you missed the big event of the century. You weren't there when Jesus appeared to the rest of the disciples! Write a letter to Jesus—as Thomas—that expresses what you feel, what you are thinking, why you doubt that this really happened, and what you need in order to believe.**

Let youth share the letters with the group. Take up these letters and keep them until CONNECTING.

OPTION 1

Why Do I Doubt?

PREPARATION: Make signs that read: *What I hear makes sense to me; I need more information; I want real proof; Someone I respect disagrees; People lie; I believe something else.* Hang the signs around the room.

Challenge older teenagers with this option. Point out the signs hanging around the room.

Ask:
▼ **What reason do most teenagers give for doubting something?**

Direct youth to walk to the statement that is closest to their answer or to stand in the middle, if they have another idea.

Ask:
▼ **What statement best expresses the questions you have about the Bible? about God? about Jesus? about your faith?**

OPTION 2

The Great Thomas Debate

Divide the group into two teams for an informal debate. One side will argue that doubting is wrong and that Thomas shouldn't have doubted. The other side will argue that doubt is good and that there was nothing wrong with Thomas' doubt. The basis for the debate is the Scripture lesson from John 20:24-29.

Give both teams three minutes to do research. Then, for one minute, have each side present its

CONNECTING

How Does Doubt Happen?

PREPARATION: On index cards write the phrase: *Christmas, Easter, I wondered about, I feared Jesus.* You will need enough cards for every pair of youth in your group.

Divide youth into pairs. Assign each pair a different age range (5-6 years old; 7-8 years old; 9-10 years old; 11-12 years old; 13 years old; 14 years old on up to the age of those in your group). Hand each pair an index card. Tell each pair to decide what they believed about the different topics on the card at the age assigned to them. Call for a time of sharing. Point out that doubt can be the catalyst for growth and maturity, rather than something we should allow to stifle and paralyze us.

Ask:
▼ In what ways has your understanding of the following changed since childhood: the church? Christian celebration? prayer? God? Jesus?
▼ How has your faith changed?

Say: **Just as our understanding of the world changes and matures as we grow, so does our faith. What we believed as a child may seem foolish to us today. And yet those millions of questions we asked as children may be the reason for greater knowledge and deeper faith today. Ask your questions! Express your doubts and concerns! Search for answers! And know that this is a place where that is O.K.—where we will struggle together to grow in faith.**

The Letter Answered

Divide youth into teams of four and divide among them the letters written from Thomas to Jesus. Ask each group to come up with responses that Jesus might make to the questions and comments in the letters they have been given. Using these responses, create a role-play in which Jesus comes to visit Thomas to answer his questions in person. Encourage youth to explore how Jesus might deal with Thomas' doubt and how he might try to strengthen Thomas' faith. Give the groups a few minutes to work out their role-plays and then present them to the group.

OPTION 2 (Continued)

position. Give the teams three minutes to come up with counter-arguments to the opposing team's presentation, then have each team present a one-minute rebuttal of the other team's position.

Ask:
▼ **What role did doubt play in Thomas' faith?**
▼ **What role does doubt play in our faith?**
▼ **Has doubting something ever helped your faith?** *(Encourage examples or stories).*

Say: **Doubt is a normal part of life and of faith. Doubt can have a very positive influence if we allow it to challenge us to ask questions, to seek answers, to grow, rather than to paralyze us.**

OPTION 3

The Thomas Box

PREPARATION: Clearly label a box or bag "The Thomas Box." Place the box or bag in the middle of the room.

Give youth blank index cards. Tell them that they have the opportunity to let the group deal with any questions, doubts, or other issues they do not understand. Let youth anonymously write unanswered questions or doubts they have about their faith on their cards, and place them in the box.

Shake the box, then draw a card out and read it. Let everyone discuss the issue and give any insights or thoughts they have. This allows the entire group to become a resource for helping the person who wrote the card deal with the issue. (If you think you might be uncomfortable dealing with these issues and questions without time to prepare answers, invite the pastor or other knowledgeable adults to be present for this portion of the session.)

Closing

PREPARATION: Duplicate the following litany and read it as a closing prayer.

After discussing each question, ask:

▼ **How can this question or doubt help our faith?**

Repeat this process with other cards for as long as time allows.

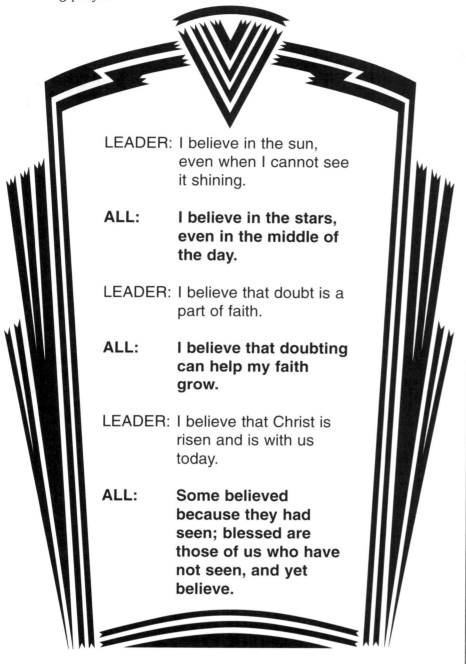

LEADER: I believe in the sun, even when I cannot see it shining.

ALL: **I believe in the stars, even in the middle of the day.**

LEADER: I believe that doubt is a part of faith.

ALL: **I believe that doubting can help my faith grow.**

LEADER: I believe that Christ is risen and is with us today.

ALL: **Some believed because they had seen; blessed are those of us who have not seen, and yet believe.**

 **CHECK OUT**

How would you explain the value of doubt to a friend?

! 43. FREEDOM! FREEDOM?

Exodus 6:2-9; 11:1; 12:29-33; 14:30-31

Focusing on how, when, where, and why freedom happens, and what freedom includes.

✔ CHECK UP!

Exodus 6:2-9 affirms Moses' call at a time when the Hebrew people were critical of his leadership because Pharaoh had increased their workload. Moses is to announce to the Hebrews that God intends to liberate them and lead them into the Promised Land. God will redeem the people and make them God's own.

Moses obediently reports to the people what God has said. However, the Hebrews are not receptive to Moses' report. In their oppressed condition they are unable even to imagine a different way of life.

God sends nine plagues to afflict the Egyptians over an unspecified period of time. First, all the water in Egypt turns to blood. Next, the entire country hops with frogs. As Pharaoh remains obstinate, God sends swarms of gnats, then flies, followed by deadly disease that kills livestock. The people and the animals are plagued with boils. Then there is thunder and hail. During the eighth plague, God sends locusts that eat the crops of the Egyptians. Next, the entire land, except for where the Hebrew people lived, becomes so dark that people cannot even see one another.

You would think that Pharaoh would understand God's power by now, but he still refuses to free the Hebrew slaves. God responds by sending one last, devastating plague. An angel of death passes over Egypt and kills the firstborn child and livestock belonging to each Egyptian family. Ancient peoples attached a special significance to firstborn children, especially sons. Thus the death of firstborns was considered particularly tragic and devastating.

Exodus 12:21-36 records both a description of what happened and a prescription for the celebration of Passover in perpetuity. The blood of the Passover lambs smeared on the doorposts had no special power, but was understood to be a sign. When God saw the sign of blood, which symbolized life, God would not allow the angel of death to enter that house. Thus God "passed over" the Hebrew households.

After the tenth plague strikes each Egyptian family, the Hebrews leave Egypt, taking with them the Egyptians' silver and gold jewelry. Exodus 13:17–14:31 recounts the Hebrews' escape from the Egyptians. As the people begin their flight to freedom, they take Joseph's bones with them, marking the end of their sojourn in Egypt.

Pharaoh quickly decides to dispatch all his forces to overtake the Hebrew slaves and return them to Egypt. The king's victory seems

✔ CHECK LIST

STARTING
❏ Prepare case studies.

EXPLORING
❏ Prepare the index cards.
❏ Scramble the cards.

CONNECTING
❏ Large sheet of paper, markers.

OPTION 1
❏ Paper, pencils.

OPTION 2
❏ Video camera.

OPTION 4
❏ Pencils, paper.

WHEN GOD SCRAMBLES YOUR PLANS

ensured. His army and charioteers corner the Hebrews as they camp beside the sea. Ahead of them lies the body of water; behind them, the Egyptian army. The Israelites seem to be hopelessly trapped.

God does not act alone, for Moses plays a central role in this salvation story. At God's direction, Moses stretches out his hand over the sea to divide it. The people miraculously walk across dry land while walls of water tower on both sides. God's people are free at last.

 CHECK IN

STARTING

Freedom with Consequences

PREPARATION: Write each of the following case studies on a sheet of paper:

> **Role-play 1:** Blair's parents expected to return home from a meeting about ten o'clock. They told him not to use the other car in their absence. He decided that he had plenty of time to run to the mall to get a tape he wanted. They would never even know he had been gone. On his way back, he swerved to avoid a dog and hit a fire hydrant. Blair's parents returned home and found out what happened. Role-play a scene between Blair and one or both of his parents.

> **Role-play 2:** Lynn has been wearing her sister's clothes without her permission. Lynn launders the clothes and puts them back in the closet before Kim discovers that they have been worn. When Lynn washed the laundry, she was shocked to see that everything turned pink! Kim was furious when she saw her items of clothing that were ruined. She immediately reported the mishap to their mother. Role-play a scene between Kim, Lynn, and their mother.

> **Role-play 3:** Jeff cleaned out his locker, dreaming of a leisurely summer. Then he noticed his report card stuck in his English book. When he opened it, the words *unfinished homework assignments, failed tests,* and *cut classes* flashed before his eyes. When Jeff got home, his parents had already received a call from the guidance counselor. Role-play the scene between Jeff and one or both of his parents.

Divide youth into three teams. Give each team a case study. Tell youth to role-play one or more endings for their team's case study. After the role-plays,

Ask:

▼ What freedom did each young person have?
▼ How did they abuse that freedom?
▼ What if each teenager had not been caught?

• Suppose Blair had gone to the mall and back without incident. Would that have made his behavior acceptable? (Blair was still disobeying his parents.)

OPTION 1

Circles of Freedom

Hand out pencils and paper. Say: **When you were little, your parents defined your freedom by the size of your playpen. When you got bigger, you were free to play inside your fenced backyard. Draw circles to indicate the amount of freedom you have in each of these places: at home, at school, with friends, in this city, at church, with your feelings.** After naming a place, allow time for youth to draw their circles. Remind them to label their circles. Say: **In each circle write one or two freedoms you have.** As you call out each place, let volunteers share the size of their circles and the freedoms. Explain that in the Bible study today youth will see the importance of freedom.

- Suppose Lynn's "borrowing" of her sister's clothes had remained a secret. Would that have made her behavior acceptable? *(The way Lynn slipped the clothes back in the closet indicated that she knew she was doing wrong and feared detection. Her sister had a right to know the truth.)*
- Suppose Jeff had been promoted even though he wasn't learning. What could be the ultimate consequences of his actions? *(Jeff may not learn how to function in the adult world.)*

EXPLORING

Rocky Road to Freedom

PREPARATION: Write each event on an index card:

- *God promised to be the God of Abraham's descendants.*
- *Joseph moved his family (the people of Israel) to Egypt because of a famine.*
- *A new Pharaoh turned the Israelites into slaves.*
- *God heard the slaves' prayers for freedom.*
- *God promised to free the Israelites from the Egyptians through Moses.*
- *Moses told Pharaoh to let the people go.*
- *Pharaoh refused.*
- *The water in Egypt turned to blood.*
- *Frogs took over the country.*
- *Gnats, then flies, brought deadly diseases to Egypt.*
- *Boils afflicted people and animals.*
- *Thunder and hail beat down crops and houses.*
- *Locusts ate the Egyptians' crops.*
- *Thick darkness hung over Egypt.*
- *Still, Pharaoh refused to free the slaves.*

Help youth understand the background events that led to this flight for freedom. Place the cards on the table or the floor in random order. Tell youth to put the cards in chronological order. Compare their results with the list above. Be sure they understand these events.

Incredible News

Read Exodus 11:1; 12:29-33. Say: **Imagine how our modern news media would have reacted to the story of Pharaoh and the Hebrews. Reporters from all over the world would have converged on Egypt to talk with Pharaoh, interview parents whose children had died, and get reactions from Hebrew slaves who were about to gain their freedom.**

Direct youth to work in teams of four, and to be prepared to present a newscast that includes the following persons: a reporter, Pharaoh, a grieving Egyptian parent, and one or more Hebrews. Tell each reporter to make up questions such as these:

1. How would you describe what happened about midnight?
2. What or who do you think brought about these tragic events?
3. How was the God of the Hebrew people involved in this incredible incident?
4. What would you say about this God?

OPTION 2

Incredible News Option

Go outdoors for the news presentations in "Incredible News," if space and weather permit. Videotape the newscasts and then replay them at the end of the session.

OPTION 3

Sense the Story

Say: **As I read the story, pretend you are experiencing these events. Think about these questions:**

1. *What kinds of sounds do you hear?*
2. *What kinds of sights do you see?*
3. *What can you taste?*
4. *What sensations do you feel?*
5. *What emotions are you experiencing?*

Assign half the youth to listen as if they are Israelites, and the other half to listen as if they are Egyptians. Read Exodus 12:29-33. Then, call for youth to share the sounds, sights, smells, tastes, and emotions they felt. Point out how each group experienced different feelings.

Allow enough time for each team to rehearse and present its newscast in the interview format. If any large misunderstandings of the Bible story surface, address those issues.

Ask:
▼ How did these people measure freedom?
▼ What did these freedoms include?
▼ How was God a part of their freedom?

Read Exodus 14:30-31.

Ask:
▼ What can we learn about freedom from this story?

CONNECTING

Freedom Wall
PREPARATION: Write *Freedom* on a large sheet. Hand out markers to youth and tell them to write brief definitions or words that relate to freedom. To help them,

Ask:
▼ Who gives you freedom?
▼ How can you gain more freedom?
▼ Where does responsibility fit into freedom?

Accepting Responsibility
PREPARATION: Designate one wall as *responsible* and the opposite wall as *not responsible*. Tell youth to move to one wall or the other, after each comment, deciding if it is responsible or irresponsible.

Say:
1. Since I was doing the driving, I refused to drink a beer that the other guys offered me.
2. I stayed out later than my curfew because I was having such a good time, and also because the friends I was with said, "Don't worry about it."
3. I made three personal long-distance telephone calls within the last several weeks. Let me know when the bill comes so that I can pay my share of the charges.
4. Yes, I did agree to participate in the mission project; but that was before I knew that the homecoming dance at Terry's school would be that same weekend. Sorry, but I won't be going with the group. Did I forget to tell you?
5. I had no way of knowing that the woman I ran into in the drugstore did a lot for my family a long time ago. I guess I shouldn't have been quite so rude to her.

✔CHECK OUT

Think of a time when you had unexpected freedom. How did you handle it?

OPTION 4

Freedom Prayer
Say: **God responded to Israel's prayer for freedom. Once they gained their freedom, God set reasonable boundaries to help them live with one another. We call those boundaries the Ten Commandments.** Tell youth to write a prayer, thanking God for the freedom they have.

44. GETTING A SECOND CHANCE

Romans 5:6-14

> Seeing how forgiveness and reconciliation with God and others provides a second chance.

✔ CHECK UP!

Paul's message in Romans 5 is that we have been reconciled with God. Considering the fact that we often fail to be the persons God intends for us to be, this is extraordinarily good news. We have the complete and welcome assurance that God will grant us complete forgiveness for our sins. We are not mired in guilt over our past and present actions, attitudes, and behaviors. A completely clean slate appears before us. We have a chance to begin life anew.

Without Christ's amazing love and sacrificial death, the ever-increasing weight of our sins would defeat us. We would never find a way to get out from under the burden of past guilt and the present momentum of sin.

But that weight and that momentum have utterly vanished because of what Christ has done for us. God does not threaten us with God's anger. Instead God cherishes us with God's love.

Paul's claim that Christ died for the ungodly (bad and immoral persons) agrees with what we know of Jesus' own teachings. For example, look up John 8:21-30. Even so, does it make sense to you that Christ was willing to die for bad persons? After all, Paul accurately observed that "rarely will anyone die for a righteous person—though perhaps for a good person someone might actually dare to die" (Rom. 5:7).

In Romans 5:12-14, Paul talks about the sin that came into the world with Adam, the prototype of humanity and of our human nature. This passage and others like it gave rise to the doctrine of original sin—that no human being can avoid sinning because of a moral defect passed along by Adam to later generations.

Experience and observation do show us that human beings, left to themselves, inevitably tend to give top priority to satisfying their own desires. However, Paul's emphasis is not so much on how crushing original sin is, but rather on how Jesus Christ redeems and salvages our life.

✔ CHECK LIST

STARTING
❏ Paper, crayons or markers.

EXPLORING
❏ Regular and Bible dictionaries, chalkboard, poster board.

CONNECTING
❏ Prepare case studies.
❏ Paper, markers.

OPTION 1
❏ Chenille strips (pipe cleaners) or clay.

OPTION 2
❏ Paper, pencils, markers.

 CHECK IN

STARTING

A Hero's Certificate

Pass out paper and colored crayons or markers. Tell youth to design a certificate for one of their heroes. On the certificate, encourage youth to list three or four reasons why this person deserves the title "hero." After a few minutes, let youth share the certificates they designed.

Ask:

▼ **What makes a woman or a man into a hero? Name some heroes from books or stories, from TV or movies, or from real life** (cartoon superheroes don't count).

▼ **What qualities do you see in these persons that help make them into heroes? Do they have any characteristics in common?**

▼ **If you were to create your own hero, what qualities would you include? Would this person give his or her life for somebody else?**

Say: **Among the characteristics heroes usually have is their ability to place a cause or the needs of other persons ahead of their own interests. This selflessness often instills in heroes a courage that permits them to face danger and death. Indeed some heroes such as Abraham Lincoln and Martin Luther King, Jr., met an untimely death because of the cause they advanced.**

Explain that as youth look at the Bible study, they will see how Jesus didn't die like a hero. Jesus didn't even die just for heroes. Jesus died for the worst of us, too.

EXPLORING

Understanding the Scripture

PREPARATION: On a chalkboard write *justified* and *reconciled.* Make a poster with *reconciled* written down the left side of the page.

Read Romans 5:6-8 aloud. Ask youth to call out words or phrases that indicate how Jesus was a hero.

Ask:

▼ **Why was Jesus willing to die for sinners?**

▼ **How does that make you feel to know Jesus died for you, no matter how you have sinned?**

Provide regular dictionaries and Bible dictionaries. Tell half the youth to look for a definition of *justified* and the other half to define *reconciled.* Read Romans 5:9-14 aloud. When you get to *justified,* call for that definition. When you get to *reconciled,* call for that definition. Remind youth that part of reconciliation includes forgiveness.

Display the poster on which you've written *reconciled.* Lead youth to use each letter to begin a word or short phrase that identifies or describes the meaning of reconciliation. Suggest they look for words and phrases in Romans 5:6-14. (If you have a large group, divide youth into teams of no more than eight, letting each team work on a separate acrostic.)

OPTION 1

Hero Symbol

Distribute chenille strips (pipe cleaners) or modeling clay and ask youth to construct an image of a hero. This activity allows youth to express their ideas in a graphic, creative way. After youth share their "heroes," use the questions and discussion under "A Hero's Certificate."

CONNECTING
Reconciliation in Relationships
PREPARATION: Write each case study on an index card.

1. You thought it would be great fun to play a practical joke on Karl, one of your classmates at school. So the day before the big science test, you hid his notebook. He frantically searched for it at school and at home until ten o'clock that night, and never found it, of course. Karl just learned that the notebook was not accidentally misplaced, but that you hid it as a joke.

2. You had thought you were good friends with Rachel, Jamal, and Bobby Joe. The four of you spent time together every school day before homeroom, and again during study hall. You also did something together most weekends. Rachel and Bobby Joe did not know you were on the stairs behind them when you overheard them say that they wished you would not hang around with them quite so much.

3. You do not know Darrin all that well. He seems to appear on the fringes of different groups and yet is not really included in any of them. He is not the kind of person who makes a big impression. You don't exactly dislike Darrin; you just never had the occasion to get to know him. Even the few times that Darrin showed up in your Sunday school class, he hardly said anything and you didn't say much to him either. The first thing you heard when you arrived at school this morning was the rumor that Darrin had been arrested the day before for shoplifting.

4. As soon as you get in the car, you notice that your mother is upset. You close the door and she drives for five minutes in utter silence. Finally your mom says she just heard from Calvin's mother that you are using drugs. Convincing your mother that you don't "do drugs," that you have never done drugs, and that you never will do drugs takes three hours of serious conversation. Even so, your mother says that from now on you have to be in by ten o'clock in the evening, "for your own good."

Divide youth into four teams. Give each team a case study. Tell youth to answer these questions:

1. What relationship or relationships have been disturbed or broken or were not strong or healthy to begin with?
2. What caused the problem in each relationship?
3. What are some possible options and reactions that don't necessarily involve trying to save the relationship?
4. Which responses would most likely help renew or repair the relationship?
5. In addition to the option or options you have selected, what else might be necessary to bring about a reconciliation?

After a review of the case studies, ask these general questions:
▼ **What did you learn about relationships and reconciliation?**
▼ **Does the renewal of a relationship depend on the response of only one person? What role does God play in bringing about reconciliation between persons?**

Second Chance Certificate

Pass out paper and crayons or markers, again. Direct youth to think of a situation in their relationships that needs reconciliation. This might be with parents, brothers or sisters, boyfriends or girlfriends, teachers, school buddies, someone in the neighborhood, or with God. Direct them to design a "Second Chance Certificate" that identifies what they need to do to bring about reconciliation. Depending on the age and willingness of youth, volunteers may share. Urge youth to keep this certificate until they have been able to reestablish the relationship.

 # CHECK OUT

If God gives second chances, why can't we just do what we want, ask for forgiveness, and be given a second chance?

OPTION 2
Reconciliation for Me

Instead of using previously created case studies, older youth may prefer to write their own. Give every three youth pencils and paper. Let each trio decide on a reconciliation situation, writing down basic information. This could be something they've experienced in the past, or are currently facing. They can also write about a friend's problems with an unreconciled relationship. Suggest youth change names. Tell each trio to pass its case study to another trio who will suggest ways to bring about reconciliation.

45. MOVING BEYOND THE INFLUENCE OF OTHERS

Numbers 13:25-28, 30-31; 14:6-9a, 28-30; Joshua 24:15

Understanding the importance of making decisions without being influenced by others.

✔ CHECK UP!

As the Israelites approached the Promised Land, Moses selected a scout from each tribe to look over the territory. These men were to determine whether the land was desirable and how strongly it was held by its inhabitants. The spies reported back that the land was good and extremely fertile but that its inhabitants would be strong opponents. (The phrase "flows with milk and honey" was a way of saying that the land was lush and rich.) A variety of different tribes lived in the large, fortified cities. One group of inhabitants, "the descendants of Anak," were thought to be unusually large people, perhaps even descended from legendary giants.

Only two of the spies—Joshua and Caleb—were confident that the Israelites could take the land. They were aware of the difficulties, but they also believed in God's power. The other spies could see only the power of the enemy. They did not believe the Israelites were strong enough to conquer the new land.

True to the way they had reacted to difficulties at other times during their journey, the people of Israel believed only the worst. They abandoned their faith in God's promises and power. Once again they got angry at God and wanted to go back to Egypt. Moses and Aaron, who "fell on their faces," knew that the people were blaspheming against God. (Tearing one's clothes was also a sign of mourning or sorrow.) Caleb and Joshua remained faithful to God and spoke words of faith to the people. They knew that God had promised to give the people the land.

Much later, after Joshua successfully led the Israelites to conquer Canaan, Joshua called all of Israel together at the city of Shechem and confronted the people with the necessity of making a decision for or against complete loyalty to God. Joshua reminded the people of the many things God had done for them, including making possible the conquest of the Promised Land. God had blessed the people with a rich land they did not toil for.

On the basis of God's mighty deeds, Joshua urged the people to be loyal to God and to put away all false gods. Joshua offered his own example of unswerving loyalty, declaring that he and his household would serve only God. After hearing Joshua's powerful arguments, the people enthusiastically proclaimed their loyalty to God.

✔ CHECK LIST

STARTING
❏ Pencils, paper.

EXPLORING
❏ Post the sign.
❏ Butcher paper, markers.

CONNECTING
❏ Make the poster.

OPTION 1
❏ Prepare the slips of paper.

WHEN GOD SCRAMBLES YOUR PLANS

✔ CHECK IN

STARTING

Basic Decisions

Hand pencils and paper to youth as they arrive. Tell them to write down the decisions they have made today. Remind them to include small decisions (when to get up, what to wear, what to eat for breakfast), as well as more important decisions. Say: **Every day we make choices.** Call for youth to share some easy choices. Say: **Some decisions are more complicated.** Ask youth to share a couple of complicated decisions they face.

Ask:
▼ **Who influences your decisions?**
▼ **How do others exert their influence?**
▼ **How much influence do your friends have on your decisions?**

Explain that today youth will see how the influence of a few changed the direction of the nation when it came time to make a crucial decision.

EXPLORING

"Do Not Enter" Experience

PREPARATION: Post a "Do Not Enter" sign on the door of another room in the church. (Notify appropriate personnel ahead of time of your plans.)

Act as if you have suddenly remembered something that the youth are supposed to do. Say: **I just remembered. Something special has been planned for our group.** Then have everyone go to the room with the sign on the door. Note the "Do Not Enter" sign and say, **I thought we were supposed to meet here. I guess we will just have to go back to our room.**

If anyone raises objections, try to convince them that returning to the room is the best course of action. (You might pose questions such as these: What could happen if we ignore the sign on the door? What might be wrong with the room that would make it unwise or dangerous for us to go inside? What if we disturb other people or classes?)
Lead everyone back to the room.

Ask:
▼ **What was your reaction to being told that something special had been planned? How did you feel when you saw the "Do Not Enter" sign?**
▼ **Do you think we missed anything? if so, what?**
▼ **How do you feel about possibly missing out on something?**

If no one objected to returning to the room, ask:
▼ **Did everyone agree with the decision to return to our regular room?**

OPTION 1

Yogurt or French Fries

PREPARATION: On several slips of paper write, *Try to convince others that yogurt is more nutritious than french fries.* On several slips write, *Argue that french fries are more nutritious than yogurt.* On the remaining slips of paper write, *Form your own opinion.*

Distribute the first two sets of slips to the majority of the youth. After everyone has a slip, open the discussion with this question:

▼ **Are french fries more nutritious than yogurt?**

Invite each person to express an opinion in accordance with the instruction on her or his slip. After a few minutes of discussion, take a vote on the question. Then ask those who received a *Form your own opinion* slip to identify themselves.

Ask:
▼ **Did the opinion of the majority influence your vote? why, or why not?**

Say: **You have just experienced something like what happened to the people of Israel in today's "Bible lesson." God had promised the Promised Land to the people. As we will see, things did not work out exactly as originally planned.** Next, ask a volunteer to read aloud Numbers 13:25-28, 30-31. Lead youth to compare their experience with the Bible study today.

Making a Decision

Direct youth to read Numbers 13:25-28, 30-31; 14:6-9a, 28-30. Divide youth into three teams. Make one team the Spy team, the second the Israelite team, and the third the Caleb-Joshua team. Give each team a large sheet of butcher paper and a marker. Tell them to list the decisions their assigned person or persons faced. These could include basic decisions, as well as bigger ones.

After teams have shared, ask:
▼ **When might it be a good idea to go along with the advice of the majority?**
▼ **What are some reasons not to go along with a decision just because most people seem to agree with it?**
▼ **What are some factors to consider before making up one's mind?**
▼ **What did the people fail to consider when they decided not to take possession of the Promised Land?** *(They failed to remember that God had promised to give them the land if they would be faithful to God.)*
▼ **Why do you think the people didn't consider what God had done for them and what God promised to do?**
▼ **Do we ever forget God's promises when we are making important decisions?**

OPTION 2
Reenact the Event

Assign each youth a part in this Bible story—at least one person to represent the ten spies, Moses, Caleb, Joshua, and at least one person to represent the people of Israel. As one youth reads Numbers 13:25-28, 30-31; 14:6-9a, 28-30, let the others act out their parts or read their parts from the Bible. Ask those who played Caleb and Joshua:

▼ **How did you feel being rejected by the others?**

Ask the others:
▼ **What choices did the people face?**
▼ **Why did the Israelites listen to the ten spies and not to Joshua and Caleb?**
▼ **How can others' influence be negative, instead of helpful?**

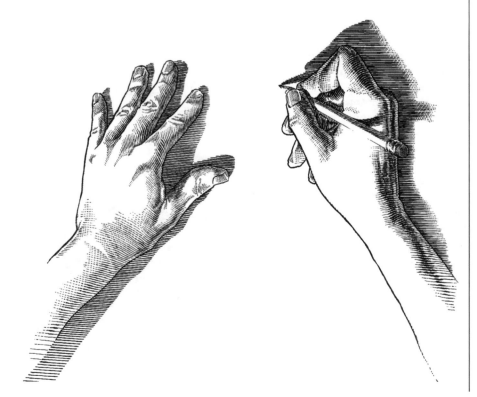

WHEN GOD SCRAMBLES YOUR PLANS

CONNECTING

Follow the Leader?

PREPARATION: Write the following on poster board.

I try to determine how many people hold a certain opinion that relates to my decision.
I consider the reasons for others' opinions.
I consider what has happened in the past.
I look ahead to what might happen as a result of my decision.
I go along with the majority.
I think about what God may have planned.
I recognize that others' opinions are not necessarily based on facts.
I realize that following God's way often looks harder than making some other choice.

Lead youth to brainstorm several decisions that they face. These might include: *drinking, going to unchaperoned parties, rolling a person's yard, smoking, doing drugs.*

Ask:

▼ How are your decisions influenced by others?

Display the poster. Ask youth to select the statement that best expresses how they make decisions.

Take a Stand

Ask a youth to read Joshua 24:15. Say: **Once the people of Israel conquered the land of Canaan, Joshua still had to remind them to choose God.**

Ask:

▼ What are some excuses teenagers give for not following God?
▼ How can positive peer pressure help reluctant teenagers follow God?

✔ CHECK OUT

How can you determine when the influence of others is healthy or unhealthy?

OPTION 3

Follow the Advice

In Numbers 14:9*a* Joshua and Caleb gave some good advice to consider when making decisions.

Ask:

▼ How would these words of advice apply to at least one situation that you have encountered or that you might face in the future?

Say: **The people of Israel rebelled. Because they were unwilling to follow God's guidance, they missed out on what God had promised.**

Ask:

▼ Do you know someone who is unwilling to follow God's guidance?
▼ What is that person likely to miss?

46. WHEN CHOOSING RIGHT IS REALLY HARD

Jonah 4:1-4

Examining why making the difficult choices is worth the effort.

✔ CHECK UP!

In Jonah 1–3 God calls Jonah to go to Nineveh to preach. But Jonah hates the Ninevites. He knows if he goes there to preach they might repent, and Jonah doesn't want that. So Jonah goes east across the desert, which is the right way to Nineveh, by sailing west to Spain. God will not accept this disobedience. A huge storm arises on the Mediterranean. The sailors try desperately to save the ship. All this time Jonah is asleep in his cabin. The sailors wake him up and tell him to pray. Perhaps his God can save him. If only they knew how ironic that statement is. Jonah's God sent the storm in the first place to get Jonah back on the right track. Finally, the sailors cast lots to determine what the problem is, and the lot falls on Jonah. Jonah finally explains that he is running away from God because he does not want to do what God wants. God catches up with Jonah, but Jonah isn't through yet. It's clear to him that the ship isn't going to get to Tarshish. God will keep the storm going as long as necessary to get Jonah to turn back and head for Nineveh. So Jonah comes up with another plan. He tells the sailors to throw him overboard, and they'll be safe. If they do, he thinks, *I'll die. I can't survive at sea in a storm like this. At least I won't have to go to Nineveh.* This is how desperate Jonah was.

The sailors throw Jonah overboard and a great fish swallows him. Three days later, covered with fish slime, Jonah is vomited up on land and goes to Nineveh. He's still not happy about going to Nineveh. His message is simple as he walks through the streets of Nineveh: Forty days and Nineveh will be overthrown. He's not excited because he doesn't want anybody to respond. God is going to get you guys, he says, which of course is what Jonah really wants. Surprise! The Ninevites repent. In fact, Jonah sets the all-time record for number of repentances in one day. And so does God. God cancels the destruction order because God is happy with everyone in the city. *Repent* doesn't mean being sorry for sins. After all, if that were the case, how could God repent? Repent means to change one's mind, to alter one's stance toward life. The Ninevites alter their whole stance toward God. And God alters God's stance toward destruction.

So why is Jonah having a tantrum? Because he knows God is a God of grace; Jonah doesn't want God to be God. He wants God to be like Jonah and hate Jonah's enemies. He doesn't want God to be

<table>
<tr><td>

✔ CHECK LIST

EXPLORING
❒ Bible, concordances.

CONNECTING
❒ Duplicate "The Prayer of Saint Francis."

OPTION 1
❒ Prepare the three role-plays on index cards.

OPTION 4
❒ Pencils, paper.

</td></tr>
</table>

compassionate, merciful, slow to anger, and abounding in steadfast love. Think about the implications of that statement. If God isn't like that, where's hope? Unless we're willing to have God give grace to our enemies, how can we ever hope for grace for ourselves?

 # CHECK IN

STARTING

The Right and Wrong

Read the story of Leila aloud. Tell youth to listen for Leila's thoughts and actions.

> Leila dragged her feet as she went back down the hall. It wasn't fair. Just because she'd found out that Greg, Casey, and Kelsey all bought their term papers from a company didn't mean that she should be the one to send them to the principal.
>
> She hated being a tattletale; she hadn't tattled since the first grade. But she was furious because she had spent hours and hours in the library doing research and had even typed her term paper herself. (She didn't own a computer.) Then here came these three, waving around laser-print papers with fancy binding, and laughing about how easy it was, about how they weren't going to waste their time in the library. So she'd sent a note to Mr. Brewer.
>
> The next morning before homeroom, Leila saw Mr. Brewer in the hallway. He said, "Thanks for your help, Leila. Dr. Sanderson talked to Greg, Casey, and Kelsey yesterday. They admitted the papers were not their own and realized that what they had done was wrong. Dr. Sanderson and I agreed to let each of them write a new paper; and if they have them in by Wednesday before graduation, they can go through the line with the rest of you. But they'll take a D for the course." Leila was furious all over again. "But you said at the beginning of the year that cheating was not tolerated and anyone who cheated would fail."
>
> Mr. Brewer answered, "That's true Leila. But they didn't lie when they were confronted; they admitted they'd done wrong and asked for another chance. They still have to write the papers, and they may fail. But when people sincerely want to make up for what they've done wrong, I like to let them try. What we've decided doesn't take away from all the work you did on your paper. Why should you be upset? They may get to graduate with you."

Ask:
▼ Did Leila have the right to be angry? why or why not?
▼ Why did Mr. Brewer have a right to change the rules?
▼ How do you feel about second chances?

Say: **Sometimes we are like the person we will study today. We don't want others to have a second chance, particularly if it seems unfair.**

OPTION 1

Caught in the Middle

PREPARATION: Write the three role-plays on index cards. On the front of each index card, write one name, and on the back of each card, write the characteristics of that role.

Mike: (a) You are best friends with Tim. (b) You will have nothing to do with Annie and will do anything to keep her out of your conversation with Tim.

Tim: (a) You are best friends with Mike. (b) You don't really know Annie. (c) You don't want to hurt Annie's feelings, but your first priority is Mike.

Annie: (a) You want to be included in the conversation between Mike and Tim and will do anything to be included.

Select three players and give each a role-play card. Allow a few minutes for the role-play to unfold; then stop the role-play and have the players switch roles. Do this until each player has a chance to play each role.

Then ask:
▼ How did it feel to be excluded from the conversation?
▼ How did it feel to exclude someone from the conversation?
▼ How did it feel to be caught in the middle?
▼ Which character was the most difficult for you to play? why?
▼ Which character was the easiest for you to play? why?

Say: **People have a tendency to form cliques and, through their attitudes and behaviors, exclude certain people from fellowship. This is what Jonah was doing to the people of Nineveh.**

EXPLORING

The Story of Jonah

Since the book of Jonah is short, divide youth into four teams. Assign one chapter of Jonah to each team. Direct youth to plan a skit acting out the events in their assigned chapter. Put the story together with each team presenting its chapter. Say: **You may use as many or as few characters as you like. Be sure to include a narrator, God, and Jonah. You could also use sailors, fish, a king, a bush, a worm, sun, and other props or people.**

After youth have presented the story, say: **Jonah didn't want God to forgive Nineveh. Jonah didn't want to do right, and he didn't want God to do right either.**

Real Repentance

Distribute Bibles and concordances. Ask the youth to work in groups of two or three to find the references to the word *repent* in the Old Testament.

Ask:
▼ **How many times did God repent?**
▼ **Why did God repent?** *(For example: In the story of Noah, God repented.)*
▼ **Do the examples of God's repenting suggest that God makes mistakes?**
▼ **What would happen if God never changed God's mind?**

Say: *Repent* **comes from a French word that means to rethink. We usually understand that** *repent* **means to be sorry, but it actually means to rethink who we are and what we're doing.**

Ask:
▼ **How does the meaning of repentance change our understanding of the story of Jonah?**

OPTION 2

A Whiner's Skit

Have everyone turn to Jonah 4:6-11. Ask for volunteers to play the parts of Jonah, God, the bush, the worm, the sun, and the wind. Encourage them to use humor and exaggerations. (For instance, the worm could grab the bush around the neck and pretend to choke it; or the sun could pretend to beat Jonah on the head.) Explain that everyone else will be the "Whiners," a voice choir expressing a variety of emotions at the appropriate points. Their cues are: *at the end of verse 6, sighs of relief and happiness; at the end of verse 7, sounds of sadness and pity; at the end of verse 8, whines and complaints followed by a huge sigh; at the end of verse 9, growl with anger; at the end of verses 10-11, a long "H-h-hu-u-u-um-mmm?" and then shout "Amen!"*

Read Jonah 4:6-11 verse by verse, as outlined above; have the players pantomime their parts and the "Whiners" offer their sound effects. Then say: **Jonah acted just as we sometimes do when we don't get our way. We complain and pout and run away and whine and even get angry to try to make others do what we want them to do. And sometimes it works—but not with God.** Have a youth read aloud Jonah 4:2.

Ask:
▼ **Why was Jonah angry at God?** *(for forgiving the Ninevites, for being God—gracious, merciful, slow to get angry, always ready to love and forgive)*
▼ **How did God win the debate?**
▼ **Do you think Jonah came to a new understanding of God's love?**

WHEN GOD SCRAMBLES YOUR PLANS

CONNECTING

Temper Tantrum

Clear a space in the center of the room. Invite volunteers to throw temper tantrums as Jonah did. They can jump up and down, scream, pound on the floor, kick their feet. (Make sure they know not to do anything that could destroy property or hurt people.)

Encourage the other youth to watch each person as he or she throws a tantrum and to be aware of behavior that might look like their own behavior at times.

Ask:

▼ What does a tantrum look like?
▼ Are tantrums attractive behavior?
▼ How did you feel being around someone who was throwing a tantrum?
▼ How does knowing that Jonah was throwing a tantrum help you understand the Bible?
▼ What have you learned about yourself?

The Prayer of Saint Francis

PREPARATION: Make copies of the following prayer.

The Prayer of Saint Francis

Lord, make me an instrument of thy peace;
where there is hatred, let me sow love;
where there is injury, pardon;
where there is doubt, faith;
where there is despair, hope;
where there is darkness, light;
and where there is sadness, joy.

O Divine Master,
grant that I may not so much seek
to be consoled as to console;
to be understood, as to understand;
to be loved, as to love;
for it is in giving that we receive,
it is in pardoning that we are pardoned,
and it is in dying that we are born
to eternal life.

From *When God Scrambles Your Plans* by Ann B. Cannon. Copyright © 1997 by Abingdon Press. Reproduced by permission.

Say: **Just as Jonah was called to enter into a ministry with God, God also invites us to become partners in ministry.** Hand out copies of "The Prayer of Saint Francis." Assign youth different phrases from the first stanza of the prayer. Say: **Name a way we can sow love, instead of hatred. Name a way we can give pardon, instead of injury.** Continue to call for ministry actions to the different phrases in the first section of the prayer. Lead youth in reading the second stanza as a closing prayer.

 **CHECK OUT**

What makes you want to escape from the presence of God?

OPTION 3

Being Right–Doing Right

Say: **One of Jonah's problems was he fought doing right because he didn't care about others as much as he cared about himself.** Tell youth to agree (thumbs up) or disagree (thumbs down) with the following statements:

• It's O.K. to cheat on a test; if I'm caught I can repent and get a second chance.
• I am responsible for my own behavior.
• It's O.K. to do something wrong if I'm trying to achieve a goal.
• I am responsible for someone else's behavior.
• It's O.K. not to do God's will if I know what I'm doing is morally right.

Ask:

▼ How would Jonah respond to those statements?
▼ How do you think God feels about those statements?

OPTION 4

A Selfish Prayer

Ask the students to write a prayer comparing the immature and selfish thoughts and actions of Jonah with the loving attitude and actions of God. For example:

Dear God of love: so often I am like Jonah. I complain and pout and try to run away from you when you don't do what I think you ought to do. But you never abandon me because you are God. Forgive me when I don't love other people and you with my whole heart and mind. Amen.

Close the session in a prayer circle, allowing volunteers to pray their prayers aloud.

47. WHEN GOD SCRAMBLES YOUR PLANS

Acts 9:1-9

Seeing how God's plans can cause dramatic changes in their lives.

✔ CHECK UP!

In chapter 8 of Acts we read how Saul ravages the church, going from house to house looking for Christians and having them put in prison. Saul is not content with the havoc he is wreaking in Jerusalem. He wants to extend his search for followers of the Way of Jesus to Damascus. It was not very far from Jerusalem to Damascus, which today is the capital of Syria. Then Damascus was an important part of the kingdom of Arabia.

What follows is probably the most famous conversion story in history. Certainly, it is a dramatic account of God's speaking to a specific person. Being knocked to the ground by a light from heaven would get anyone's attention. Then Saul hears the voice. Notice the message: "Get up and enter the city, and you will be told what you are to do."

After Saul enters Damascus, blind, not eating or drinking, then comes the forgotten hero of this story. Saul has had a powerful experience with God in Jesus Christ, but he's blind, he's refusing to eat or drink, he's in need of help in the next stage of his faith journey. So God speaks specifically to a humble member of the church in Damascus, Ananias.

This encounter with God includes a specific address: the house of Judas in Straight Street, presumably someone Ananias knows well. Ananias has a problem. He's heard about Saul, and the news is not encouraging. Ananias knows what Saul has done to the saints in Jerusalem. The "saints," by the way, are not the apostles, whom Saul apparently left alone. The saints are the ordinary people in the church, who were just trying to be faithful to Jesus. Ananias isn't at all sure he wants to help a man like that. The vision empowers Ananias. The presence of God gives him the strength to do what he is called to do. There is an important word for our world here. Youth often feel powerless as individuals. They need to hear about God's empowerment, about God giving strength to do what God calls them to do.

Ananias goes, lays his hands on Saul, and says he has come from Jesus so Saul can regain his sight and be filled with the Holy Spirit. Immediately Saul can see. For three days, lying in darkness, filled with fear and confusion, overwhelmed by what he has experienced, Saul's mind has raced and turned. By the time Ananias comes, he's ready for the next step. There is more here than the biological reality that Saul's eyes were again sending messages to his brain. Saul also saw clearly the reality of his conversion and what it meant for his life.

✔ CHECK LIST

STARTING
❏ Enlist a helper.

EXPLORING
❏ Make a copy of Jennifer's and Timothy's stories.
❏ Newsprint, markers.

CONNECTING
❏ Chalkboard.

OPTION 2
❏ Nontoxic clay, water, paper towels.

OPTION 3
❏ Paper, pencils.

 CHECK IN

STARTING

Life Scramble

Enlist a helper *(youth or adult)* to quietly write the names and order of youth who answer the first set of questions.

Ask:
- ▼ What are your plans after high school?
- ▼ When do you think you will get married?
- ▼ Where do you expect to live?
- ▼ What work do you think you will be doing?

After several youth have shared, say: **O.K. I'm going to ask these questions again, but this time the people who answered have to give different answers.** Ask each question again, letting the helper identify youth who answered the first time. After getting a second set of answers, ask:

- ▼ How would you feel if God scrambled your plans?
- ▼ How could those scrambled plans change you? your future? your family? your faith?

Say: **In this Bible study youth will study a man whose plans were scrambled by God.**

EXPLORING

Sincerely Wrong or Right?

PREPARATION: Make copies of the following case studies.

> Jennifer worked as a cashier in a fast food restaurant. She showed up on time, and she worked hard. One day a homeless man came into the restaurant. He was obviously hungry, but he had no money. Jennifer watched him for a few minutes. Then she put five hamburgers in a big bag and handed them to the man. "Thank you, Sir," she said. "Have a nice day." Then she indicated on her register that five hamburgers had been returned. Jennifer's faith taught her to feed the hungry.
>
> *What was right about what Jennifer did?*
> *What was wrong about what Jennifer did?*
> *Did the right outweigh the wrong?*
> *Do ends justify means? why? why not?*

> Timothy had many friends, but his best friend was Allen Rosenberg. Not many people at school knew that Allen was Jewish; they'd never bothered to ask. Some of the people at Timothy's school got involved with the skinheads, who believed that white Christians were superior to Jews, blacks, and everybody else. They tried to get Timothy involved in the group, but he refused. Timothy's faith taught him that all people were equal in the eyes

OPTION 1

Turn Around Game

Choose one person to be the leader (to represent Jesus). Invite the others to form two lines that face in opposite directions. Youth should stand one behind the other holding the waist of the person in front of them. One line will represent Saul, the other Paul. Tell youth to begin walking. When the leader calls, "Saul turn around," the youth in the line representing Saul should immediately turn around and go the other direction. *(Everyone should let go of the person in front of him or her, turn around, and put his or her hands on the waist of the person who is now in front of him or her.)* When the leader calls "Paul turn around," the youth in the line representing Paul should immediately turn around and walk in the other direction. The leader should vary the order in which the lines are called *(for example, he or she may choose to call "Saul" two or three times in a row),* and he or she should speed up the action until both groups are a bit dizzy from turning around. Stop the game.

Ask:
- ▼ How did you feel about having to change directions suddenly?
- ▼ Why do some people not change easily?

of God. Timothy was furious that anybody would even consider joining the skinheads, and he said so. The people who had joined the group just laughed at him.

Timothy decided to expose the group as racist. He arrived at school early one morning armed with a can of red spray paint. He painted the words *racist* and *bigot* on the lockers that belonged to the skinheads, and nobody ever suspected that Timothy had done it.

What was right about what Timothy did?
What was wrong about what Timothy did?
Was Timothy's motive a good enough reason to do what he did? why? why not?

Read aloud Acts 9:1-19. Say: **We tend to think that Saul was horrible for killing Christians, but he believed that he was doing the right thing by getting rid of a dangerous sect.**

Ask:
▼ **What do you think about Saul's belief?**
▼ **Why did believing he was right not make Saul's actions right?**
▼ **How did Jesus scramble Saul's ideas of right and wrong?**

Divide youth into two teams. To help youth see how they can be sincerely wrong, give each team one of the case studies. After a few minutes of study, let teams share their responses to the questions.

Different Points of View

Challenge youth to tell the story of Acts 9:1-19 in their own words in the following way. Using the same teams, have one team tell the story from Saul's point of view and the other group from the perspective of Ananias.

Ask:
▼ **How do these two stories differ?** *(Ananias may not know the particulars of Saul's experience of Christ, only that Saul is blind. Saul may not know the details of the conversation between Ananias and God about Saul's persecution of Christians, but he is told that the Lord sent Ananias that Saul may regain his sight and be filled with the Holy Spirit.)*
▼ **How are they alike?**
▼ **Why is it important that we hear both sides of the story?** *(One reason is that this passage includes two very different experiences of call and obedience to that call. Help youth think of others.)*

OPTION 2
Do What?

Read (or have one or two persons read) Acts 9:1-19. Invite a person to simulate being blinded. Wet the clay; make a ball of clay and gently flatten it over the person's eyes. Ask the youth to walk around the room, trying to find his or her way in the dark (remove dangerous obstacles first). Choose another person to be Ananias and to remove the clay from his or her eyes.

Ask the "blinded" youth:
▼ **How did you feel when the clay came off?**

Ask everyone:
▼ **How do you think Ananias felt about his call in this story? about his meeting with Saul?**
▼ **How do you think Saul felt about his experience on the Damascus road? about his meeting with Ananias?**

Remind youth that Ananias' plans were scrambled just like Saul's.

A New Name

Say: **Saul changed his name to Paul to further signify to everyone who had known him that he was a changed person, transformed by God's love and forgiveness. If you could do this, what name would you choose?** Let youth write their responses on newsprint, then display them to the entire group.

Ask:

▼ How did you choose or create your new name?

▼ How would this new name signify a change in your life?

▼ Does your new name reveal your identity as a Christian? If so, how?

CONNECTING

God Speaks to You

Lead youth to list events, people, and situations that might cause them to change their plans. After listing these on a chalkboard, pick out two or three, and ask:

▼ How would you respond if this happened to you?

▼ How willing are you to change your immediate plans?

▼ How willing are you to change long-term goals for your life?

Say: **God spoke to Saul in a very dramatic way. God also directed Ananias to do an amazing thing by going to his enemy Saul.**

Ask:

▼ What would it take for God to get your attention?

▼ What would it take for God to get you to change your plans for the future?

Say: **The Bible says "something like scales fell from his eyes."**

Ask:

▼ If you were given new sight, what would you want to see? why?

✔ CHECK OUT

What if Paul and Ananias had not followed God's scrambled plans? What if Saul had decided to continue persecuting Christians instead of helping to establish and strengthen churches or writing letters about faith and life that became a part of our Bible?

Tell youth to think about the next question for a few moments before responding.

Ask:

▼ What would happen if we ignored God's call today?

OPTION 3

Behavior Change Letter

Give a sheet of paper and a pencil to each person. Ask everyone to think of behaviors that they would like to *(or need to)* change. Some of these may even require a radical transformation *(such as drug use)*. Then have them list these behaviors on paper by drawing a symbol for each behavior. Assure them that their lists will be confidential and that none of their responses will be discussed.

When everyone is finished, ask youth to fold their papers in half and to write on the outside: *Dear God, I need your help to change these behaviors.* Have them pray silently for one or two minutes, concentrating on one behavior at a time and asking God's help to change that particular behavior. Close with a prayer asking God to open their hearts to the transforming love of Christ and to give each of them the courage to ask for and risk change.

Have youth fold their papers in half once again, tape them shut, and write their names on them. Collect the papers and tell youth that you will keep them unopened for several months. Encourage the youth to continue to pray during this time for God's help in changing their behavior. Several months later (3 or 4 months), return the lists to youth and ask them to reflect on how their lives may have changed.

48. WHEN GRIEF HAPPENS

John 11:1-44; 2 Corinthians 1:3-11

Exploring the role of faith in facing death
and other kinds of loss that causes grief.

✔ CHECK UP!

The John 11 passage actually contains two stories. The first one is about the events surrounding Lazarus' death, and the other one reveals Jesus' caring response to his friends' grief. These two stories form part of a pattern of Jesus' compassionate earthly ministry.

Imagine that you are watching Jesus cry as a sign of his compassion for Mary, Martha, and their friends. And then listen carefully as Jesus approaches Lazarus' tomb and, in a quiet voice, says with calm assurance, "Take away the stone."

You hear Martha skeptically groan, "Lord, . . . he has been dead four days." She knew of the superstition that the spirit of the dead remained at the burial site three days and then was gone forever.

The stone is removed anyway; and Jesus says in a loud voice, "Lazarus, come out!" Lazarus stumbles from the cave, still wrapped in the burial cloths. Jesus quietly says to the others, "Unbind him, and let him go."

As you continue to stand at the burial site, you realize that you've experienced the miracle of resurrection. A person was dead, and now he's alive again!

Jesus once again proclaimed, "I am the resurrection and the life." His meaning goes beyond physical death. Jesus spoke of the death of sin and of the new life that is ours when we believe in Jesus Christ, the Son of God. New life means just that—new vitality, new visions, and new vigor for living as new creations.

The second Scripture deals with the church in Corinth. From Paul's letters, we can tell that the church had a great many problems. At the beginning of 2 Corinthians, Paul gives a prayer of thanks to God for comfort in times of difficulties. He addressed God not only as the Father of Jesus Christ, but also as the Father of all mercies and comfort. As we benefit from God's comfort, Paul says, we gain the ability to comfort others during their suffering.

Although we don't know the exact nature of what Paul and his traveling companions had to endure in Asia, the people in the church at Corinth likely knew what the apostle meant. Whether they suffered illness, persecution, or some other kind of distress, the circumstances were severe enough to deeply depress Paul and cause him to despair "of life itself."

Apparently God came to the rescue in this alarming situation.

✔ CHECK LIST

STARTING
❏ Gather obituary notices, chalkboard.

EXPLORING
❏ Chalkboard or newsprint.

CONNECTING
❏ Duplicate the case studies.

OPTION 1
❏ Colored paper, markers.

OPTION 3
❏ Paper, pencils.

Paul goes on to say that he values his traumatic experience. Because of the comfort God provided, Paul was able to declare victory over the affliction and to pass on to other distressed persons his sympathy and God's comfort.

Paul also discovered that God's comfort brings the courage to cope with any of life's trials. When we suffer, we become participants in Christ's experience of suffering. Paul considers such an association a privilege. In addition, we have a chance to become God's helpers. When we suffer in this manner we gain the power to comfort others who are also suffering.

Paul believed that suffering reminds us to rely only on God and not on ourselves. The apostle's experience increased his confidence that God would enable him to survive any crisis that he would ever have to face in this life.

Not only did God help in the earlier situation, but Paul also believed that the prayers of the church members in Corinth sustained him as well. This is quite a statement, considering that the congregation at Corinth seemed to contain some of the weakest Christians of the time. Obviously God heeds the prayers of members of the faith community who desire to help alleviate the suffering of other Christians.

✔ CHECK IN

STARTING

Imagine the Loss

PREPARATION: Collect obituary notices from local newspapers.

Distribute one obituary notice to each person as he or she arrives. Have the youth form small teams and ask them to imagine that they are the friends and relatives of the persons described in the obituaries. In their small team they are to discuss their relationship to the persons who are now gone, and how they are dealing with their loss.

Ask:

▼ **When you think about death, how do you usually feel?** *(uncomfortable, sad, unsure, no problem)*
▼ **How do you feel when a family member or a close friend moves away and you no longer see them regularly?**
▼ **How is that like a grief experience?**

OPTION 1

Impressions of Death

Distribute the art supplies. Ask youth to think back over their life to the most troubling time they have ever experienced. Invite everyone to design a representation of their own feelings and experience.

These difficult times may include an eating disorder, the death of a parent or sibling, being the victim of violence, failing in school, addiction, moving and leaving close friends.

When youth have finished their drawings, invite volunteers to explain their designs. If appropriate, explain the symbol you created.

Lead youth to name other situations that would be difficult for teens to face. Help everyone recognize that sometimes we feel as if no one understands our feelings because others may not think a particular situation is all that difficult. Conclude the activity by asking youth to think of words that describe how a person might feel during a difficult experience *(possible answers: devastated, hopeless, distressed, miserable, desperate, lonely).*

Beyond Physical Death

Say: **There are other things that don't cause a physical death, but that can be just as difficult. These experiences can even result in the feeling of grief.** Brainstorm on what these experiences might be *(the loss of a lifestyle, of independence, of health through a crippling disease or injury, of a broken relationship, of a long-held goal).* Share a testimony of a personal grief experience that involves one of these.

EXPLORING

A Caring Christ

Have youth dramatize the scene with Jesus, Mary, and Martha as they mourn Lazarus' death. Assign one person to each role, and give the youth a few moments to review the account in John.

As you slowly read aloud John 11:1-44, tell the characters to use as many gestures and motions as they can devise to illustrate the story. At the conclusion, ask all the players to "freeze" as you go from character to character, inquiring what it was like to role-play that particular part.

Why Grief Happens

Direct a youth to read 2 Corinthians 1:3-11 while the others listen for reasons why we grieve. After the reading, ask:

▼ **How can our pain help us help others?**
▼ **How important is comfort when you are hurting?**

Lead youth to rate (1 for worst to 5 for best) which actions give them comfort:

_____ receiving a hug

_____ writing a caring note

_____ someone spending time with you

_____ someone offering you advice

_____ telling others that you are hurting and asking them to help you

_____ receiving a small gift

_____ someone saying, "I care and I'm sorry that you are hurting"

_____ someone praying for you

If you have time, allow volunteers to practice some of the suggested ways to comfort others. For example, there are several ways to "hug" someone: putting both arms around a person's shoulders, placing one arm around a person's back, or lightly patting someone on the back or the arm. Have youth also practice saying or writing actual words that may provide comfort. Ask for examples of times and places where the youth might offer comfort to others (in the hall at school, in the school cafeteria, on the phone, and so forth).

Say: **Another part of dealing with grief is learning that others can help us during grief. We don't have to trust in ourselves.** Read 2 Corinthians 1:9.

OPTION 2

EXTRA!

Say: **The news program EXTRA! is coming to interview key people about the events in John 11:1-44.** After youth read the scripture, select one youth to be the reporter. Choose volunteers to be Martha, Mary, the disciples, and townspeople. Don't forget Lazarus. Tell the reporter to interview these people about the events and their feelings.

Ask:

▼ **When you are grieving, who can help you?**

Tell youth to work in pairs or trios to think of and list sources of help in times of trouble *(possible answers: parents, friends, teachers, school counselors, church youth leaders, doctors, social service agencies)*. Invite each team to write their answers on a chalkboard or on newsprint as they formulate their ideas.

Ask:

▼ **How would it feel to get comfort from these sources?** *(possible answers: reassuring, O.K., better than nothing)*.

Ask the youth to tell whether they have ever experienced a time when they felt that they had to rely on God because there was no one else on whom they could rely. Allow volunteers to comment briefly on their experiences.

CONNECTING
Grief Notes
PREPARATION: Make copies of the following case studies.

1. You and James became good friends in elementary school. Now in junior high, James has started hanging around with an older gang. He does drugs and gets drunk every weekend. You miss his friendship and grieve over the broken relationship. What can you say or do about your grief?

2. When Erica rounded the corner near the mall going too fast, her car smashed into a tree. The fire department took three hours to free her. Erica will never play soccer again or do any of the things she enjoyed doing. What can you say to Erica when you see her in the hospital?

3. Joe worked hard toward his dream of going to college. The summer before his senior year, however, Joe's parents got a divorce. Money that would have been used for Joe's college tuition is now being used to pay legal fees and maintain two homes. What can you say to Joe in his grief?

From *When God Scrambles Your Plans* by Ann B. Cannon. Copyright © 1997 by Abingdon Press. Reproduced by permission.

Divide youth into three teams, and give each team a case study. Tell youth to share how they would respond to someone in this situation, using verses from the Scripture studied. If youth enjoy drama, let them role-play their responses.

 **CHECK OUT**

Read 2 Corinthians 1:11. How can a Christian give thanks in every situation, especially when it involves grief?

OPTION 3
Good Grief!
Invite youth to write a short advice column for a teen magazine. Ask half the youth to write a letter of advice to someone who is helping a friend who is grieving. Ask the other half of the youth to write a letter or advice to someone who is dealing with his or her own grief. After youth have finished, call for volunteers to read their advice columns aloud.

49. WHEN LIFE IS THE PITS, HOPE HELPS

Psalm 130; John 14:26-27

Looking beyond current crises and remembering God's offer of forgiveness, and help.

✔ CHECK UP!

Think of this psalm as moving in three acts. The first act, in verses 1-4, portrays the worshiper's experience of abysmal pain and separation from God. In the biblical tradition, the depths typically refer to the waters of chaos, which God mastered and swept back at the time of Creation. The metaphor of chaotic waters is easy to understand. Human beings often feel threatened on all sides by turbulent, meaningless confusion. Many young people know this feeling too. They often find it difficult to articulate such dark feelings. The singer of Psalm 130 voices the basic human fear that life has spun dangerously out of control. In verse 3 the psalmist is honest enough to state that a primary reason for our uneasiness stems from the realization that our sin has divorced us from God.

If God, who is perfectly holy, were to keep a tab on human disobedience, then none of us could come to God. We are drifting at sea and have thrown away our only life preserver. A shift occurs at verse 4 and sets the stage for the tone of the rest of the psalm. With God there is forgiveness. God is more powerful than the chaos around us. God is mightier than our sin. According to the psalmist, such a realization elicits reverence, better translated as fear. Why fear? Because if we are honest, we know that human beings cannot stand before the majesty of God's forgiveness without trembling. God does not forgive our sins because we deserve it, or because forgiveness is God's business. God's forgiveness is a free, unmerited, unconditional gift. God's awesome grace gives us much to think about.

The second act of Psalm 130 comes in verses 5-6. The life of faith has mixed into it tablespoons of assurance and hope. Those who watched for the morning were the military sentries, who stood under strain and on alert throughout the night, awaiting to be relieved from duty at dawn. The people of God are like that, constantly alert, yet confident that relief is coming. The final act of this psalm generalizes from the psalmist's individual experience to that of the whole worshiping congregation.

At least three things are emphasized in the psalm's conclusion. Stress these with youth as well. First, religious experience in the Bible is personal, but never individualistic. Our personal experience

✔ CHECK LIST

STARTING
❏ Prepare index cards and place in chairs.

EXPLORING
❏ Paper, pencils.

CONNECTING
❏ Yarn, scissors.

OPTION 2
❏ Paper, pencils.

of sin and forgiveness enlarges our sympathies, relates us to others, and points toward God's desire for a community in relationship to God. Second, stitched deep into the fabric of the universe is God's steadfast, constant, unbreakable love. In spite of life's real chaos, the world continues steadily with the heartbeat of God's love. Third, our knowledge of that love redeems us, liberates us from the clutches of human sin and despair. The last word is not ours but God's. God remains in control, and God's love and holiness will prevail.

 # CHECK IN

STARTING

Times of Trouble

PREPARATION: Write each situation on a separate index card. Place one card on each chair.

- *grades*
- *getting into the right college or finding a decent job*
- *popularity and acceptance by his or her peers*
- *pleasing his or her parents*
- *desiring financial security*
- *having the right clothes or enough money to do what his or her group is doing*
- *being too busy with school, sports, clubs, and church activities*
- *use of alcohol or other drugs*
- *a relative or friend who abuses alcohol or other drugs*
- *personal appearance*
- *being the victim of prejudice, harassment, or abuse*
- *a sexual relationship and its implications for his or her health or reputation*
- *national or global issues: the environment, peace, a sound economy, racism.*

As youth arrive, ask them to think about how the item on their card can create concern, emotional or physical pain, or even a sense of hopelessness. Call on volunteers to share their cards and ideas.

Ask:
▼ **Do you know anyone who faces a hopeless situation?**
▼ **How is that person handling the situation?**
▼ **Why is there no hope?**
▼ **What would it take for them to experience hope?**

Encourage youth to listen closely to the Bible study today. Say: **You may find out how to deal with hopeless situations in your own lives, as well as how to help your friends.**

OPTION 1

Dear Diary

Read the following "Dear Diary" note to youth.

> December 26
>
> Dear Diary,
>
> I hate Christmas! Shuffling off to be with step-brothers is definitely not fun. Mom gets all worked up about putting too much on the credit cards and buying gifts for people who don't need anything. I'm tired of hearing my stepdad complain because he can't spend time with his *real* kids, which means I don't count anywhere. I never get what I want at Christmas, and sometimes I'm not even sure what I want that I don't get. But I know it's not under the tree.
>
> Peace on earth, goodwill toward all. What a joke! No peace here, and for sure no goodwill.
>
> O God, I shouldn't have done what I did. I didn't mean it. I knew it would only make the situation worse and make me feel worse.
>
> They say more people call suicide hotlines during the holidays than at any other time of the year. I can see why.
>
> —John

EXPLORING

Pick a Problem

Divide youth into teams of three or four. Based on the discussion of hopeless situations in "Times of Trouble," let each team select a problem from those written on the cards. Hand out paper and pencils. Tell each team to turn to Psalm 130 and read it as a team. Then, direct each team to write a paraphrase of the psalm using the specific situation they chose. After a few minutes, call for the paraphrase. Briefly share the ideas behind the three parts of the psalm (*pain, yearning for God's forgiveness, praise for God's love*).

Ask:
▼ The psalmist expresses his yearning for signs of hope by comparing himself to a person who, during the long night, waits for morning. How does being in the depths of despair feel like a long night?

The psalmist finds hope in God's steadfast love and says that God doesn't keep a record of our failures and mistakes.

Ask:
▼ Did you know that God loves us and doesn't keep a record of our sins?
▼ Do you believe this?
▼ If you don't, what would help you believe?
▼ If you do, what has helped you believe?

Hope with Christ

Read John 14:26-27. Say: **Let's see how Christ can be a comfort to us in hopeless situations. I'll read a statement; you explain how Christ and his promise can help.** Read each statement pausing to let youth respond. There are no pat answers. Remind them of God's forgiving love. Encourage youth to think how they can be a part of the healing process. The statements are:

● Hopeless situations are sometimes said to be the consequence of sin.
● Hopeless situations surprise us.
● Hopeless situations paralyze us; we may have a hard time taking any action.
● Hopeless situations overpower us because we feel we can't do anything.
● Hopeless situations make us aware of our weaknesses.

CONNECTING

All Tied Up

Provide a skein of yarn. (If your youth group is large provide one skein for each group of 12.) Have the group or groups sit in a circle and begin by having one member wrap the yarn around his or her wrist. Explain that you will give a topic and the person with the yarn is to speak briefly on the topic (a thought, opinion, idea, feeling, and so on). Then this person is to toss the yarn to another member of

Ask:
▼ What was John expecting for the holiday? Were his expectations realistic?
▼ Why did he feel hopeless? Why was he despairing?
▼ What did he do that made things worse? Was he trying to find a way of expressing his despair and hopelessness?
▼ Why did he say what he did about suicide hotlines?
▼ What are things John might do to get past his despair, disappointment, and anger?
▼ How might forgiveness help John?

Say: **Many of us struggle with situations that appear hopeless. Today we will look beyond hopelessness for real hope.**

OPTION 2

Reverse Paraphrase

Hand out paper and pencils. Say: **Write a reverse paraphrase. Reverse each statement in the psalm so that it says the opposite of what it normally says. For example, if you were to do a reverse paraphrase of Psalm 23, you might begin, "The Lord is not my shepherd, I want . . ."** Call for youth to share their paraphrases.

Ask:
▼ What is the real truth of this psalm?

Continue with the questions under "Pick a problem."

OPTION 3

I Can Do It By Myself

Have everyone sit on the floor so that no one is touching anyone else. Give the following guidelines for youth to follow, then challenge them to try to get up.

the group. The new person wraps the yarn around one wrist several times, and speaks to the issue. Have several persons speak to each issue, then give a new one. Use the following list to get you started, but feel free to add more:

1. Describe a time when you felt hopeless.
2. Describe a time when another's actions frustrated you.
3. Describe a time when the surrounding events seemed out of control.

Continue the process until everyone in the group has the yarn wrapped around his or her wrist several times.

Beginning with the person who has the yarn wrapped around his or her wrist the most times, have an individual group member do the following:

1. Try to shake hands with someone sitting across from you.
2. Say something to someone not sitting near you that no one can hear.
3. Try to leave the group without detaching or breaking the yarn.

Ask:
▼ How did the yarn restrict what I asked you to do each time?
▼ How is this similar to how some of our actions restrict us in real life?
▼ What are ways that we tie ourselves up through what we do or say?

Cutting Loose

Ask everyone to pull their hands back and put tension on the strings *(but not so tight that they cut off their circulation)*. As someone reads John 14:26-27 aloud, have another person cut the strings that have been restricting movement, so that everyone is free.

Ask:
▼ What did it feel like to be cut loose?
▼ How is this similar to what was read in the Scripture?
▼ What does God's forgiveness cut us free from?

Rope Prayer

Have everyone form a circle for a closing prayer. Once in the circle, have them form a human "rope" by locking elbows with the persons on either side. Go around the circle and have each person say a one-sentence prayer. This is strictly voluntary. Close with a prayer asking God's forgiveness. Pray also that the members of this group might have the strength to throw a rope of forgiveness to one another when it is needed.

 CHECK OUT

What have you done in your life that still bothers you? What would it be like if you felt completely and utterly forgiven?

Say: **Sit on the floor with your legs extended straight out in front of you. Your hands and arms cannot touch the floor or anything else. You cannot roll sideways. Your feet must remain in front of you.**

Give youth several minutes to try to stand up. It is physically impossible, so if anyone does it, he or she broke one of the rules. Let each person get a partner. Have them sit back-to-back. The pairs should follow the same rules as before, except this time they can use back-to-back pressure. This time they should be able to stand up. Have everyone form a circle and ask:

▼ How did you feel the first time you tried to stand?
▼ What was the problem?
▼ How did you feel the second time?
▼ What made the difference?

Read John 14:26-27.

Ask:
▼ How does God help us get up when we've fallen spiritually?
▼ What role does forgiveness play in this?

50. WHEN YOU BLOW IT!

John 21:4-17

Examining life to discover the need of God's forgiveness.

✔ CHECK UP!

There is something mysterious about the appearances of the resurrected Jesus. He appears to the disciples at the close of a night of fishing, yet they fail to recognize him until he tells them where to cast their nets. They catch a lot of fish. Even after the beloved disciples recognize that it is Jesus, none of them dared to ask, Who are you? because they knew it was the Lord. This could be described as uncertainty in the midst of assurance. There is obviously something about the presence of the risen Jesus that confuses human perception. Of course, we recognize that the disciples are experiencing what no human had ever experienced before nor has since, the resurrection of one who was crucified, dead, and buried.

Although it is said that love is blind, we have here an instance of love that gives sight. It was the disciple whom Jesus loved who made the identification of the stranger on the shore. This suggests that the issue in the recognition of Jesus may lie, not so much in the identification of physical details, as in the depth of the relationship the disciple has with Jesus. Could Jesus' thrice-repeated question to Peter, "Do you love me?" relate to the fact that Peter did not recognize Jesus as he stood on the shore? Another aspect of Jesus' questions to Peter lies in the terms Jesus and Peter use in their exchange. Jesus asked Peter, "Do you love me?" using the Greek term *agapao*, the deepest of all kinds of love. This is a love of consecration to the beloved. Peter replies, "Yes, Lord, you know that I love you," but uses the term *phileo,* the love of friend for friend. The second time the exchange is exactly the same, with Jesus using *agapao* and Peter using *phileo*. In the third exchange, however, Jesus shifts to *phileo,* almost as if to say to Peter, "I will meet you on whatever level of commitment you will make to me. If *phileo* is the full extent of your relationship with me, I will meet you there."

It is interesting that Peter was grieved when Jesus changed from *agapao* to *phileo*. The writer indicates that it was not because Jesus asked Peter a third time that Peter was upset, but because Jesus asked him on the third time *"Do you phileo me?"* instead of *"Do you agapao me?"* Even then, Peter could not respond with *agapao;* he remained with *phileo*. There's a wonderful honesty in this. Were this some kind of contrived account, a skilled writer would have had Peter change to *agapao* at this point to bring closure to the story. It's

> ✔ CHECK LIST

STARTING
❏ Enlist a reader.

EXPLORING
❏ Enlist a reader.
❏ Prepare Scripture references.
❏ Chalkboard or butcher paper, markers.

CONNECTING
❏ Fish-shaped crackers, cups, juice.

OPTION 2
❏ Prepare slips of paper, tape.

unclear from the account what Jesus means when he asks Peter, "Do you love me more than these?" Does it mean more than the other disciples? Does it mean more than the fish, the occupation of fishing, and all that goes with it? Does it mean more than the bread and fish that Jesus provided for their breakfast? All three possibilities seem to be present in the account.

Finally, Jesus had just fed Peter and the others with fish and bread. He now calls Peter to become the one who feeds and cares for others. In Jesus' question about "loving him more than these," Jesus may be asking Peter whether he is completely consecrated to him or are these other things in the way.

 CHECK IN

STARTING

MegaMistake

Invite a youth to read "MegaMistake" aloud to the others.

MEGAMISTAKE

Jesse would have given anything to avoid walking up to his front door with the two police officers. He watched the door open and saw his mom and dad silhouetted against the light in the hallway. Then he saw their faces. He expected them to be angry, but they looked sad, disappointed; he would never forget the looks on their faces. "I'm sor—" he started but his mom interrupted and told him to go sit at the kitchen table. "We'll be in to talk with you in a few minutes."

He moved heavily into the kitchen, weighed down with guilt and too much alcohol. He heard an officer explain the procedure to his parents and tell them that he had cooperated completely. The officer even reminded them that they'd been young once themselves.

When the officers left, Jesse's mom and dad sat down across from him. He wanted nothing more than to put his head down and sleep. "O.K., Jesse," said his mom, "tell us what happened." So Jesse explained that he'd decided, just this once to have a few drinks with some of his friends. He'd never had more than one or two drinks before. When Tom was taking him home, the police had pulled them over. It didn't take the officers long to discover that they were both drunk. Jesse's parents listened, then sent him to bed.

The next day his mom and dad told him how he would be disciplined. Not only was he grounded for two weeks, but he'd lost his parents' trust and this made a curfew necessary. His parents explained that trust takes a long time to build up, but that it can be destroyed in an instant, with one mistake. He argued with the

---

OPTION 1

Time to Eat

Lead youth to name times when families get together to eat.

Ask:
▼ Why is it important for us to share food with our families? with our friends? with our church family?
▼ What difference does eating food or a meal make in our fellowship today?

Say: **The Gospels frequently portray Jesus at the table with his disciples and others, teaching them and explaining God's word and will for their lives. Christians in the early church made mealtime a time to remember Christ's sacrifice in the breaking of bread and the drinking of wine. Eating together was an important part of life for these people—a time to remember and to witness, a time that brought them closer together and strengthened their faith.**

curfew because his independence was important to him, but arguing was of no use. He went back to his room. If he could only take back the night! Sitting on his bed, he wondered how long it would take for his parents to trust him again.

After the reading, ask:
▼ How did Jesse blow it?
▼ Even though Jesse is sorry, why does he have to live with the consequences?
▼ How can Jesse regain his parents' trust?

Say: The disciple Peter made a megamistake by denying he knew Jesus. Today we will see how Jesus, after his resurrection, responded to Peter's megamistake.

EXPLORING

Lights! Camera! Action!
PREPARATION: Recruit a youth to read John 21:1-17. Also, recruit several volunteers to play the parts of Jesus and his disciples. (See John 21:2 for the cast of characters. If you have a small group, assign the parts of Jesus, Peter, the disciple whom Jesus loved, and as many disciples and fishermen as you have youth.)

Group the disciples together and encourage them to pretend that they are fishing. (Chairs may be placed around them to suggest a boat.) Place Jesus some distance away. Ask the reader to read verses 1-5 aloud. Then stop the action and ask each of the "disciples" to identify which character they are playing and to imagine what that character is thinking at that moment in the story. Ask the reader to read verse 6; then stop the action and again ask each disciple to report his or her thoughts.
Ask the reader to read aloud verse 7. Have Peter come out of the boat and tell what he or she believes Peter might be thinking at that point. Then have verse 8 read and invite the other disciples to leave the boat and report their thoughts. Ask the reader to read verses 9-14 aloud and invite all the players to state what their characters might be thinking. Then have the reader read verses 15-17, stopping after each verse to let Peter and Jesus report their thoughts.

Peter's MegaMistake
PREPARATION: Write the following Scripture references on the chalkboard or butcher paper, leaving space after each to write a sentence or two: *John 13:36-38, Mark 14:32-42, John 18:15-17,* and *John 18:25-27.*

Form four groups and assign one text to each group. Ask them to discover what Peter did in each of these readings. (Notice that in Mark 14:32-42, the disciples fell asleep not once, but three times. Could the repetition be for emphasis' sake?) As each group concludes its task, ask a representative to write the actions of Peter that they discovered next to the appropriate reference on the chalkboard or paper.

OPTION 2

Basic Elements
PREPARATION: Write these words "Who," "What," "When," "Where," and "How" on the five slips of paper (one word per slip). Tape the slips to the underside of five of the chairs where youth will be sitting. (To ensure that these chairs will be used, set up fewer chairs than you will need and then bring out additional chairs as more youth arrive.)

Ask for several volunteers to read aloud John 21:1-17, with each volunteer taking turns reading one verse. When the whole story has been read, have everyone look under his or her seat. Ask the person who has the "Who" paper to name the persons the story is about *(Jesus, Simon Peter, the disciple whom Jesus loved, and some other disciples).* Next ask the person with the "What" paper to give a brief description of the action that took place. Allow the people who find the other three papers to tell "When" *(just after daybreak, one morning shortly after Jesus was raised from the dead),* "Where" *(by the sea, where the disciples were fishing),* and "How" *(by the power of God).*

WHEN GOD SCRAMBLES YOUR PLANS

Ask:
- ▼ How do you think Peter probably felt about these actions? *(perhaps ashamed, unworthy, or confused)*
- ▼ If you were Jesus, would you have given up on Peter?
- ▼ How do we know that Jesus did not give up on Peter? *(Jesus appeared to Peter after his death and emphatically charged Peter with tending to his people.)*

Say: **In Jesus' time, to share a meal with someone who had hurt you was to offer forgiveness.**

Ask:
- ▼ Do you think Jesus might have prepared food for Peter as a way of offering him forgiveness?
- ▼ How can sharing a meal with someone you have wronged improve relationships in our culture?
- ▼ How did Peter become courageous and faithful after this meeting with Christ? *(Peter was a great preacher and an important leader in the early church; tradition says that he was martyred for his faith.)*
- ▼ How can Christ's presence in your life empower you to be a faithful disciple?

CONNECTING

When You Blow It!
Say: **We've all done it. We've all had times when we've blown it.**

Ask:
- ▼ How do you feel after you've made a megamistake?
- ▼ Do you blame another person?
- ▼ Do you want to try harder next time?
- ▼ Do you feel guilt? anger?
- ▼ How does God help you deal with megamistakes?

A Second Chance Meal
Distribute fish-shaped crackers and small cups of juice. Say a prayer of thanksgiving for gifts and abilities, full nets of health and happiness, and the gift of Jesus Christ in our lives. Celebrate second chances!

✔ CHECK OUT

Jesus asked, "Do you love me?" each time he asked Peter to feed his sheep. The key to feeding the sheep (living with others) is to first love the shepherd (Jesus). How can his idea help you when you blow it?

OPTION 3

Peter's New Job

Ask:
- ▼ What would a job description for "catching people" be like?
- ▼ What was Peter's primary responsibility? why?
- ▼ Was his job different from that of the other disciples?

Tell everyone to read John 21:15-17. Say: **This was Peter's new job description.**

Ask:
- ▼ What was his primary responsibility?
- ▼ Did he have other responsibilities?
- ▼ Was being made a shepherd a promotion or a demotion from being a fisherman?

BIBLE PASSAGES

WHEN GOD SCRAMBLES YOUR PLANS